THE GREAT RON PAUL

*The Scott Horton Show Interviews
2004–2019*

The
LIBERTARIAN
INSTITUTE

The Great Ron Paul
The Scott Horton Show Interviews
2004–2019

© 2019 by The Libertarian Institute
All rights reserved.

Edited by Scott Horton

Cover art by
Sarah DeYong
SarahDeYong.com

Cover design by
TheBumperSticker.com

Published in the United States of America by

The Libertarian Institute
612 W. 34th St.
Austin, TX 78705

LibertarianInstitute.org

ISBN-13: 978-1-7336473-1-1
ISBN-10: 1-7336473-1-7

For Larisa

Contents

Preface i

2004

May 30, 2004 1

October 16, 2004 11

2005

December 17, 2005 21

2006

December 13, 2006 31

2007

April 3, 2007 38

August 17, 2007 48

2008

March 6, 2008 60

September 26, 2008 65

November 21, 2008 73

2009

February 18, 2009 82

April 22, 2009 94

May 29, 2009 101

September 23, 2009 108

2010

January 21, 2010 115

March 4, 2010 127

May 12, 2010 132

June 18, 2010 137

August 27, 2010 142

November 23, 2010 147

2011

February 24, 2011 155

April 1, 2011 161

April 22, 2011 165

June 3, 2011 170

November 23, 2011 175

2013

April 26, 2013 179

June 10, 2013 185

August 22, 2013 191

2015

February 12, 2015 196

July 3, 2015 204

2016

April 12, 2016 214

June 8, 2016 221

2017

March 15, 2017 229

May 15, 2017 234

October 2, 2017 243

December 1, 2017 251

2018

April 18, 2018 257

November 15, 2018 266

2019

January 18, 2019 276

June 14, 2019 282

About the Host/Editor 295

About the Guest 296

About the Libertarian Institute 301

Preface

Ron Paul is the greatest politician in American history. Not that he ever passed much legislation in his long career in the U.S. House of Representatives. That was never the point. Dr. Paul carried out his job as congressman differently than the rest. As an angry citizen once complained to the *Houston Chronicle*, all the congressman did on Capitol Hill was "write articles, give speeches and vote 'No.'"

That he did. And those articles, speeches and votes? They were all for liberty.

His presidential runs in 2008 and 2012 were the greatest speaking tours ever given on behalf of liberty. Millions of Americans and people from around the world were shown a better political philosophy, above the petty squabbles of the left and right in their fight for control; against control itself. Freedom is what is right. Freedom is what works best to bring people together and to provide for society. Freedom is all we need. Believe it.

We do.

Today Dr. Paul continues the fight for peace, freedom and sound money from his indispensable Institute for Peace and Prosperity, and on his essential daily YouTube show, *The Liberty Report*, co-hosted with Daniel McAdams and Chris Rossini.

Dr. Paul's libertarian individualism represents the great principles of the American Declaration of Independence, distilled and perfected. It's the unified theory of freedom.

His good name is sure to live on into future human history for centuries among the greatest American champions of individual liberty.

The following interviews were recorded on my various radio shows between May 2004 and June 2019.

In them Dr. Paul talks about war and peace, torture, spying, economics, the financial crisis and debt, whistleblowers, and the great Ron Paul Revolution of 2008 and 2012, during his runs for the U.S. presidency.

The interviews have been lightly edited for clarity, as well as for some of the redundancies in the introductions, but not subject matter. So we do talk about "blowback" and letters of marque and reprisal a few different times, but don't worry, it's better each time.

(By the way, I'm really not that bad on everything. I often try to play devil's advocate to get the best out of my guest is all, you understand.)

Scott Horton
August 2019

"If you love liberty, you hate empire."
— Ron Paul

May 30, 2004

This interview was conducted in person at the 2004 Libertarian Party national convention in Atlanta, Georgia.

Scott Horton: Alright, everybody. Welcome to the *Weekend Interview Show*. The guest today is an obstetrician by trade, a former flight surgeon and apparently, he's the only congressman who gives money back to the Treasury at the end of every term. I am truly honored to introduce "Dr. No," Congressman Ron Paul.

Ron Paul: Good to be with you.

Horton: It's an honor to have you on the show, sir.

Paul: Thank you.

Horton: My first question is a hypothetical. I hope maybe you can have a little bit of fun with it. If somehow the majority of the House of Representatives came to their senses and made you the house speaker, what would be the new agenda for the House of Representatives?

Paul: Of course, the House can't do a whole lot by itself. You have to have the Senate to go along, and also a president that will sign your bills. But if we thought about the most important thing we could do if we had like-minded people in the Senate and somebody that would sign the bill — or you think we can get it passed, I'd work on a constitutional amendment, get the states to pass it — that would be the Liberty Amendment.

The Liberty Amendment means that you get rid of the IRS, repeal the 16th Amendment, and the federal government has three years to stop doing everything it's doing that is not explicitly authorized in the Constitution. They have to cease and desist and quit. Then we would get back to constitutional government. But that is a hypothetical and a dream, and it's not something we'll hold our breath for.

Horton: But the power of the purse strings is all in the House of Representatives, so as house speaker, you couldn't necessarily pass a lot of legislation, but you could stop a lot of unconstitutional things from being funded, right?

Paul: Yeah, you could really bottleneck it up if you go through the expenditures. But the tragedy, of course is the current Congress, they have given up all their prerogatives, whether it's on the issue of war, or whether it's the issue of writing regulations that become law or what they allow the courts to do. If we had the control, you literally could stop the funding and stop these unconstitutional programs that I'd like to ban.

But it would cause chaos if you didn't have the Senate to go along with that. The Vietnam War was finally stopped by Congress cutting the purse strings and stopping funding it. That would be one way to do it. But a speaker by himself can't do it. You have to have a majority vote, because if you were the only one who thought that way and you were an accidental speaker, they would kick you out of office the next day. You're only going to have a libertarian speaker when you have a libertarian Congress, and you won't have a libertarian Congress until the people want a libertarian Congress.

Horton: You filed a bill in October 2002 to declare war against Iraq, and then you voted against it. Why is that?

Paul: It wasn't actually a bill. It was an amendment. The resolution giving to the president the option to do whatever he wanted in Iraq came through the International Relations Committee on which I sit. When it came up, I had the chance to amend it, so I offered a substitute amendment, which was a declaration of war. When I presented it, I said, "This is a declaration of war, and I'm going to depend on you, the rest of the committee, to make sure it doesn't get passed, because I'm not going to vote for it."

The reason I did that was to remind them that war should only be fought on declaration and with congressional participation. But the resolution was not doing that at all. The resolution was citing the United Nations and then saying to the president, "If you want to go to war, it's okay. If you don't want to go to war, it's okay. When you want to go is up to you." It was giving to the president the authority to do what only Congress should do. In many ways, what we did as a Congress is, we transferred power from the Congress to the executive branch, which is unconstitutional. That was the reason I introduced that and made them vote on it. Of course, the vote was 43 or 44 to zero.

Horton: How does that make you feel when you see these congressmen now demanding accountability and complaining that they don't know what's going on when they've passed all their authority away?

Paul: I don't say too much. I let the events speak for themselves. But one member… I was on a committee this week on international relations, and the individual that was sitting next to me leaned over and he says, "Ron," he says, "don't you ever feel like sending out a press release saying, 'I told you so'?" I thought that was pretty neat because he suggested it. If you say it yourself, it doesn't sound so good. But at least he was thinking about it.

Horton: Now that it's proven there's no weapons of mass destruction, there's no links between the former Hussein regime and al Qaeda, the people apparently don't seem to think they're very liberated over there with the latest polls that I've seen of the opinion of the Iraqi people — I wonder, do you think that those were the real reasons that we went to Iraq? And if there were other reasons that were not so publicly discussed, what do you think those might've been?

Paul: Those were the reasons many members voted for it, believing what they were told. Of course, now we find that that information was wrong. The question is, did they do it deliberately, or did they just blunder? Or what were their ulterior motives? It's probably a lot of all of that. I think there were other ulterior motives.

Horton: Such as?

Paul: I have a lot of members admit to me, even though they wouldn't say it in public, that we do need to protect the oil. What are we going to do if we don't have this oil? We depend on this. So they recognize this as being important.

Horton: That's the other members of Congress. What do you think were the real goals of the administration?

Paul: I think oil probably was a major issue, although they would never admit it. Because when they went into the Persian Gulf the first time with George Bush Sr., he publicly said immediately, "We've got to go over there and stop Saddam Hussein to protect our oil." They were talking that way.

Of course, there's the neocon approach of remaking the Middle East. They're very sincere about that. It's a philosophic position that they take.

Horton: You wrote quite a long thing, I'm not sure if it was a speech that you gave, but a friend of mine got in the mail her *Liberty Report* that was called "Neo-Conned."

Paul: Yeah, I gave that. It was a speech I gave on the House floor demonstrating how this war was planned for a long time. Matter of fact, the basic authority was passed in 1998 under Clinton. We had a resolution come up on the floor. It was under suspension, which means they didn't expect any opposition. If they bring a bill under suspension to the floor, if both parties are in support of it, an individual like myself can demand the time in opposition. I was so outraged in '98 that they were moving toward war that I went down and took the 20 minutes. There were only 40 minutes. I had 20 minutes and the other two parties, the Democrats and the Republicans, had 20 minutes. We debated this issue, which I said is going to lead to war.

But that was the original authority saying the intent, the policy of the United States, is to get rid of Saddam Hussein, to have regime change. It's cited quite frequently. It's called the Iraq Liberation Act or something like that, but it was in 1998. They hide behind that and say, "Oh, Congress said this, and Clinton believed it." That is true. But this was pushed by the neocons.

Of course, immediately after President Bush took office, they were talking about the war and planning. That was what Paul O'Neill wrote in his book. He said the first month they were there, they were talking about the war.

Horton: How unprecedented is it, the invasion of Iraq, in terms of what they call a preemptive strike? But, of course, it's not the first time that we've attacked a nation that never attacked us, is it?

Paul: No, hardly. But it is a significant event, where we went in with a huge army to change the government and to occupy the country. We've done it in the South American and Central American countries not too long ago. Panama was a regime change.

In modern times, it started in 1953 when Eisenhower sent the CIA over to Iran to get rid of an elected leader, Mosaddegh. They kicked him out and put the Shah in, who was a ruthless dictator. They remember that. Now, who are we fighting over there right now? The Iranians who probably orchestrated this whole thing in getting the information to the Congress and gave it to the CIA and all this…

Horton: Through Ahmed Chalabi.

Paul: Yeah, through Chalabi. It never goes away. But I think the fact that we did that led to the rise up of the radical Shi'ites and the overthrow of the Shah with the Ayatollah in 1979. So it goes on and on. Then we became his ally — of Saddam Hussein — against Iran. They remember that too. This just goes on and on and on. That's why there's a pretty good argument for nonintervention. Stay out of there. Stay out of the affairs of other nations.

Horton: You wrote a weekly column a few months back called "Keep the UN Out of Iraq — and Out of the U.S." Now that the transfer of power seems imminent and we have a UN official — I forget what his name is — is picking the new government over there. I wonder, what degree of control do you think that the UN might end up having in Iraq? And why out of the U.S.? What do you mean by that, as a secondary question?

Paul: I didn't use the term "out of the U.S." I just said we ought to be out of the UN.

Horton: Oh, maybe I got that one backwards. I'm sorry.

Paul: I was jokingly saying also that… They asked me what the solution is, and I said, "Turn the whole mess over to the UN. Then we should get out of the UN, and the UN will have to deal with it." No, the UN eventually will be involved. Even though Bush was sort of obstinate about getting UN approval, final approval, he used the UN as justification. Some people argue that he really was putting backbone into a UN resolution that wasn't being enforced. They made the resolutions and then decided, "We don't want to invade as a UN army." So Bush says, "We've got to go in there anyway." The UN is alive and well. At the same time, we're backing UNESCO, which put us back in UNESCO, and that's cost us a lot of money.

Horton: Their new treaty on civilian ownership of light arms, too, as well, right?

Paul: That's right. They're talking now about international taxation on the internet and arms control.

Horton: What does it mean when conservatives in America are angry at the UN for not doing enough and for being obstinate? I thought that the conservative critique of the United Nations was that it did anything at all.

Paul: I think there still are a lot of conservatives that sort of listen to some of the rhetoric and say, "That's good. We're going in on our own." They like that. But in the administration, there are some who sort of would like not to be hamstrung with the United Nations. They don't mind the United Nations too well, but they want to have total control of the United Nations. It's sort of made up of a mixture.

Paul: I still think the majority of the American people still think it's good to be in the United Nations. But there's a growing number of people disenchanted, and right now much so over this issue of the corruption of the oil-for-food programs. This could turn out to be one of the biggest scandals in the history of the world.

Horton: Do you regret voting to authorize the use of force against Afghanistan? That was not a declaration of war.

Paul: Regret voting not to...?

Horton: Afghanistan, I said, not Iraq.

Paul: Oh. I voted for the...

Horton: You voted for the invasion of Afghanistan, correct?

Paul: It wasn't listed as Afghanistan. Right after 9/11, we had a resolution to vote to give the authority to the president to take action against those individuals who were responsible for 9/11.

Horton: Is that any more constitutional than the one against Iraq?

Paul: Yeah, I think it is. I think that is much closer to the type of authority that... Because it wasn't to go into and occupy. It was to go after the al Qaeda. It was the equivalent to what Jefferson did when he went to the Congress six or seven times to get explicit permission each time he did something to deal with the piracy on the seas. He would get permission. He recognized the importance of the Congress. He didn't have, again, back then anybody to declare war on. They were pirates on the high seas. So he would get explicit permission. And he did it each step of the way, fully recognizing that Congress authorizes the use of force.

We did authorize the use of force. But then you have to sort of trust the president to do what is instructed, and the instruction was to go after the al Qaeda. It didn't say, "Take over and do nation-building in Afghanistan." Besides, later on, some of that money that was authorized for that war was secretly used to start to go into Iraq. I think his judgment, at least, was different than what I would've expected. Because I think specifically, they sort of ignored the al Qaeda after that.

I also at the time suggested that the Congress should've been even more explicit and issued letters of marque and reprisal, where you literally permit private companies to go and get certain individuals.

Horton: Only individuals, not groups? They would have certain names on...

Paul: No, they could be groups. You could designate... It depends on how the Congress would write it. But only Congress can write letters of marque and reprisal. It's a lot different than assuming that the president can decide how much money can be used for a reward for the CIA to go in and bump somebody off. It was a little more honest about it.

I think we should have spent our time going after the al Qaeda. I'm sorry that he overstepped the bounds of what was intended there and went into Iraq and a few other things. But no, I think it was very hard to vote against that. I remember my statement on the floor, because I considered it a tough vote. I said that, "I'm not satisfied with this resolution. I don't like it. I think we could do a better job. But the alternative of doing nothing under these circumstances is unthinkable." Otherwise you would have to be practically an anarchist if you say the president can't have any authority to do anything about it.

Paul: Of course, I would've liked to have all our presidents for the last hundred years doing a lot less. Then we wouldn't have to be facing these kinds of problems. But that's history, and we have to deal with the violence that's going on right now.

Horton: What do you see as the future of the so-called War on Terror, about how it will be fought when, like you say, we're fighting pirates who are actors less than states? Do we have to overthrow every nation that has al Qaeda in it and create democracy there?

Paul: I'm afraid that's the direction we've been going, and I think it's the wrong direction. I just think it creates more terrorists and recruits for the al Qaeda, and occupation is certainly one of the worst things that we could've done for our own benefit. I see us as less secure now than before. I think we should be concentrating more on trying to protect our people back at home.

The whole idea that our Coast Guard right now... We've had lots of

Coast Guard members in the Persian Gulf, because they're over there protecting terminals and things. If we're thinking about the responsibility of the federal government protecting us, why wouldn't we have the Coast Guard in the Gulf of Mexico around our ports, checking on unusual things? I think that the emphasis should be, are we protecting our country or are we policing the world?

The whole philosophy we've been following — it's just not this administration, it's been going on for a long time — it has led us to a situation where we have made a lot of enemies by aggravating people and being in the Persian Gulf, having troops on what they consider holy land, and then it ends up that we weren't very well protected. We've exposed ourselves. Seoul, Korea was probably better protected on 9/11 than New York City, because we had planes there, and if those North Koreans ever dare do anything, they would've been prepared. But not in this country. I'd much rather emphasize protecting ourselves here. I'd bring our troops home and spend a lot less money.

Horton: Commentator Gary North, who writes for LewRockwell.com, wrote a column where he said, "The American empire ends on June 30. This is a complete disaster. Iraq is such a failure that all your fears that America is going to go crazy and be an empire — Don't worry about it. Because after this, everybody's coming home pretty soon." What do you think of that?

Paul: We're just not cut out to be empire builders.

Horton: It seems from my perspective, sir, that the American people really don't want to have an empire, and that, I believe, is why the executive branch always lies to us to get us to go fight their wars for them.

Paul: That's right. I think the American people are good-hearted and they get talked into... Even if we have sinister motives, we tell the American people we're going there for good motives, and we're going to help people and take care of them and give them democracy and give them freedom. Of course, when we look around and see all the inconsistency, it becomes a joke. But I think he's probably on to something, which is probably good for us.

I tell people in Washington, everyplace, that I will win this argument about what we should be doing. But not because all of a sudden, I'll be persuasive. I, or we — those who believe this way — will win because we're going to run out of money. Gary, I guess, figures we're going to run out of credibility and ability to police the world and be an empire builder once they see what'll happen after June 30.

Horton: This is a question from a friend. Why don't the members of the Republican Liberty Caucus vote with you? It seems that they would have little excuse since you get elected by a bigger margin every term, what is their excuse to not vote constitutional? If they are the Liberty Caucus, surely they've at least read the Constitution, unlike most of the House, probably.

Paul: They're very sympathetic, and they do tell me that. There would be some disagreements. Nobody would agree on all the issues. But a lot of them will tell me that they agree with me, but they think it would hurt them back home. But that's been one of my goals, is always to get reelected by sticking to my guns and voting what I consider the best I can following the Constitution. We've been able to always do better.

Horton: In fact, last time you were reelected by the biggest margin ever, right after voting against the war in a very Republican district in South Texas, correct?

Paul: That's right. Went up to 68 or 69 percent in November 2002.

Horton: Pardon me, but before I forget, I used to live right on the edge of District 10, or almost in it. Now I can't even see it anymore. I think it's gone.

Paul: District 14?

Horton: District 14, pardon me. I wonder what happened to your district?

Paul: It was pushed toward the Gulf Coast, and they've done it again. Even though I've had a new district for between 2002 and 2004, this year it will even be much smaller in geographic area, because they've given me the city of Galveston. Galveston, of course, will be a much more liberal, Democratic city.

Horton: And they took all your conservative rural votes away, or most of them.

Paul: They took a bunch of them away.

Horton: That was Tom DeLay and Rick Perry and the boys who engineered all that, right?

Paul: Yeah, but they were designing it to get more Republican seats. Mine is still a Republican-leaning district, but it's probably the worst Republican district out of the 22 that they want to win.

Horton: If there's only one of you in the House of Representatives — which, I watch a lot of C-SPAN and I don't see too many more Dr. Pauls there — I wonder what real hope do we have to have the old republic and not the new empire and the total state that we're marching towards now?

Paul: I work on the assumption that none of us know what exactly will come tomorrow. Before 1989, 1991, in that era, how many people were saying, "You know, it's going to be a new world. The Soviet Union's going to disappear"? That was pretty magnificent. I saw predictions philosophically on economics, that they couldn't be sustained, and they weren't. But all of a sudden, they disintegrated. Things can happen beyond our imagination.

You can't get a whole lot of encouragement by being in Washington. But when you leave Washington, there's a growing number of people who are becoming aware of what's happening. I think we're making progress. I think, like Gary North assumes, that there will be some kind of major change, a recognition that we can't sustain the empire after June 30. I've been predicting all along that because of the finances of this country, something major has to give.

But that's why it's so important to spread the message of freedom and get as many people to understand as possible. This is why a radio show like yours is so important, that you talk to people and try to get them interested. The government generally reflects the people's attitudes. I know there are dictators and all, but once the people really, really get sick of even dictators… Of course, as bad as Stalin was, the USSR lasted a limited amount of time. It finally had to go. Now it doesn't exist.

Attitudes are very important. I think our job is not to worry about tomorrow, but just to work on the job of trying to change people's minds, to tell them that there's a tremendous amount of benefits if we follow the Constitution and defend freedom.

Horton: Thank you very much, sir, for your time tonight.

Paul: You're welcome. Thank you.

Horton: I sure appreciate it.

October 16, 2004

Horton: I am honored to welcome the man Anthony Gregory says makes James Madison look like Alexander Hamilton. He is the most honest — and most modest — member of the U.S. House of Representatives. As the congressman representing District 14 in South Texas, his votes are always favorable to individual liberty, free markets, peace, national sovereignty, and the U.S. Constitution. Listen up my friends, it's Dr. Ron Paul. Welcome to the show, sir.

Paul: Thank you. Good to be with you.

Horton: It's great to have you on, sir.

Paul: Thanks.

Horton: Dr. Paul, two of this year's presidential campaign issues are whether America should fight unilaterally, or multilaterally, overseas, and also at what point does a threat or humanitarian crisis demand American intervention? Your thoughts?

Paul: Overseas is going to be very, very rare. I think the national security of this country has to be either directly threatened or very imminent, and it has to beyond doubt. Unless we have been attacked, it has to be with permission of the Congress. But, in the Cold War, if the Soviets were known to have unleashed some missiles, it's very obvious from the very start that the president does have authority to respond and protect this country. But I think you're alluding to getting involved in fights, and skirmishes, and civil wars, and disputes, and nation-building overseas. I think it's pretty safe to say that it's almost never necessary or proper for us to do that.

Horton: What about the issue of multilateralism, and whether — when we do go to war — whether we have allies involved or not?

Paul: I think that's interesting, because when you hear the president talk, sometimes he says things that sound a little bit like what we might say in that we don't take our marching orders from the UN. We shouldn't get directions and resolutions that we have to enforce. He was talking out of both sides of his mouth on that, because at one time, he says that he wanted the authority to go to war in Iraq because he had to enforce these resolutions to make and keep the UN strong. At the same time, he wants it both ways, and he says, "Well, I am not..." Then he found out the UN didn't want us to go. He says, "I don't take my orders from the UN," and therefore he wants to be a unilateralist.

I think what I talk about and others talk about in a more peaceful foreign policy is not unilateralism as much as independence, a strategic independence where we take care of ourselves, we mind our own business, and we don't depend on anybody else. But this arrogant unilateralism isn't what we want, because it would be better for the world if we intermingled with the world, and not antagonize them, and call them names, and put on sanctions. What we want to do is be friends with the world, with anybody who wants to be friends, and trade with them. The more we trade with them, and communicate with them, and travel with them, the less likely we are to fight with them.

Horton: So the United States should be unilaterally at peace.

Paul: I think that's it. That is our position, that we should never be the aggressor, and I'm afraid in these last several decades it's become rather clear after Kosovo — that was a token effort, even though there were other governments involved, and NATO was involved — sort of set the stage for this more latent preemptive war, saying, "Well, for our benefit, we have to start this war, and we think there are some problems over there." And now it turns out the problems didn't exist.

Horton: We have a problem with terrorists now, whether past interventions created the problem or not. There's a band of pirates who wants to kill us, and there are different arguments about exactly how that should be handled. Most of them, obviously, take place within a pretty narrow spectrum of argument, but you do believe that al Qaeda must be dealt with in some fashion, don't you?

Paul: I do, and if you look back even at all my votes after 9/11 — although essentially I rejected the direction that we went in — immediately after, I voted for the immediate authority for the president to respond to those individuals that attacked us. So, in that case, I did endorse the notion that our government had the authority to go after the al Qaeda. I didn't interpret that, nor should anybody have interpreted that, to mean that we should do nation-building and take over a government in Afghanistan, as well as Iraq. So, yes, I do, I think we should have and still could have, but there's a lot of different ways of doing it than perpetuating the problem that we have.

Ultimately, I don't think we can become more secure until we back away from our aggressive, antagonistic, interventionist foreign policy, because that's the source of the hatred and the frustration, and yet I also understand the argument, "Well, what does that mean? You mean you just pack up the troops and be home in two days, and say, 'You terrorists, you've won,' and we're not going to do a thing?" I don't think you can do that, but you could start backing off as quickly as possible, and you could target only those individuals that have committed the crimes. For all the $200 billion we've been spending over there in Iraq — first bombing it to smithereens and then rebuilding it — I would say that money could have been spent much better in targeting the al Qaeda, as well as having better security here in this country, and better border patrol, which I think is legitimate, so that we know more about the people who are coming in.

But that also has to be done cautiously. I believe you really can do that without the sacrifice of personal liberty. I just really believe it. I think some of our problems on 9/11 was the lack of liberty, rather than too much liberty. For instance, the freer a country is, the more the individual and the businesses and corporations are responsible for what they do. So the airlines, instead of assuming more responsibility for the protection of their passengers, they have less than ever. If we would have had a greater emphasis on the Second Amendment before 9/11, and the airlines knew that, by golly, they better protect these passengers at all costs. But instead, here we had an interventionist government here at home that said, "Well, if you are ever hijacked, never fight them, and also you cannot have guns on the airplane to protect yourself." Absolutely bizarre.

I think we should have had an announcement on 9/12/01 by a president that just invoked the Second Amendment and said the federal government should have no restrictions on companies protecting themselves with their own weapons.

Horton: That's very interesting. Back to the so-called Global War on Terrorism for a moment, sir. The president of the United States, in his debate — I think in the second debate with John Kerry — said that Kerry's mistaken understanding of the War on Terrorism was that we have to just go after al Qaeda, and what Bush understands, which makes him such an invaluable leader to us, is that it's not just stopping al Qaeda, but it's stopping the proliferation of weapons of mass destruction that people like al Qaeda could someday eventually get their hands on, and that that proliferation must be stopped at all costs. How does that square with simply hunting individuals in al Qaeda, and withdrawing the rest of the way?

Paul: I think it's over-expansive. I don't think you can declare war against the potentiality of building weapons. Besides, it's almost like the argument about the pro-Second Amendment people domestically. It's not the guns that commit the crime, it's the criminals that commit the crime. If tomorrow Canada all of a sudden had 30 nuclear weapons, who would care? We get along with them, so the relationship between the two countries are much more important, and this whole idea that it's only the weapons you deal with doesn't make a whole lot of sense, since we went through a period of time — certainly in my lifetime — where these weapons were rather prevalent around the world through the Cold War, but we never felt like we had to get rid of every single nuclear weapon that the Soviets had, or the Chinese had, or the Indians had, or the Pakistanis had — or the Israelis have.

They have weapons. It's the relationship that is much more important. I don't think the notion that you go after the potential building of a weapon as being the enemy, rather than the individual who has attacked us, should be the target.

Horton: So George W. Bush is kind of on an international gun control crusade.

Paul: In that way, he's assuming that it is the United States' responsibility. I give leeway to the argument that even in the Middle East, I am absolutely neutral there, and see that as part of our problem, that when we give weapons, and money, and guns, and munitions to Israel, that doesn't help us. That makes us less secure. But in the same sense, if Israel were to be an independent nation, not dependent on us, I would not complain a whole lot about it if they had decided to bomb the nuclear reactor in Iraq, like they did in the early '80s, saying, "Well, we're doing this for national security."

That to me is somewhat similar to our responsibility, and I thought Kennedy had the absolute right to confront the Soviets when they were 90 miles off our shores. That's getting a little bit close. Actually, I think that was resolved rather correctly — and I was called up into military duty during that time. It's that not only did he confront them, and say, "Don't mess around or you're going to have trouble." He immediately agreed to take the missiles at the borders of the Soviets. We took our missiles out of Turkey. So, in some ways, even at the time of 9/11, I had made the suggestion that we should look to Kennedy, how he resolved that crisis, rather than declaring war on everybody.

Horton: When and how should the U.S. military leave Iraq?

Paul: You know, there's no easy way. Even some of the people who opposed going in now say, "It's so bad, and it'll be so chaotic if we stay, and therefore we have to stay." And too many who opposed the war were the internationalist UN types, which I'm not, and it isn't easy. But the difficulty in getting out isn't my fault. The question is: Is it correct to get out? If it was wrong to get in, it's wrong to stay. I would literally get out as soon as I could, and just see what happens. There's so much chaos there now, and they say, "What do you want to do? Have us go back to Saddam Hussein?"

This idea that he was the most evil person in the world… Morally, he may have been, but the conditions that existed didn't happen to be the most evil. Right now — today — we heard four or five Christian churches being bombed. Christians can't even live in Iraq, yet under Saddam Hussein they were able to.

Horton: Yeah. So the question is, if we leave and Iraq splits into three, and they have a giant civil war and all that, you don't think there's a way that maybe we could set it up so that that doesn't happen, before we go?

Paul: No. Well, they're having a civil war now. We have created a civil war. It's the U.S. troops, and the troops we have hired, against the insurgents, and there's a civil war going on. So the civil war would probably continue. Yes, I think you could leave by saying, "This is what we're suggesting," and even draw the traditional line where the Kurds live, and say, "This is Kurdish territory, this is where the Sunnis live, and this is where the Shi'ites live in the south," but there's so much involved, there's no way our government — or the UN, or Kerry, or anybody else — would concede to that, because they really are giving up the loot. They're giving up this oil loot, and control of that region, so they're not about to do that, because they'd immediately say, "Well, there's going to be war up in the northern part with… The Kurds are going to have a battle with the Turks, and the Shi'ites in the south might align themselves with the Iranians," and to tell you the truth, that's always possible.

But I'm still not to the point where those difficulties would say that it's a good idea for me to send my kids over there, and have their lives taken for this fight. Just think of how those kids just yesterday felt when they decided they didn't want to take that truck on that convoy, where they thought they were going to get their hides blown up. Yeah, they didn't obey the law. They didn't obey a command — and they're supposed to, if you're in the military — but can you imagine how many members of Congress or in the administration would send their kids on that trip? That's the litmus test.

Horton: The soldiers called it a "suicide mission."

Paul: Would those neocons send their kids on that trip up there, hauling that fuel?

Horton: Congressman, the National Intelligence Director bill is now in conference committee. How far do the different versions go in altering the relationship between the national government and the individual?

Paul: You're talking about HR 10?

Horton: Yeah, the 9/11 Commission regulations bill.

Paul: Yeah, well, I have to confess. I don't know exactly what's going to happen in that commission. I didn't support the bill. I don't think either one's going in the right direction. I'm critical of the whole system that existed before, and I think once again, they're going in the wrong direction, just as they did after 9/11. Instead of going away from government dependency, they went toward more government dependency. I think on this gathering of intelligence, they're doing the same thing. They're making it bigger, and more bureaucratic, and some of the differences aren't as critical to me as the idea that both sides seem to be going in the wrong direction.

Horton: Well, the *Washington Post* and the *Toronto Star* reported that the White House had actually intervened to make sure that there was something in the House version legalizing the export of Americans to foreign countries to be tortured.[1] There have been reports of U.S. military and CIA "ghost prisons" on Navy ships in the Indian Ocean, bases in Central Asia, and as *Haaretz* reported last week, in Jordan. These prisoners are in a situation that's often described as a "legal black hole."

Paul: I wouldn't be surprised that some of that is coming. Much of this

---

[1] I do not know what this was a reference to, but it must have been overstated or misinterpreted. -ed

can come even with executive orders, just look at Abu Ghraib, or what happened there, and also in Guantánamo, these things happen. And they're pretty blatant about the national ID card in this. They're institutionalizing that, so we can all expect that our driver's license will be a national ID card from now on.

Horton: Isn't it Congress's responsibility to rein in the power of the executive branch?

Paul: Yeah, but for some reason, for 50 years the U.S. Congress has been derelict in their duties. There have been some of those individuals in the universities and elsewhere who say that it's only been one problem our last 20 or 30 years and that there has been too much power left in the hands of the U.S. Congress, which is exactly opposite of my belief, because I want very little power in the hands of the executive, and it usually gets out of hand, and Congress only wakes up when a lot of harm has been done, and then finally they realize they do have the control of the purse. But I think they've just been derelict in their duty, and they are reflecting a philosophy that's been taught to them by our public school system, as well as our universities and the prevailing wisdom — so-called wisdom — of our government and media.

They just pump this out, that we need a strong president, we need this. Just think of all the presidents they hold up as our great heroes, they're always the ones who want to undermine the representation in the Congress and build the power of the executive.

Horton: Yeah, and have a war somewhere overseas.

Paul: Right.

Horton: Well, after the House defeat of Charlie Rangel's conscription bill last week, do you think that there's much chance of it being revived?

Paul: Yeah, that was all a charade, and Rangel really was — I don't think he, deep down in his heart, is for that. He was just making that as one of those racial statements. He was antiwar, and whether there had been a draft or no draft, he would have just taken the opposite position, saying, "You know, there's racial strife in this country, and that's the basic problem." But yes, I think there's going to be a draft, because they're not going to change the foreign policy, whether we have Kerry or Bush. I think there's less likelihood to have a draft if Kerry wins, but neither side is against the draft. If they had been against the draft, if they did not endorse the principle of draft, they would have passed my bill to do away with Selective Service registration.

And some of those individuals who called that vote up and who were for that bill on the draft, actually also supported my bill to get rid of registration. That's what we ought to be doing.

Horton: Alright, hang tight one second Dr. Paul. [*Commercial break.*]

Sir, I'm sorry, when we went out to the break, I had to interrupt you at the end there, and you were saying that you think that conscription probably can't be avoided, as long as the American foreign policy doesn't change.

Paul: Yes, that's my belief. In time, that doesn't mean that there's going to be conscription in January, or February, or March, but we just don't have enough troops to maintain the foreign policy that both parties have endorsed. I hope I'm wrong on this, because maybe they'll come to their senses and decide that they don't need to take on Syria — and Iran, which I'm afraid that they're getting ready to do right now — and they just don't have the troops. Then if you have some type of a skirmish, or something breaks out in Korea, we just know they're not going to back away.

The presidents would think that they would be seen as just surrendering, and therefore they're going to call up a lot of troops. That's why it's so important to try to rally the troops in this country, and that means the American people, to the position that nonintervention, and a more peaceful foreign policy — and following the traditions of this country, and the Founders, and the Constitution — is the only out for us, to keep us from getting involved in so much more fighting and killing.

Horton: If the people's minds don't change, is there any chance that the American empire can run out of gas before it drives off a cliff?

Paul: Yeah, but we don't know when, and we don't know how much killing is going to happen before that occurs. The ultimate limitation will be the debt that we build up, and it is growing rather rapidly. And then the currency collapses. With both parties fully endorsing the entitlement system and the interventionist policy overseas, this is going to take us rapidly to a financial crisis, and then we run out of money. Other empires have done that before. They have to quit, because they can't afford to pay for it. We'll print the money for a long time. As long as the world accepts our dollar, we're going to continue to do it, and they're still taking our dollars, but not as readily as they were a year or two ago.

That's, of course, the reason why you've seen the gold price go up and the dollar go down, and oil prices going up. This is all related to our foreign policy, as well as our financial situation.

Horton: Dr. Paul, on your website right there on the front page is a video of a speech that you gave called "Can the Constitution Be Saved?" And it's a speech that you gave on the House floor, and you said something in that speech that I don't think many people often get a chance to hear, particularly, that liberty works. Is that your view, that from a strictly utilitarian point of view, principle aside, that individual liberty is really the best way to accomplish public goals?

Paul: I think that's what America has proven. We've been a great country. We still are. We still have a lot more freedoms than most. We're still very prosperous. What we have done, though, is undermine those basic liberties, and we have spent beyond our means. So, if we look to our history, and look to the principles that the country was founded on, we realize that freedom does work. The freedom that we've had in the past was imperfect, and there's no reason why it can't become better, instead of giving up on it, saying, "Well, it didn't work. People got poor and didn't get medical care, and we've got to solve the problems of the world."

Instead of saying that, say, "You know, maybe they were on the right track." We should concentrate on freedom, not only because it's morally correct that government shouldn't be telling us how to live our lives, and we don't have a right to tell other countries how to live, but for the very practical reasons that if you want peace and prosperity, you have to vote for liberty. Our big problem today is, if you ask President Bush and John Kerry if they're for liberty, or if you ask any member of Congress, how many of them would say, "Oh no, we're not interested in that anymore"? They say, "We are the champions of individual liberty. We are the champions of the Constitution and peace, and we just want to get rid of all the bad guys."

So their concept is quite different than the concept that I think the Founders had, and so many of us now, who have been trying to revive these ideas.

Horton: Sir, the last time we spoke, I asked you if there was any reason to have hope, since you were the only libertarian in the House of Representatives. I loved your answer, and so I hoped you'd answer that question again for us today. Is there reason to have hope for American liberty in the near future?

Paul: Well, my answer has always been, and hopefully it'll be close to what I said before. I tend to be an optimist in that there is hope, otherwise I wouldn't be in politics, and I wouldn't be running for Congress, and when I go around the country and talk on talk shows, and the people that you even reach, this is so much different than it was in the 1970s. We see the internet. The internet is just great. The Antiwar.coms, and LewRockwell.coms, and the various organizations, they're just great, so there's a large number of people — the Remnant, those individuals who were the true believers — I think the Remnant is getting very, very big, and yet it is not reflected yet in Washington.

You can't judge what's happening in the country by what's happening in Washington. Matter of fact, usually the opposite is happening. I think the country is way ahead of Washington, and there will be a crisis, it will be a financial crisis, but that's when we will be tested to find out if we have reached enough of the people, where the majority of the American people say, "Yes, what we want to do is have more liberty, not more dependency and government security." And that'll be the test.

Horton: Have you noticed people in Congress coming around to your point of view at all? People who were already there?

Paul: I think every day, at least behind the scenes, I get encouragement. I have a little committee called the Liberty Committee, and I have 23 members, and they at least want to identify with what I do. They don't hide from it. They don't vote with me all the time, but they do identify with me, and there's more and more people voting correctly, so it's slow but sure.

Horton: Alright. Everybody, Dr. Ron Paul. Thank you so much for coming on the show today, sir.

December 17, 2005

Horton: I want to go ahead and introduce my next guest. He's a leading voice for libertarianism and Austrian economics in the U.S. House of Representatives. His strict adherence to the Constitution has earned him the title "Dr. No" in Washington, D.C., and he's the author of the books, *Challenge to Liberty*, *The Case for Gold*, and *A Republic, If You Can Keep It*. Representing District 14 around Surfside, Texas, Dr. Ron Paul. Welcome back to the show, Dr. Paul.

Paul: Thank you. Nice to be with you.

Horton: It's great to have you on again, sir. I was researching about you and obviously mostly on this show I like to talk about foreign policy, the police state, gold money and that kind of thing. But I realized there's really not too much available on the internet about you personally and where you come from, and how you became the Dr. Paul that we all know and love. I wondered if perhaps you could tell you a little bit about where you come from and how you became a libertarian and that sort of thing.

Paul: My claim has always been, I must have been born that way, because I can't remember when it started. I think there were a lot of natural instincts for a lot of us, to just enjoy the fact that we ought to be left alone. But I think in some ways, that natural tendency was knocked out of me by public schools and public education and through college. It wasn't until I discovered Austrian economics, reading Hayek, and Mises, and Rothbard, and getting to Leonard Read at the FEE Foundation, that I realized that there were a lot of people who seemed to be writing about what I agreed with. I was delighted to find people I thought were very intelligent, defending the position I've held. All of a sudden, the whole philosophy came together.

I was born and raised in Pennsylvania in the Pittsburgh area. Went to college in Pennsylvania and then to medical school in North Carolina. While I was in my training up in Michigan after medical school, I was drafted into the Air Force and ended up in Texas and stayed in the Air Force for five years and then went back and became a specialist in obstetrics and gynecology and settled in Texas.

But because of the reading in economics, and more than anything else,

I, as a lark, ran for Congress in the '70s and didn't expect much to happen and was elected. Economics in the '70s were very tumultuous, with the breakdown of the Bretton Woods system and runaway inflation and stagflation that they had. It was giving me a chance just to talk about economics. I really was surprised I ever got elected. I've been in and out of politics ever since.

Horton: Now, when you were drafted, that was during the Vietnam era. You didn't have to go to Vietnam though?

Paul: No. I was called up. Actually, it was a little bit before Vietnam got really moving along. It was in the Cuban Crisis, which would have been '62. By the time I actually got into the service — the crisis didn't last that long, but I still had to stay. I was in for two years on active duty and then I stayed in the Reserve after that.

I was there up until I guess 1968 — '63 to '68 — but did not have to go to Vietnam. I traveled a lot as a flight surgeon to Korea and different places, but fortunately for me, I didn't have to go to Vietnam.

Horton: I guess you were lucky. You had already finished medical school before you got drafted, so you got to have a job where you didn't have to carry a gun, huh?

Paul: Yeah, that was interesting. I do remember World War II and Korea very well, because one of my teachers was re-drafted and went off and got killed. Even early on, I always knew that I couldn't shoot and kill people in war. I think it helped motivate me to go into medicine.

During World War II and Korea, it was just thought that we'd grow up and be drafted. And sure enough, I was, but I was determined that I would be on the medical side of it rather than on the shooting side of it. I think that helped push me in that direction and helped look into the libertarian views on foreign policy as well.

Horton: Not only did you end up being a flight surgeon and helping to save lives during your time in the Air Force, but after that, you became an obstetrician and now you help bring lives into the world. Quite the opposite of being a solider.

Paul: In many ways, I think it was. It had to do with my personality, I think as well as it fit the philosophy, too. It just never made any sense to me that we should be fighting so many of these wars. The more I studied it and studied the history and looked at what Wilson did with World War

I and how that led to World War II. It just is so much nonsense and so much foolishness. It's foolishness and so much death and destruction that need not be. It's just a matter of, I guess, trying to educate people and wake people up to our foreign policy. Hopefully, we'll make some inroads. Right now, though, we still have a lot of work to do.

Horton: This is an older conservatism that you seem to hold here. Modern-day conservatism has it that being a tough guy and kicking butt is more appropriate and more admirable, I guess, than anything else.

Paul: Yeah. The one really disturbing aspect of some of this modern-day conservatism is done in the name of Christian values, too. There was somebody on the House floor just the other day in this debate we had on a resolution yesterday, is that we had to support this position of continuing to fight in Iraq because of the Beatitudes, "Blessed are the peacemakers." And I thought, "What a distortion." They were claiming to hide behind the Beatitudes in support for this war of preemption and the war of aggression.

Horton: A war in which all the Iraqi Christians have been forced to flee.

Paul: That's right, that's right. What did we do? We turned the country over to — likely, it'll be that way — a radical Shi'ite theocracy aligned with Iran. We have the unintended consequences of the policies. Even if you want to try and give them the benefit of the doubt that they're well-intended, there's always the unintended consequences that seemed to be in opposite of what they claimed they were trying to do.

Horton: Iran is the big winner of the elections. That's the headline from the *Financial Times* this morning.

Paul: Yeah. It'll just lead one to another. Here, even yesterday, we had a vote on a resolution, just stirring up trouble with Syria. That's why I dwell not so much on just figuring out who to blame precisely for where we are at this moment, but to try to look at overall policy. Because even those who have become critical of the administration endorse what the administration wanted and gave them the authority. And now, they want to play politics and they blame him and the president for doing things.

At the same time, they're all endorsing the policy of interventionism and military force, and it looks like they're stirring up trouble with Iran and Syria.

Horton: You're absolutely right about that. Just in the last week, when George Bush gave his speech at the Woodrow Wilson Center, surely these are the people who blame him for not carrying out the war properly, I guess. But when it came to broad topics, in terms of preemption and democratizing the poor backwards people who need democratizing, there were standing ovations all around at the Woodrow Wilson Center.

Paul: Yeah, that can be pretty discouraging.

Horton: Something that you've often emphasized in your writings, in your speeches, is the relationship between foreign interventionism and big government here at home, the idea that we can't really have a Department of Homeland Security unless there's a foreign war going on so that they can say, "Hey, don't you know there's a war on?"

Paul: I think this is pretty much what has happened throughout history, if the wars are going on overseas, government forever grows at home, and abuse of civil liberties and excessive spending and inflation. It just seems like it's over and over again, and we're doing the same thing.

When I talk to groups, both conservative and liberal groups, I always acknowledge and say, "You may well disagree with me on this. But I'm going to win the argument. Not so much that I'm going to convert my colleagues here in the Congress about the foreign policy, but we're going to run out of money."

Eventually, empires just collapse, as did the Soviet system. They collapse because they can't economically be supported, and finally, they just run out of wealth. That's what will happen to us.

Horton: I think it was a rude awakening in my childhood to realize that most congressmen, really, they're just up there worried about their day-to-day and how they're going to get by and how they're going to make a million-dollar deal when they get out of office, and that kind of thing, as opposed to really being mindful that this is history in the making here. Every law they pass, every war they start, especially, this is the history of the world going on here.

When you say all empires fall, Dr. Paul, we all know that. From the time we're little children, we know that. If America stays a limited constitutional republic, it can last another five hundred years. If we go down the road of empire, we'll destroy ourselves. We all know that. Even little children understand this.

Paul: We still have a lot of naïve people in our country that still don't even understand that we're an empire. They still see us as doing this wonderful service to the world of spreading goodness and democracy through war. That's part of the educational need that we have, but some days I think it'll come before they even wake up and realize what's happening.

Horton: For the average person in my neighborhood to not really understand is forgivable. But for the Congress to not understand is unforgivable. These are the people who are responsible for the future of this nation. If they're driving us over a cliff and they're as ignorant about foreign policy and economics as my next-door neighbor, then what kind of hope do we have? If we've got maybe Ron Paul and his three or four friends up there who even understand how these things work.

Paul: It does sound rather dismal, but I think we also can look on the positive side that we're probably making more inroads than we did fifteen or twenty or thirty years ago. Washington doesn't reflect it, but with the use of the internet and certain radio programs, I think we are reaching a lot of people. The internet's been a real help to us.

I think the educational efforts are well in place and we don't have to worry about converting and educating 50 percent of the people. We just have to get more of the individuals who are in position to influence opinions, and our teachers — you know how the Mises Institute works in bringing about new teachers and universities. Those kinds of things are happening, so, in some ways, we should look on the positive things as well. Although, we better be prepared for the difficulties ahead, too.

Horton: Right. That's a really good point. They say there's, what, fifty neoconservatives and forty of them are newspaper columnists.

Paul: Yeah, that's it. If all the libertarians would've been in the position of the neocons… The neocons really proved the point. They had a philosophy and a belief, and they got a position of influence and they became very, very effective. How many people in the country even know what neoconservatism is? But because they were well-placed, they were able to use the propaganda machine and affect policy. Hopefully, our views will prevail, and we will have an influence on policy someday.

Horton: I really appreciate that optimism. I'm reading Justin Raimondo's biography of Murray Rothbard right now, *An Enemy of the State: The Life of Murray N. Rothbard*. He talks in there about all these different times where literally there was Murray Rothbard and a couple of guys at the Foundation for Economic Education. That was about it. They were the only libertarians in the entire country. They couldn't find a single journal to write a single article for. They were having to go and make alliances with extreme left-wingers and extreme right-wingers, and were trying to do something to go against the *National Review* grain. They had basically nothing.

It made me think, if Murray Rothbard was alive today and could see Antiwar.com and LewRockwell.com and Mises.org and see just the number of unique visitors a month going and exposing themselves to this kind of information, I think he'd be absolutely out of control with delight.

Paul: Oh, yeah. I think he would be. We have to make the best use of it, too.

Horton: Alright, everybody, I'm talking with Dr. Ron Paul. He's a Republican, although he may not sound like it from his antiwar stance. But it's definitely true. I want to save the PATRIOT Act stuff, I guess, until we get back from this break, because we have all kinds of new news coming out about the PATRIOT Act and the National Security Agency tapping Americans' phones and that kind of thing.

But I wanted to ask you real quick about the Republican Congress and how they seem to do just nothing but carry water for George Bush. I was talking with Jeff Deist, your aide, yesterday. He was telling me how basically they just issue resolution after resolution, just to browbeat the opposition, just to waste time and pass a resolution that says, "Anybody who disagrees with us is terrible"

Paul: That's right. If he needs a little bit of support, they put these resolutions in just to do whatever the president thinks he needs. But the other day, in one way, it backfired. The Democrats forced the vote on torture and accepting the Senate language, McCain's, in opposition to torture.

The Republicans, of course, didn't want this and they worked real hard. They couldn't win the vote, but they had 100 or so who voted to support torture. Then the next day, Bush changed his position and decided that he was against torture, too. All those Republicans were hanging out there trying to support Bush, and Bush deserts them.

Most of the time, it doesn't work that way. But we got a little bit of a chuckle out of there, because the diehards tried to help him, but it didn't work out very well.

Horton: Making a list and checking it twice.

Paul: Right.

Horton: Dr. Paul, big news yesterday, or, two days ago, I guess, about the defeat of the PATRIOT Act or major portions of it. I was wondering if you could tell us exactly what happened there.

Paul: What happened is when they brought the conference report to the House, it passed pretty easily. But when it got to the Senate, the filibuster killed it yesterday. But the president, this morning, had his radio message on this very issue, really chastising the Democrats and the few Republicans that supported the filibuster, and he was urging them to compromise and change it. Here it is, Saturday evening. We'll be in tomorrow, but I do not think they're going to be able to revive it. I don't think it's dead, but it sure is dying. It's a great issue. I have always argued that the American people finally did speak out. Think of all the resolutions sent up here. I kept thinking, "All these resolutions, if we have… members of Congress should respond." And, of course, the House did better. I think we had 17 or 18 Republicans vote against it this time. The first go around, we only had three Republicans.

So this is some progress there, although it doesn't look like it's going to pass in the next day or two, unless they pull up something tomorrow and have some type of a compromise on it and make us vote on it. But I'm afraid if they do get a vote, they might only get it where the sunsets are put back in there, and some of those horrible provisions are sunsetted for four years instead of seven or ten, which isn't a major victory. It's a minor victory, because in many ways, if something is bad… This is why I argue with these guys, is if something is so bad that you think it should be sunsetted, you shouldn't even be doing it at all.

But they say, "Oh, no. Well, it's bad, but we need it. We'll look at it again." That's a little bit better than not sunsetting, but not a reason why I'll support it, I'll tell you that.

Horton: Well, how many more days do you have before y'all come home for Christmas?

Paul: Right now, it looks like we'll finish by Sunday evening. Tomorrow evening, we should be done. There's still this possibility that it would come up.

Horton: Well, now, if there's any good news that could be mixed with this, it's the fact that the *New York Times* has broken the story about the National Security Agency spying on Americans.

Paul: Oh, absolutely.

Horton: That is, the military.

Paul: And that probably pushed three or four or five over into the filibuster anti-PATRIOT Act column yesterday and provided that vote, so that was a story that was very helpful.

Horton: Here's something they don't hear me say very often: Thank you, *New York Times*.

Paul: Even if they were a year late.

Horton: Yeah, they waited a year. They sat on this story for a year, and it turns out they had good timing when they finally did publish it, anyway. I saw Saxby Chambliss, a Republican senator from the South somewhere, I forget, on *Hardball* yesterday. He was saying that before the PATRIOT Act, they didn't even have the NCIC, the National Crime Information Center, and it was almost impossible for a police officer or an agent to type a name into a computer and find out if they were a terrorist or not.

And I thought, that's funny, because I think I first heard of the NCIC in 1995.

Paul: Well, that might tell you about the efficiency of government. Who knows?

Horton: Yeah, right? Yeah, maybe they proposed it then and they only got it in place more recently.

Paul: That sometimes is a saving grace, that they have a lot of bad desires, but maybe they'll never be efficient enough to do the harm they'd like to do to us.

Horton: Right. Is it your opinion, sir, that the executive branch had all the power they needed to fight terrorism before the PATRIOT Act?

Paul: Oh, sure.

Horton: Most people who oppose it say that, "Well, there are certain provisions of it that I don't like, but overall, it's not that bad."

Paul: If it would've been cut in half, I might have been able to support it. But most of the ones that they really want were totally unnecessary. What's the big deal about following the rules that we have followed before, and get search warrants and get a judge to look at that, and do it through a normal process instead of having torture and secret prisons and reject habeas corpus? All these things that they've gone through, and now spying on Americans. I'm afraid that that's just the tip of the iceberg. I think they've been doing plenty of that for a long time, but fortunately, this story did come out at a crucial time.

Horton: This also brings up the question of, what if the PATRIOT Act is dead, at least those parts that are scheduled to sunset on the 31st. If they do sunset on the 31st, can't the government basically just do whatever they want anyway, regardless of what the law says?

Paul: I unfortunately do think so. And the Congress is so complacent. We allow presidents to do what they want in foreign policy. How long's it been since they've declared war? And Congress is sort of, "Oh, you have a war going on. How much money do you need?" That's how bad they are.

And presidents, they're rather arrogant about it, too. "I'm going to do this. I will make the decision. I will decide when the war starts. I will decide on who will be spied on." In this case, we have to give credit to a lot of members of Congress who have finally perked up their ears to this story. I guess our views are somewhat alive. I hope we keep them well.

Horton: They're coming up on an election year, so all these House members who've been supporting the president no matter what, now, all of a sudden, they have their own interests to look out for. Hopefully, we can coerce them or compel them one way or another to erring on the side of liberty.

How many close allies would you say you have in the House of Representatives?

Paul: It's hard to say. I have the Liberty Committee and I have 22 members. About half of them are pretty darn good voters, but I tell people that everybody's an ally and nobody's an ally. It depends on what the issue is. When it comes to civil liberties and war, you know I work closely with Democrats. On economic policy, you have to work closer with Republicans.

Paul: The main goal is to get people out there in America sending messages to their members of Congress to come over and help me out on some of these issues.

Horton: Yeah, got that right. Alright, everybody, that's Ron Paul.

December 13, 2006

Horton: The Baker Commission has released their report providing a fig leaf for American withdrawal from Iraq. So far, all indications are that the president means to stay the course. Who decides? To help us answer that question today, Dr. Ron Paul. Welcome to the show, Dr. Paul.

Paul: Thank you, Scott. Good to be with you.

Horton: Good to talk to you again, sir. Yesterday on Antiwar.com your article was the Spotlight article. It's called, "Who Makes Foreign Policy?"[2] And I believe your point was there, sir, that the Constitution grants all legislative powers to the Congress and that the president's job is only carrying out what you tell him to do. Is that right?

Paul: That's basically the theme of the article I wrote. We have to start with pointing out though, the words "foreign policy" don't exist in the Constitution. So this whole idea that people say, "Oh, the Constitution gives the power of the president to run and do whatever he wants in foreign policy" — And, of course, the president, and this president isn't the first one to do it, they all assume they have this tremendous power. But if you read the Constitution carefully, it's up to the Congress to declare war, to ratify ambassadors and treaties. We're responsible for raising an army and dictating to the president. He is the commander in chief, if we decide there is a war to be fought, then he can maneuver and command the troops. But that's all that meant. But, to say that he has full control over foreign policy is completely wrong.

Horton: Well, now in the actual text of Article II, there are only two powers related to the president that have to do with foreign affairs at all, and that's the power to negotiate treaties, which don't have effect unless the Senate ratifies it, by supermajority. And he has the power, as you say, to execute the war once Congress has decided to have one, right?

Paul: Right. That's it.

---

[2] Ron Paul, "Who Makes Foreign Policy?" Antiwar.com, December 12, 2006, https://original.antiwar.com/paul/2006/12/12/who-makes-foreign-policy/.

Horton: Is there anything else in Article II? About his foreign policy powers, that I'm missing?

Paul: Not that I know of. If somebody else can dig them up, they can tell us. But, no, he has essentially very limited powers and the Founders were intent on making the president a weak president. And, of course, systematically from the very beginning of our country, there were always those who wanted to increase the power of the president. The Hamiltonians originally, very early on, wanted to do that. But I think that side is winning. The power of the executive branch has continued to grow. To me the most disturbing thing is not so much that the presidents have yielded to the temptation of using and wanting more power. It's the unbelievable willingness of Congress to give up their prerogatives, their responsibilities. It just seems like they go out of their way to diminish their importance.

Horton: Well, and that is sort of a common symptom of empires, right? As more power gets centered in the executive branch, the congressmen know that really their power comes from being close to the president, rather than standing their own ground against him?

Paul: Yes, and that was really the basic problem that's happened to the Republicans in these past six years and why the Congress got wiped out. They didn't stand on their own two feet, and they believe everything came from the president, the president was powerful and got all the attention, and it was all over and if you didn't support him, on the issue of war or all these great draconian pieces of legislation passed after 9/11, that they would be hurt in the polls. But lo and behold, by them pandering to the president and supporting him on everything, they themselves lost out as well as the president. The president couldn't be reelected today, he sort of snuck in his second term. But long-term it doesn't work, in the short run, it seems to help by pandering and following the party line. But I think the American people will eventually want somebody to stand up and believe in something and fight for those beliefs.

Horton: Now back to that commander in chief clause, quickly, where it says that the president shall be the commander in chief "when called into the actual service of the United States." According to Justice Department legal theorist John Yoo — or I guess former Justice Department legal theorist John Yoo — that means the president can do just about anything, as far as I know, probably up to and including abolishing Congress. Because he's the commander in chief. Is that not correct? During war time?

Paul: His interpretation is so broad, and so scary, that the commander in chief could do just anything by executive order. Of course, when he set up these prisons and started torturing people and carrying out all this surveillance on private American citizens, you know, fortunately the courts said that he's gone too far; that the commander in chief title does not give him this power.

And the courts rule reasonably well, and so what happens? The president comes back to Congress and the Congress is like a puppy dog. They concede to the president everything he had been doing and actually exempts the people in the executive branch from breaking any previous laws and they can't be taken, and in the bill, on the military commissions bill, they've actually said that this law can't be reviewed in the federal courts. That's yet to be tested, but no, that's a very dangerous interpretation. Every day it seems like we get closer and closer to a dictatorship. But I always remain hopeful that the American people will wake up and finally put their foot down and say enough is enough.

Horton: Do you have much hope that the new Democrat majority will repeal the Military Commissions Act, recently passed by the Republicans?

Paul: No, not a whole lot. Just as you'd think they would do something to curtail the war. But it looks like they're about ready... They said that they would vote for $160 billion in additional funding. So, no, I'm not too optimistic.

Horton: Well, I hate to say this, but it is the typical argument, and I'm sure you have an answer for it. Everything changed on September 11th, Dr. Paul. This is not the era of the 1900s when our oceans protected us. Now the terrorists can come and get us, and our president needs this kind of power to keep us safe.

Paul: The American people unfortunately bought into this and they believe that they can't be saved without giving up some of their freedoms and depending on the federal government; I've come to the opposite conclusion. The more freedoms you give up and the more power you give the president, the less free we are. I mean even 9/11 — You can argue from a freedom point of view, that 9/11 might not have happened if the airlines had been responsible for their property and their passengers, and had guns on the airplane, and really ran security like an armored car division might run their security.

I would say that the American people are naïve in believing that they are going to be a lot safer by giving up more of their liberties. That's like saying, "Aha! What we need to do now is totally get rid of our Second Amendment, and we're all going to be safer." But giving up our privacy and all the things that we do on airlines and how the government now monitors everything that we do financially, medically and on the internet, all effects law-abiding American citizens. If you happened to be a terrorist, it wouldn't take you very long to work around these restraints. We punish the American people.

It's the old saying that the conservatives have always said that, if you have gun registration and restrictions on gun ownership, you take the guns from the law-abiding citizens and you give them to the criminals who always have them. I think this is true on all this type of invasion of our privacy and this effort by the federal government to make us safe. So it's the loss of faith that the people have both in the free market economy, as well as taking care of themselves, that they become dependent on the federal government.

Horton: And then, your argument is that leads to even less security in the end?

Paul: That's right. You end up with less freedom and less security. And I think that's where we are today. Because although there haven't been any attacks on us by terrorists domestically, every day we have attacks on our people, because we're in their backyard. Why should they worry about coming over here, where they can undermine us over in Iraq and Afghanistan? They're delighted to have us over there and bleed us. I don't think the Iranians could get a better deal than what they've gotten. Where they have us over there, they're not directly involved — indirectly, probably — but the al Qaeda and the different groups who would like bleed us, are delighted with us being there and weaken us. And of course, making us financially in much worse shape.

Horton: Well, clearly you didn't support the invasion and don't support the occupation of Iraq. What would be the proper way for a president to handle September 11th in a libertarian, Jeffersonian fashion, rather, than a George Bush one?

Paul: It's always tough to solve a problem that was created by conditions that we would have never endorsed. But once it's happened and you say, "Well, can you do nothing?" Almost, almost you could. I had no objection to go after the head of al Qaeda, once it was decided the al Qaeda was responsible for the attack. Take out the head guy and go after Osama bin Laden. But not to invade and occupy a country and take over Afghanistan and going into Iraq was completely foolish and had nothing to do with it.

But to target one individual... I even suggested why don't we look at the letter of marque and reprisal and get a small group of people all the authority to go and do that.

Horton: Well, and for people who don't understand, what exactly is a letter of marque and reprisal?

Paul: Well, in the original day — I think Jefferson used this a good bit — they used this against pirates. Instead of having a strong navy and going out and making attacks and settling these disputes when these ships were being attacked on the high seas, the Congress could write a letter of marque and reprisal and give a certain group or a ship, or an individual authority, in the name of our government, to go and attack and destroy certain individuals. So it was very limited, it wasn't presidential, it was by Congress. They saw this a way of taking care of an enemy, without having to declare war.

And this to me seemed like an opportunity for that, because this was a stateless attack on us. We can't declare war against Afghanistan. I mean Pakistan was as friendly to the Taliban and to Osama bin Laden, and they're probably still harboring them. But we didn't declare war against Pakistan, and we shouldn't have occupied Afghanistan. So it would be a limited answer. But there's a lot of other things that we could do. I was drafted into the military during the Cuban crisis, and everybody said that it was a total victory for us, because we stood tough. And I think we did, and it was probably quite proper, we had nuclear missiles pointed at us from Havana.

But the one thing that Kennedy did, he went and talked to the Soviets behind the scenes and said, "What do you want?" And they said, "We want those missiles out of Turkey." And the American people would have been furious at the time if they had known that Kennedy agreed. He said, "Alright. You take your missiles out and we'll take ours out of Turkey." So, in one way, why couldn't we have talked to these guys? What's your big beef? Well, our biggest beef is that you have military bases on our holy land and in Saudi Arabia. Fine, that doesn't sound like a wise thing to do, we're coming home, and just agree to it and get out of there.

Instead, we did the opposite, even though we did close the base down in Saudi Arabia, we decided to build an embassy that's going to cost us a billion dollars in Baghdad, and build fourteen more major bases, right in their holy land. And Iraq is considered Muslim holy land as well. So we should have changed our policy, told them what we were going to do, come home. Also, at the same time you could have, in a very limited way, gone after Osama bin Laden. Possibly Tora Bora would have come out differently. Instead of walking away from that and going into Iraq, maybe that would have ended that, and then it would have been a good excuse to say, "Hey, look. We took care of everybody who attacked us, and now we're going to have a different foreign policy."

Horton: Well, now, if we had declared an actual war, because you said the letter of marque and reprisal was an alternative to declaring war in the Constitution. But, of course, what Congress decided to do in the case of Afghanistan and Iraq, of course, is to pass an authorization for the president to do what he wants.

Paul: Right — and that is where the real problem comes. On the resolution giving the president power to go into Iraq, Congress was ducking their responsibility, but they gave two reasons for it: that Saddam Hussein was a threat to our national security — which was an absolute joke, misinformation, and possibly a lie — and the other one was to enforce UN resolutions, because they claimed Saddam Hussein wasn't following the UN resolutions. Of course, there's been other countries that have not followed, but nothing seems to happen. But the irony there was that we were unilaterally enforcing a UN resolution against Saddam Hussein and when the UN was asked about supporting this enforcement, they said no they wouldn't do it. So here we are, using an international body to enforce one of their laws that they themselves didn't care whether it was enforced or not. So it doesn't make a lot of sense.

Horton: Well, and you said before the war, that this is what Osama bin Laden wants. That was part of your reasoning for opposing it, back in 2002. Is that not right?

Paul: Yeah, we couldn't have done him a bigger favor. I think the success of the planes was far beyond what they expected. And then, our response, was more than they expected. They probably figured we would do like Clinton did, bomb a few places. But the fact we literally took over two countries, this fell into their lap. Now their recruitment is way up, and we're doing what the Soviets did, and what finally bankrupted the Soviet Union, and may well bankrupt us, because by now, I don't see an end coming to this. Ironically, it's more likely we're going to send more troops than less troops, even after the Iraqi Study Group's report.

Horton: Dr. Ron Paul, thank you very much for your time today, sir.

Paul: Thank you. It was great talking to you.

Horton: Alright. Take care.

April 3, 2007

Horton: Alright, a very special guest today on *Antiwar Radio*: Doctor Ron Paul, congressman representing District 14 in South Texas and new presidential candidate — although that's all I can say about that because Antiwar.com is a non-profit and the government has rules about such things. But we can talk all about what Dr. Ron Paul believes and that's really what I'm interested in anyway, so welcome back to the show Dr. Paul.

Paul: Thank you, Scott. Good to be with you.

Horton: You have the most consistent antiwar record of any congressman from either party. If one goes back and reads your speeches from years and years ago, they're just the same as the ones today, taking the strict antiwar position. This is obviously due to the fact that you have some very strong principles about such things. So, Dr. Paul, what are your first principles of American foreign policy?

Paul: Well, first I think it's in our best interest to mind our own business, provide for a strong national defense, and stay out of the affairs of other nations. I don't believe in internationalism of this sort where we go to war under the United Nations. Those are my personal beliefs, but at the same time the most important promise I make is the promise to uphold the Constitution. If you read the Constitution carefully, we find out that there is no authority to do those things. So I personally abhor getting involved when we don't need to be and getting in wars that are unnecessary. At the same time, we're told that we're not allowed unless there's an explicit declaration of war, and since World War II we've totally ignored those guidelines.

Horton: And now, I think probably the mainstream policy establishment would say that that makes you an "isolationist" then, is that right?

Paul: Yeah, well, they use that term all the time and they do that to be very, very negative. There are a few people in the country who say, "Well that's good, I sort of like that term." I don't particularly like the term because I don't think I'm an isolationist at all, because along with the advice of not getting involved in entangling alliances and the internal affairs of other countries, the Founders and… It's permissible under the Constitution is to be friends with people and trade with people and communicate with them and get along with them but stay out of military alliances.

The irony of all this is they accuse us, who would like to be less interventionist and keep our troops at home, as being isolationists, and yet if you look at the results of the policies of the last six years we find out that we're more isolated than ever before. I claim the policy of those who charge us with being isolationists are really diplomatic isolationists. They're not willing to talk to Syria, they're not willing to talk to Iran, they're not willing to trade with people who might have questionable people in charge — we have literally isolated ourselves. We have fewer friends and more enemies than ever before, so in a way it's one of the unintended consequences of their charges. They are the true isolationists, I believe.

Horton: The original term for it, back in the 18th century, was "independence," right?

Paul: That's right, and it's a much better term, but they don't want to use that. It really probably came out in World War I and World War II, when there was a drumbeat to get involved in wars even then that were unnecessary, so they had to paint those who didn't want to go as being somewhat unpatriotic and isolationists and not caring about the world.

Horton: I'd like to get your criticism of the Bush Doctrine as it stands, its three main sections: preemption of threats before they occur in order to prevent catastrophes like what happened on September 11th; unilateralism and doing what America thinks is right regardless of international opinion and the United Nations; and then third, obviously, being regime change and deciding who is fit to run other people's countries.

Paul: Right, and of those three, the one that I talk about the most, and I think is the most dangerous, is preemption. We've been involved much more so than we should have been for many, many years — even before World War I — for over one hundred years we've been doing way too much. Our CIA has been involved on numerous occasions, even in the 1950s, getting involved with overthrowing the elected leaders in Iran. But, today it's much more blatant and it's not sort of backdoor stuff. It's not sneaky. It's not using the CIA secretly to get us involved when we shouldn't be. It's a blatant, open, declared policy: "Well, if we think it's in our best interest and we don't like them, we should go and start the war."

That's what preemption is all about. We have never been so bold as to say we should start wars and at least we have pretended we weren't involved in starting wars. So I think that is the most significant and most dangerous change in our foreign policy.

I think unilateralism is a tricky term, because in some ways militarily I'd just as soon be unilateralist. But I think that if you are a unilateralist in your military, but you are willing to talk with people and be friends with them, it would be a more natural internationalism. Of course, that would require an international sound commodity standard of money, such as gold or silver, which would allow much more conducive trade with everybody. Going it alone, at the same time bragging about being the powerhouse, and saying "If you don't listen to us we can take you on," I think is very, very, very dangerous.

The other one is very tempting, and that is a lot of American people succumb to the temptation of saying, "Well, when you really have a bad guy, we have to get rid of him because he might become worse." So they get tempted and they support this idea of "We've really got to get rid of a Saddam Hussein, or an Ahmadinejad" without seriously thinking that through. Because in some ways I think it's a disaster. Here, Bush says, "Well, that boiled down to, well, we got rid of this really, really bad guy. We got rid of Saddam Hussein, and that means it's worth it." That means Saddam Hussein, that one person, was worth 3,200 American deaths and 25,000 casualties. I don't think the guy was worth that much. He wasn't going to attack us, so I think he put way too much value on Saddam Hussein, insisting that we have to have regime change.

When we know that a certain regime is powerful enough that it might do some harm to us, all of a sudden, this noble goal of getting rid of bad guys doesn't exist. We didn't go after Stalin and we didn't go after Mao Zedong in China, and Pol Pot, we just let them be, and, of course, even today we deal with a lot of bad people. So that is just a pretense for the American people, once we say, "Well, we've got to rile the people up to go get rid of Saddam Hussein," when in reality they're probably thinking more about the oil than they are about Saddam Hussein.

Horton: September 11th did reveal an actual threat to the lives of American civilians that must be faced one way or another. I wonder if I could get you to address the War on Terror, specifically if possible, in a context of you being a conservative, Christian, Texas Republican, and whether you think September 11th heralded the "clash of civilizations" and a real long-term struggle that America needs to win victoriously, or whether you think this is the kind of thing that could be settled by other means.

Paul: I think there is a pretty significant clash, but I think very few people in America understand that because they have been told so many lies about why they want to attack us here, and why we have to go over there and fight them over there so we don't have to fight them here. I think that is so misleading. I think the whole mess in the Middle East started many, many years ago — hundreds, a thousand years ago — where the fighting was going on between Christians and Jews and Sunnis and Shi'ites and Persians and it's just been going on forever. In recent years, I see this as a civil war within the Muslim world, the Shi'ites and the Sunnis. We'd prop up Sunni governments around the world, and those Shi'ites would then like to attack us. So the War on Terrorism is real, and there is a clash, but I think we would be out of danger if we would have never imposed our will on them by going over there and being in their face.

I happen to believe most everything that Osama bin Laden wrote about why they attacked us, and it was nothing more than blowback for our policies over there, having bases in their holy land. I think we would be a lot better off if we just had a more neutral policy and the War on Terrorism probably would fade. Zawahiri has been reported as writing in an email that he hopes and prays that we don't leave Iraq, because it is a very good thing for them to rally their troops and motivate their fighters and recruit suicide bombers. If all of a sudden, we would leave, it would be very detrimental to their policy. I believe that is the case and I'd like to hurt their policy by leaving.

Horton: And when you talk about American forces occupying the Arabian Peninsula as Osama bin Laden's motivation, that's not to justify what he has done, just to explain it, right?

Paul: Well, yeah, I think that is the explanation. He had some other reasons, but that was the biggest one — the fact that we had military bases in Saudi Arabia. The other thing is some people think that, "Boy, I think we actually closed that base down in Saudi Arabia," but then we invaded two other Muslim countries as well. We are in the various countries like Kuwait and all around on the Arabian Peninsula. The whole peninsula is, to them, holy land. This provides a tremendous motivation for them to come after us because they see us as attacking them. Whether or not we are involved in a clash, or whether or not we're over there really taking them on, doesn't matter, because probably 90 percent of the Muslims believe we are over there for the wrong reasons and that we are out as an enemy of the Muslim people. Therefore, it serves as a motivation for them to be continuously willing to attack us.

Horton: Besides ceasing poking the hornet's nest, what is to be done about the followers of Osama bin Laden as they exist already today?

Paul: Our policy now creates more, not less, of them. Immediately after 9/11, I was supportive of the authority to go after those responsible. Of course, those truly responsible were all dead — the 19 — were dead. It certainly didn't mean that we should go into Iraq. It meant that we could go after Osama bin Laden himself, but we should have maybe taken a closer look at Pakistan and Saudi Arabia if we were really looking for the source of our problems. Unless we change our policy, we are going to have a difficult time solving this. I just don't think that our administration has been willing to look at it objectively, and there's too many other factors involved.

Horton: What sort of changes to our policy towards Saudi Arabia and Pakistan do you have in mind?

Paul: Just leaving them alone and not propping their governments up. I thought it was rather amazing that King Abdullah in Saudi Arabia announced that we were occupying unnecessarily and dangerously the country of Iraq. That to me is pretty amazing, the fact that Saudi Arabia is actually talking to the Shi'ites in Iran. I think they should sort this out. I think we should come home. The Arab League over there could solve a lot of those problems. Israel is willing to talk to Syria and we interfere with that negotiation. I think if we weren't there, Israel would have a much different motivation to talk to moderates over there. If we have Sunnis and Shi'ites talking to each other in spite of us over there trying to stir up this hornet's nest… I would think if we left, there would be a great deal more willingness on the part of these factions to talk to each other. It would be far from peace and tranquility, but look at what it's like since we've been there.

I think the most important thing is to come home. People say there still could be some chaos; if there is chaos, it's because we went in there and messed things up. There wasn't nearly this type of chaos before we went in. Our answer should be what is best for America. We shouldn't pretend that we can nation-build and pick regimes and make all these decisions and pretend that we are the policemen of the world. That is where the big mistake has been. It is going to contribute to a major bankruptcy of this country.

Horton: Now when you talk about the interests of America, it seems often that what takes precedence over the interests of America, is the interests of certain Americans, say, for example, stockholders in some of the military-industrial complex corporations. William S. Lind for example has characterized Washington D.C. as merely an "imperial court" where there are so many people sucking off of the United States Treasury and pushing these policies that are bad for America as a whole, but good for them in the short-term, that it is almost impossible to have it undone. We know how much it takes to run for office — a lot of money — and only rich people can afford to bankroll politicians and it seems more and more rich people have their interest in sucking off of the U.S. Treasury, rather than having a free enterprise system where they can make their ends their own way.

Paul: I think the money tells you a whole lot. The fact that some of these candidates will be able to raise $100 million to run their campaigns tells you that as far as companies are concerned it's a good investment. A Halliburton has a lot of incentive to pump in money to the campaign. What about a drug company who gets monopoly control over sale of drugs? They must think it's a good investment as well. There are many companies involved in the military-industrial complex. The real evil isn't the spending of somebody's own money to help a candidate. The real evil is the fact that the government is so big and has so much to auction off, and there is such an incentive and there are so many benefits by being friendly to the people who are in power, that government is bought on a continuous basis.

The big question is whether the American people will wake up and try to combat this or will they just go along with another candidate who has a lot of this money and can put some fancy ads on television. Hopefully, a few people will wake up one day.

Horton: If we can switch gears here a bit to worries about a war with Iran. You may have seen the headlines this morning: "Washington Hurting British Bid to Free Crew." The Iranians have captured fifteen British sailors and marines and apparently the United States is interfering in their negotiations with the Iranians to get these sailors back. Your comment, Dr. Paul?

Paul: I guess we shouldn't be surprised because it seems like the neocons have always said, and I guess they believe, that chaos is a benefit to them. Out of chaos they can gain a certain edge. They don't want the Israelis, like I said, to negotiate with Syria. They have to paint them in a certain fashion. They don't want this thing to be settled too easy with Iran because we are looking for an excuse to go in there and bomb them, and cause chaos there, and have regime change. So it to me is a real mess, and the Iranians, at least, I think would be a lot more reasonable in their dealings with the British. But hardly anybody is talking about the five hostages that we hold, the diplomats from Iran that we picked up. There are some who believe this is nothing more than retaliation for us holding their diplomats, and that's compounding the problem with the British. Unless the British can talk the United States into releasing those diplomats, they are going to have more trouble getting their fifteen men back.

Horton: And it may be a portent of things to come in Iraq. Perhaps a warning from Iran, look how easy it is for us to get at your guys. This is what is to look forward to if you do bomb us.

Paul: Yeah, I think that is the case. They're not stupid. Our reaction would have been a lot different if they would have captured fifteen Americans. They're picking on a softer spot. Blair speaks tough, and wants to do whatever Bush tells him to do, but I don't think the British people are nearly as supportive of Blair as Blair is of Bush.

Horton: There was a provision in a recently passed authorization for funding of further war, which included the "benchmarks" and time tables and so forth, and that provision basically, I believe, reminded the president that he does not have the authority to initiate a war with Iran, and yet Speaker Pelosi took it out. What does that reveal about the Democrats' leadership? The Democrats who were elected to their majority in the House and the Senate by an antiwar American population last November?

Paul: I think it shows that they're trying to appease the antiwar position at the same time I don't think they are truly antiwar. You look back to 1998 it was Clinton who signed the Iraq Liberation Act into law, which was to have regime change in Iraq. As bad as this administration has been, these plans have been in place for a long time. The removal of this is really pretty sick. First, it seemed like it should be unnecessary because it should be automatic that a president can't go to war and start bombing another country without permission, but under the conditions of today, everybody realized that he might. So to put that in seemed reasonable, as a matter of fact, it was a bill that I was an original co-sponsor of that we attached to the budget deal.

But the explicit removal of this is almost like saying to the president, "We really don't care. We are not going to tell you that you are not allowed." To me that looks so bad, and it's something that indicates that the president probably is going to have a free ride. If the excuse is there, I am afraid the bombing and the attack on Iran will happen, and unfortunately if the incident that precipitates our bombing is strong enough, the American people, unfortunately, will probably go along with it.

Horton: What do you think the likely consequences of an American war against Iran might be? We talked about their ability to get at our guys in Iraq. What else do you foresee as likely consequences if we do start another war?

Paul: Probably $200 per barrel for oil, and four to five dollars for gasoline. That is one economic consequence. I think it will mean that a lot more of our men are going to be killed in Iraq and there will be a call for doubling the number of troops over there. Before you know it — although, there are no plans right now for us to invade Iran — somebody will say, "Well, let's not be hamstrung, we can't let them hit us and run back over into Iran." They will have to send a lot more troops over and that's going to, who knows what it will do after that, how this war might spread. Right now, we have ups and downs. Today happens to be a down day. That is, there is probably not as much friction right there now, in hopes that the British and Iranians will work something out, but that could change within hours.

Horton: Of course, bombing Iran and perhaps even changing the regime there is exactly what Osama bin Laden would want us to do, isn't it?

Paul: Boy, that's for sure. We tend to want to get rid of their enemies. We've fallen in the trap of supporting Iran. We got rid of the Taliban, so we have helped the Iranians, and Osama bin Laden has been helped in his recruiting. The al Qaeda was pretty weak six months, a year, after 9/11, but it looks like they're getting all their strength back. The motivation is that our troops are in the various countries over there. So far it looks like we're in for a long fight. I am not so sure that we are all of a sudden going to have a change in policy, but I do think there is a chance that this country will become so poor over the dollar crisis that we won't be able to afford this empire anyway.

Horton: Dr. Paul there's a story that has been very little covered, and it's something I was hoping you could help explain: the John Warner Defense Appropriations Act that was passed last fall, the same day, I believe, as the Military Commissions Act, apparently changed the authority over the state national guard units and gives the president power to nationalize them without seeking the permission of the governors. The state governors' association sent a unanimous letter signed by all fifty governors protesting this, and yet, apparently, they've lost the fight. I wonder if you can tell me if I have characterized that accurately and what that might portend for our federal system.

Paul: I'm not sure, but that may be related to the changes that occurred in the modification of the Insurrection Act, which means that the president can call all these troops up at will. It doesn't even have to be a military confrontation, or a real insurrection. It could be a big flood someplace; the president could actually do this. I believe it is also related to the modification in the Posse Comitatus Act, which means the president has a lot more authority to declare a national emergency and actually impose martial law. It has gone through, and those changes have gone through subtly and quietly. Long-term, this is not very good for us as citizens, not very good for the principles of the republic.

Horton: And it does reveal, doesn't it, that principle that war is the health of the state, that while we have an overseas empire our domestic government grows bigger and bigger as well.

Paul: That's probably the most dangerous part of it. When you look at all the laws that have been passed domestically, everything from the PATRIOT Act to the Military Commissions Act. The whole works, the idea that we can be monitored, everything that we do, warrantless searches, and another very, very serious change is this attitude about habeas corpus — the fact that we can be held as an American citizen without getting into court as a suspected terrorist. As long as we're a suspected terrorist, we don't have any rights left. Although that has been not used so much with American citizens as of yet — although to a slight degree, once that principle is established it's very hard to reverse — it's very dangerous.

Horton: And we've seen kind of the farcical nature of the Guantánamo Bay tribunals, when this man David Hicks, who has been in the news for years and years because he is an Australian citizen, a state that is closely allied to us. They made a plea bargain and gave him nine months. So how dangerous could this terrorist have been all this time?

Paul: Well, our courts are politicized. The sooner we close down Guantánamo, though, the better. I don't know how you can solve that mess down there. That is just so un-American.

Horton: Do we give these men trials in American federal courts, Dr. Paul?

Paul: I don't know the full details of every single person they ever captured, but there has to be some type of a court, whether it is a military court, or a court here. I guess a crime committed in another country, I don't know whether that means you can bring them here and justify it, but there has to be something better than secret courts and secret holdings and extraordinary renditions and having prisons all around the world. That process has to end.

Horton: Dr. Ron Paul, he represents District 14 in South Texas, a libertarian Republican congressman. Thank you so much for your time today, Dr. Paul.

Paul: Thank you, Scott. Good to be with you.

August 17, 2007

Horton: Ron Paul is here. He's a former Air Force flight surgeon, and an obstetrician by trade. He's a ten-term congressman from District 14 on the Gulf Coast. He's the author of the books *Gold, Peace, and Prosperity*; *The Case for Gold*; *Mises and Austrian Economics*; *Freedom Under Siege*; *A Republic If You Can Keep It*; and *A Foreign Policy of Freedom*. He's currently running for president of the United States of America. Welcome back to the show, Dr. Paul.

Paul: Thank you, Scott, nice to be with you.

Horton: It's so good to have you back on the show, and I have to tell you, we're all very excited about all the hype. I don't know what else to call it, all the thousands and thousands, maybe millions, of people who are being turned on to the message of liberty, due to your recent efforts. I guess my real question is in terms of your presidential campaign so far is, are you having fun?

Paul: It is. It's really rewarding to know that there's so many people interested. I'd like to take all the credit for it, but to tell you the truth, I think there have been a lot of seeds planted over the last decade or two to get so many people interested, but now that we're getting some attention for this message, it's very, very pleasing to find so many new people willing to come in. Sometimes it's young people bringing in their parents and vice versa, so it is really exciting.

It is a tedious job, but we've been at this before, and it's always been at a much lower key. Since I've been doing this for thirty years, we've never quite seen the interest expressed by so many people. I think the internet has a lot to do with that, and, of course, talk shows. Radio is helping out a whole lot, and maybe one day we will get the mainstream media talking about freedom and the Constitution.

Horton: Well, as far as spokesmen for individualism and liberty and limited government in this country, you are the best of them, and you shouldn't sell yourself short. It has a lot to do with the messenger, and people can tell that you mean what you say, and you're consistent. You follow the principles that you preach, and people can tell that you really mean it. That's why they take you so seriously.

Paul: Well, thank you.

Horton: Now, let's talk foreign policy. The last time we spoke, you mentioned repeatedly that the costs of the wars were going to come back and haunt us. Is that what's beginning to happen now?

Paul: Yeah, I think so. Those of us who remember very clearly the '60s and the '70s — of course, I was in the Air Force during the '60s — and back then Johnson reassured the public, in that he said that it doesn't matter; you can have guns, and you can have butter. In other words, you can run a huge military operation and a welfare state and expand it, and don't worry about it.

Well, he was completely wrong, because the '70s were very, very hectic, and we had a lot of inflation. We had a very weak economy, and the dollar was on the ropes and was rescued at the end of that decade, barely, but all the metals and commodity prices were soaring. Then, things have settled down, but once again, in the last ten years we've been back at it again. I mean, conservatives have been elected to cut back on the size of government, and government keeps expanding. The entitlement system is exploding.

And now we have this ongoing war in several places, like both Afghanistan and in Iraq, with the threat that it may spread to Iran. The markets now are starting to react, because we have paid for it temporarily by borrowing money and by inflating. That is, literally, we have permitted our Federal Reserve to create money to buy Treasury bills in order to pay these bills. But that doesn't work. That's just a delay in payment. The eventual payment comes when the dollar gets weak, and prices go up, and markets get shaky, and we're starting to see the beginning of a real, real serious shakeout, with the nervousness that we're seeing on Wall Street today.

Horton: Do you remember in 2002 the deputy secretary of defense testifying that the oil sales from Iraqi oil will pay for the war, the "revenue-neutral" war?

Paul: Yeah, and remember Larry Lindsey predicted how much money it might be, and his was a modest prediction. Of course, he got fired from the administration. And a general — I think it was Shinseki — said that we'd need a lot more troops if we really want to win. Of course, he got set aside. So anybody that tells the truth about the real cost of this war, whether it has to do with money or the number of troops or the quagmire that has occurred, you're not received very well. People don't want to hear the truth, if you're trying to do something that the American people actually don't understand or really don't want.

I think that it turned out like many had predicted. It wasn't like nobody was concerned and made predictions that this would be very costly, and that's what's coming about. I mean, the oil is not paying for it, and we're still there. Billions of dollars that we appropriated are still being spent. There's no end in sight.

Paul: They talk about 3,600 men and women killed over there, but another thousand contractors have been killed, and it's unknown how many wounded and sick we have. They claim maybe 30,000, but there could be twice that many, when you look at all the illnesses and the post-traumatic stress syndrome and brain injuries that aren't yet recorded. It is unbelievable what this cost is going to be, and it's endless, and yet there seems to be no serious attempt by anybody in Washington to change policy.

Horton: I'm so glad you mentioned the wounded soldiers. We've seen so many stories about guys with post-traumatic stress disorder told to drink a beer and chin up and be a man and quit complaining. We've seen articles about soldiers who are literally physically wounded, who are being told that they have some sort of personality disorder that disqualifies them from medical care. I know you're an opponent of socialized medicine, but these are American soldiers, who've done their duty and are wounded. It seems like the Bush administration is just turning their back on them.

Paul: Yeah, and this is a high responsibility of ours to take care of those men, so I don't put that in the category of socialized medicine. That's a responsibility, because our policies have caused these problems to occur. If something doesn't happen, these numbers are going to continue to grow. We just saw this week the statistics on suicide on military, higher than ever. This is something which I don't think is surprising. I'm surprised it's not worse, and it's not just being wimpish. It's the fact that governments ask their young people to do things that aren't normal.

If you take a normal individual that's a teenager or just past teen age and turn him into an individual that shoots and kills strangers that he never knew of or had never done any damage or threatened us, it contradicts everything that I think is natural to our psyche. And yet we do. We tell them that we do this in the name of patriotism and saving our Constitution and protecting our liberties. It's a schizophrenic type of operation, so this produces a lot of stress. In one sense, the government is saying you're a noble hero to go over and kill people. At the same time, they don't have it in them to do this, and because of that conflict, it leads to depression, which is not abnormal. It, to me, seems to be a normal reaction for decent people to become depressed over this conflict of interest.

Horton: Right, and then the government doesn't want to really acknowledge how bad the problem is with the post-traumatic stress and so forth because then they have to admit this is the results of their policy.

Paul: No, they want to hide it, just like they hid the Agent Orange problems that came out of Vietnam and the Persian Gulf War Syndrome was hidden for a long time, and veterans couldn't get treatment. Now, of course, there's a lot of depleted uranium floating around and lying around over in Iraq, and people are going to get sick from that. It might not be immediate, but maybe in five or ten years, and it'll be hard to measure, and the symptoms will be different for each one, and there'll be cancers caused by this. Our government will stay in denial, and yet we have these hundreds and thousands of people who will be suffering.

Horton: Which also brings up the question of our responsibility to the people of Iraq. It's our government that's covered their country. Our guys eventually, hopefully, will leave that place, but their country is going to be covered in depleted uranium dust for how long to come? The indefinite future.

Paul: It's morally reprehensible, but it poses a difficult solution. Do you further tax the American people that had nothing to do with the decision-making to pay for this and help these people that we've literally harmed? It would be nice if justice could be levied against those who promoted the war. You know, if you were a warmonger, and you promoted this policy that has led us to such a disaster, it'd be nice if we could require that they personally assume some responsibility, but that, of course, is an impractical proposal.

Horton: Sounds nice, though, sure does. You've said before, "We just marched in. We can just march out." You know the war party's talking point number one is that, "No, Dr. Paul, we cannot do that, because things will get worse." Do you think that that's right, that things will get worse, and you're saying that, well, we're not going to be able to make it better anyway, so if things get worse now, they'll still get worse if we leave ten years from now, or are you saying that there's a chance things will get better if we leave?

Paul: Well, I don't think anybody knows exactly what'll happen. Let's say we take the next six or eight months, and we just leave, because you can't walk out in one day, just physically you can't. Let's say we're out of there in eight months. We do not know exactly what would happen the year following that. One thing we do know is no more Americans would die, and that we would save a lot of money, and maybe there would be an incentive for the various factions in Iraq to come together and talk to each other.

People say, "Don't we have a moral responsibility to stay there forever, because we've messed it up? Now we have to protect these people from what we're doing." I think our presence there is the incitement for al Qaeda and the incitement for the civil war and everything else. My bet would be that things would get better, even though I wouldn't know exactly when that would happen. But I recall in the '60s all the predictions about how we can't possibly leave Vietnam, because there would be the domino effect, where the communists would take over, and China would rule the whole Southeast. Yet, the only thing that's happened in that area is that they have become more capitalistic. Not only Vietnam trades with us — and we visit with them, we invest in Vietnam — but the Chinese, it looks like they're learning capitalism pretty well. They're our bankers, so I guess they know something about buying and selling and lending.

So it never turned out like they predicted. Those who have these dire predictions of what will happen in Iraq are the ones that said that it would be a cakewalk, and that it wouldn't cost us anything. Why should their predictions be listened to? Why don't they go to those experts that claimed that this would not go well, the generals that advised against it? There were some people in the State Department. There were some people in the CIA. There were some people in the administration, in the finance area, that all said it was a dangerous thing to do. We should ask them what they think will happen if we leave, instead of just listening to those who proposed the war.

Horton: It also seems that the current policy is to arm the factions that are fighting in the civil war, the Iranian parties, and now arming the Sunni insurgency, rather than backing the nationalists, who are trying to work things out.

Paul: Yeah, and I think the weapons are multiplying. They're coming from all areas, and we want to be in the arms trade. We're promising more and more weapons over there, not only to all the Arabs, but to Israel, as well. You wonder about this whole idea that — Could it be that the military-industrial complex has a voice in this? Obviously, I think they do, because whether we're in there fighting, or repairing the weapons that we leave, or arming more and more countries, there's only one group that's really making a lot of profits, and that's the war industry.

Horton: You mentioned earlier the possibility of war with Iran, in terms of further economic consequences. It does seem that the accusations against that country are getting more and more serious. Is there some kind of congressional grapevine where you get the background chatter whether they really mean it this time? We've been really worried about impending strikes against Iran at a few different times over the past few years. Is this really it?

Paul: Well, we don't know. The people I've listened to, that I consider experts, claim that it'd be very difficult for them to believe it won't happen before Bush leaves. He may wait a little while longer, toward the end, but he just does not believe — I guess he has a conviction about this — he does not think he should leave unless he destroys these sites that he has conjured in his mind, where they're going to build nuclear weapons.

I don't have any inside information from the administration, but I just think, from observing what they do and what they say, and their beliefs, that it still worries me a whole lot that something will happen, but I can't say that it's imminent. I think that something has to galvanize the American people into support of it, and maybe they're waiting for some type of a major incident that they could blame on the Iranians. Every day, you read stories about why the Iranians did this, and the Iranians sent the weapons in, and the Iranians are teaching this. They have actually some people, and we, the Americans called them — "Oh, there are foreigners coming into Iraq," like they have a dozen or so. Yeah, I mean, I think they are interested in their neighbors.

It's sort of like what would we be doing if Russia was in Mexico? Do you think we'd have a legitimate interest in what was happening there? It seems to me like some of this would be very legitimate. Anyway, I think it's going to be twisted. I think eventually it'll be turned around, and there will be an excuse. Tragically, I think the American people will see this as a reason to rally behind the president and even impose the draft, because there sure has been a lot more talk in Washington about the draft.

Horton: Wow. So, you mentioned before, economic consequences. I wonder if I can get you to elaborate on what you think the economic consequences of war with Iran might be, and then, I guess, further consequences for our liberties here at home, including conscription.

Paul: Well, always when there's a war going on, it's the excuse to undermine our liberties here. Just look at what's happening since 9/11. The War on Terrorism and the war on Iraq has been an excuse to really practically destroy our Fourth Amendment and our total privacy. A war with Iran is going to just keep that going and continue to undermine our freedoms here at home, but I think financially it's going to be devastating. It will cost a lot more money. I don't think anybody thinks they can invade Iran. We don't have the troops. They'd have to draft another million people to do it, and they're running out of money. They'll run out of credit pretty soon.

Paul: I think the most significant event would be, if we attack Iran, they're capable — according to some of my friends in the military and in the CIA — they're capable of literally blocking the escape route for our 160,000, if not 260,000 if you add the contractors, out of Iraq. They can't fly all of them out very quickly, and they can't come out. They could be boxed in in the Persian Gulf. Then you're going to see oil not being $70. We went over there to secure oil, and, of course, oil is more than two times the price it was when we went in. I think if that would happen, I think overnight you'd see oil not only $100, but probably in not too long, it could go easily to $200 a barrel, which finally would catch the attention of the American people, what's happening. I just hope and pray they come to the conclusion that our bad foreign policy has led us down this path, and if we'd just wise up, we could change it all.

Horton: In terms of securing Middle Eastern oil, if we had a completely noninterventionist foreign policy, and the U.S. Navy was not in the Persian Gulf "securing" those shipments, if our government was not giving all these billions of dollars of weapons to the Saudis and so forth, would the price of oil be much higher? Do we need to have our government secure these oil flows for us?

Paul: I don't think so. I think probably the oil would come down in price, because even if the Iranians ended up with more control, their main goal would be to sell their oil. All of a sudden, Iraqi oil and Iranian oil would come onto the market in a much more plentiful state than it is today, so I think oil prices would come down if we walked away from there, maybe not the first week or month, but I think that's the way to get the oil prices down, is for us to get out of there. This whole idea that we have to secure our natural resources is a mercantilist approach to economics, that you have to have the natural resources, because they will never be bought on the market. But I don't think Japan sits around every single day and wonders where they're going to buy oil the next day. There's still a market out there. They'd probably go to Amsterdam and buy their oil from there. I mean, the oil gets up there.

The markets would handle this. No matter how powerful they are, the market is even more powerful. Remember in the 1980s, oil had gone up to $40, and then under Reagan there was some freeing up of the market, and people thought oil was going to $80. Well, it went down to $10, and OPEC used to meet every couple weeks, trying to drive the price up, but they couldn't do it. Even these cartels can't do it, if the market is allowed to operate. That's what would happen if we got out of there. The market would be much more operational, and I believe the oil prices would come down.

Horton: Now this is kind of a legal question here on the… Back to Iran specifically. The State Department has reclassified Iran's Revolutionary Guards as an international terrorist group. Could that possibly be used to put an attack against Iran under the original authorization to use force against bin Laden and the international terrorists after September 11th?

Paul: I think they wouldn't hesitate to do that, and they would use it. I think it would be very, very deceptive and immoral, illegal, still unconstitutional, and every member of Congress should be outraged for that stretch to decide that would be the reason they could go in and claim they have justification for it. There was one bill that was a supplemental bill a few months ago that we had. In that, Bush could not do anything against the Iranians without explicit permission of the Congress, and yet that was removed by the Democrats in the conference report, so even the Democrats did not want to leave that in there. That's why we haven't seen any significant change in policy, even after this last election.

Horton: Yeah, it's really too bad. I think a lot of people had their hopes up.

Paul: They were voting for change, but they didn't get it.

Horton: What's your assessment of the situation in Israel and Palestine? Can there be peace there in our lifetime?

Paul: I think there could be. The Palestinians and the Jews and other Arabs have a history of living next to each other and getting along. It seems like when outsiders come in and stir things up and send in weapons and pick sides and intimidate and take over their policies — I think our taking over Israeli policy is detrimental to Israel and certainly to us and to the Palestinians. I think if we weren't there, Israel would have a real incentive to get along with their neighbors.

They've had overtures towards Syria. They'd like a peace treaty with Syria. I think things would work out, but we get in the way. We say, "Oh no, you're not allowed to do that, and you're not allowed to do this with your borders." Israel has sold out their sovereignty to us, but they also are inhibited from doing the things in their self-interest. I think they would work with the Arab League. They talk to them, even now, but I think they would have an incentive for them to deal with their Arab neighbors. I mean, there's so many more Arabs, there's a self-interest in this. But once we get over there and start passing out weapons to both sides, it just distorts everything.

Horton: So you think if America stops intervening, rather than unleashing them against the Palestinians, making it okay, or basically giving them a blind eye of permission to expel the Palestinians from the West Bank or what have you, you think it would go completely the other way, that they would realize that, well now that America is not there to protect them, now they have all the incentive to really try to make peace?

Paul: Yes, and there's a lot of Israelis that would talk like we do about foreign policy, and that's the liberal party. I mean, if you say that here, or if a Jewish community group here talks like that, they're called un-American and anti-Israel and anti-Semitic. Yet, there's a large number of Israelis who would like to have peace. Matter of fact, some of their soldiers are refusing to fight. I mean, they're tired of it all. They're being drafted, and they're sent down there to try to settle these disputes between the settlements and the Palestinians. They just know it's a real mess. I think that'd be a great incentive, and we would probably hear more from those who do not support the militant approach, and we'd hear more from the liberal party in Israel on what they would like to have done.

Horton: Dr. Paul, it seems like the promise of a new friendship with Russia at the end of the Cold War is fading away. What's happening?

Paul: Well, it seems like some people didn't want to really have peace and friendship with Russia. Our whole policy, once again, of going right up to their borders and putting anti-ballistic missiles up there and claiming that we're protecting Europe and the United States from Iran, I mean, nobody believes that. We just are provoking problems with Russia. They're no angels, but we aren't especially angelic either.

I think this whole principle of noninterventionism means that we shouldn't provoke people. We shouldn't. We don't need anti-ballistic missiles on the borders of Russia. If the Europeans think it's worthwhile, let them do it, but they're a lot less worried about it than we are. I would think that they would not want us there, because if we provoke the Russians, they're in between us. I have no idea what they think is a good reason to be antagonistic to the Russians, other than if you're totally cynical. Some people like cold wars, and sometimes hot wars, because they keep the weapons industry flowing.

Horton: Yeah, well, let's hope they don't make a war with Russia a hot one. They still have tens of thousands of nuclear weapons, right?

Paul: Right, they do. We essentially won the Cold War without a military confrontation. That's why I think it's so silly that some people think that we have to militarily confront people because they're a danger to us, and they don't even have a weapon. They used this as a reason to go into Iraq. It was just obscene what they were trying to make us believe, and they're doing the same thing with the Iranians.

Horton: In the news this week, Russia and China are doing joint war games. Do you feel like American foreign policy is pushing them together, healing that old Sino-Soviet split?

Paul: I think so, and I wouldn't be surprised if India and some other countries, and, of course, Southeast Asia, too, Kazakhstan, and the other "stans" in that region, won't be joining there, as well. Once a giant gets on the ropes, our influence can dwindle quickly, and that will affect the value of the dollar. The dollar is artificially held up, because we're the economic and military power, but as we weaken, as our economy weakens, and as our military weakens because of these protracted wars, I think you'll see more of the alignment with Russia and China and other countries getting together and saying, "You know, we're sick and tired of America telling everybody what to do."

I think the whole process will be reversed, because I think we get some free benefits because we have that position that we are the only superpower. After a while, people get tired of that. That would be very detrimental to us, and even more injurious to our freedoms here at home.

Horton: Well, we already have a proxy war in Somalia, and there's some who want to intervene in Sudan. I've seen in interviews, where you've pointed out before, it's funny how those are two African countries that have oil resources there. Of course, some have written that that's the real goal there is to try to keep those resources out of the hands of the Chinese, but I guess what you're saying is it's much more expensive to do all this intervention than to just let the Chinese produce it and sell it to us.

Paul: Yeah, that would be it. You could sit back. They would have tremendous incentive to do so. People have no understanding or confidence that markets work, and that you don't have to resort to this idea that you have to militarily control natural resources. It doesn't mean everything will be perfect, and others will try to intrude and take over, but eventually people have to sell products. I mean, Switzerland I don't think sits around and worries about where they're going to get their stuff to live, you see? Right?

Horton: Right.

Paul: Yet, although they're mountainous, they're really in the heart of Europe, but have been able to avoid all these wars going on. I think it's fantastic, and it's a great example of what another country could do. It's sort of sad that we embark on these programs of sanctions and embargoes and wars and bombing and threats. It's just so needless.

Horton: Well, what about humanitarian crises, like what's happening in Darfur with the nomads versus the farmers, and hundreds of thousands of people apparently have died so far. Is there any room for American intervention to stop a genocide or mass-scale slaughter like that?

Paul: You know, a lot of liberals and Democrats are very sympathetic to what I'm saying on foreign policy, but then they always assume, "Well, you will go into Darfur." My answer is no; I wouldn't do that either. I don't have the authority. I don't have moral authority. I don't have legal authority. I don't have authority under the Constitution. In a practical way, it doesn't really work. You send food and aid over there. The military takes it over. They're in the middle of a civil war, so it sometimes does exactly the opposite. Instead of ever getting to the people who are starving, it gets in the hands of one faction over another.

I just say that it's not in our best interest. It shouldn't be that we don't care. I think ultimately what they need is an understanding of how freedom works and how the marketplace works. We certainly should never inhibit people who want to go and help and send goods and products — if it's truly aid — and food. I mean, we have a willing country here, and if we were a lot wealthier than we are today, literally billions of dollars would be used to help people like that. I do not advocate taxing people or using the military force to even do these humanitarian adventures, because sometimes what they do in the name of humanitarianism doesn't end up helping people very much.

Horton: Well, I sure appreciate your time today. Everybody, that's Dr. Ron Paul, congressman representing District 14 on the Texas gulf coast and Republican candidate for president of the United States. Thank you, again, very much, sir.

Paul: Thank you, Scott.

March 6, 2008

Horton: Alright, my friends, joining us on *Antiwar Radio* live from the nation's capital, Washington, D.C., it's my favorite politician in American history, Dr. Ron Paul. He recently won his primary race for District 14 to go back to the House of Representatives at the very least, even if he's not going to be our president. Congratulations Dr. Paul and welcome back to *Antiwar Radio*.

Paul: Thank you, Scott. Good to be with you again.

Horton: And it's great to have you here. Now, I wanted to ask you first of all about the Bush administration's assertion that Congress basically has no more role to play in deciding Iraq policy. Sounds like, although I guess Bush has never gone as far as saying that he can go ahead and pay for the war himself, as some of your competition in the Republican primaries had asserted, his administration is basically saying that they don't need the consent of Congress to create long-term treaties of alliance with the new Iraqi government. Your take on that, sir?

Paul: Well, you know, it sounds like he learned that from his father. I don't know if you recall — I'm sure you do — but when Bush Sr. went into the Persian Gulf War, he was advised that he should ask Congress for not a declaration of war, but just to get some token approval from the Congress and he just said, "I do not need to do that. I get my authority from a UN resolution," which I thought was pretty outrageous, but he did go back and get the authority. But then this sort of reminds me of that, they think executive power is all superior, and unfortunately it seems that too many people go along with this. I really consider the Congress to be the most derelict in their duties. Executive branch officials have notoriously over all of history always wanted more and more power. Our Constitution was written to have a separation and balance and the Congress is supposed to stand up for their prerogatives, and yet it hasn't happened. So I think Bush has gotten away with so much on his searches and FISA courts and habeas corpus and all these things that he's just taking the next step that he's claiming that he can do these treaties without congressional approval.

Horton: Isn't it the case that the Democrats in the Congress, if only they would vote like you, have the power to end the war right now?

Paul: Sure they could, and they could do it reasonably. They wouldn't have to say tomorrow, this war is over and give you 24 hours to get out. They could say the funding is ending and do it safely and reasonably as possible. You have a month or two or three, whatever is necessary to do it sensibly. I think you could make the argument that it should be done more with dignity than waiting until there's a calamity. I mean the ending of the Vietnam War — I think that's what people visualize — they see the ending of the Vietnam War and it was tragic because they put it off and put it off and put it off and everybody has this vision of running at the last minute and trying to get on a helicopter. Well, if we did this in a deliberate fashion and the Democrats would stand up, they would say, "Look, this is it. You can no longer spend this money after so many months and it's a reasonable time. If we can get them out in six weeks, fine. But get them out and if not, there's no more funding."

Horton: Well, Senator McCain says that anyone who wants the American military to pack up and leave Iraq is waving the white flag of surrender to al Qaeda.

Paul: Yeah, he's used that a long time, and he probably believes it to a degree, but the reality is what we're doing is serving the interests of al Qaeda. They weren't even in Iraq before and now they are. And we've had quotes from Osama bin Laden, he says he's delighted for us to be there and we're fighting him on his sand and that will do to the United States exactly what they were able to do to the Soviets with our help and that is drag them into a prolonged war, demoralize their troops, and bankrupt the country. So I would say that the policies that McCain defends are doing exactly what he claims that leaving would do. The world would be much more peaceful. Today what the financial markets are telling us is this war will end and our empire will come down for financial reasons.

That's been my argument all along and with this dollar going down so sharply in oil prices, I mean to see oil going up five dollars in one day should alert people to some really serious problems that we face. No matter whether Bush thinks he can fund the war without the Congress and the Congress thinks they can continue to fund the war because they don't have the courage to do what is right, it's going to end, because if the dollars don't buy anything and the more they resort to inflation, the faster the dollar goes down. So they're in a catch-22. They're trapped and they will have to wake up some day. I'm just hoping we can wake them up before there's a total financial tragedy that will be so difficult to handle.

Horton: Well, Dr. Paul, yesterday the House of Representatives voted to condemn Hamas for their rocket attacks. The House of Representatives voted 404 to one. There were quite a few abstentions, but you are the only no vote. Why did you vote no?

Paul: Because it's always interference and implications and saying that if you don't do this and blaming people, it's one side versus the other, and it's always on and on getting involved when we shouldn't be. I put a statement into the record — and it'll be available I think on the internet today — explaining my position. Very simply, I abhor the violence — I abhor the violence on both sides — but when we pick one side and say all the violence comes from one side and therefore we don't care about that of the other side, I think that only encourages more violence. So we would be better off if we took a more neutral position, minded our own business, encourage people to do the right thing, even be available if they want to come to the United States and have a true discussion about how to move toward peace, but we should not be involved in the dictates of saying, "Well, do it our way or we'll bomb you. If you do it our way, we'll give you money."

Paul: That's where the real tragedy is, and these resolutions do nothing more than precipitate more problems. We are calling up those resolutions constantly and it's mainly for the purpose of endorsing policy because they always pick an incident and say, "Oh, there's been violence. Let's condemn the violence." Who can say, you can't condemn the violence? But then they always have something in the resolution that implies our responsibility for what we will do, and that in an endorsement of the policy that continues to fail.

Horton: Well, I've been reading *The Foreign Policy of Freedom*. This reminds me of what you said about Ronald Reagan's intervention in Lebanon in the 1980s.

Paul: That is right. When he went in there, he said he would never turn tail and run. I was interested in reading what he would put in his memoirs because that's exactly what he did. And he recited this quote, he says, "I once said 'I wouldn't turn tail and run,' but after I was in there, I didn't realize the irrationality of the politics of that region." So he admitted it. At least he had the courage to admit it. They talk about a lot of heroic things that Reagan had done when he was president, and some were good, and some weren't all that good. Iran-Contra was nothing to brag about. But I thought he was pretty bold to at least admit that he made a mistake and he came home. Suicide terrorism ceased when the Israelis left Lebanon and the French left, the Americans left, there was no more suicide terrorism in Lebanon. It's so dramatic, the change that occurred.

Horton: And to read your book, which is all your foreign policy speeches going back all the way through your career in Congress, it's the best, the closest I've ever been able to get to being able to keep track of whether America favored the PLO or Hamas at any given time and all the different interventions against the PLO, to save the PLO, to move them from one place to another, and all these things. This has been going on for decades.

Paul: When I put those speeches together, of course, I went back and reread some of them. I said, you know what, I could almost give the same speech on current events over there today. You know, the more things change, the more they stay the same. The same old workday.

Horton: We've switched back and forth two times since then, and now we're back again.

Paul: Yeah, there you go. It doesn't look like they're going to quit anytime soon.

Horton: Okay. Now if I can ask you one more real quick question. You brought up the wiretapping. The *Washington Post* reported two days ago that there's a compromise soon on the Protect America Act. Is that the case?

Paul: Yes, and it's from our viewpoint of protecting civil liberties, there's not a whole lot of compromise — I mean nothing. When you compromise something like this, I really don't see much room for compromise. What they've done is they've had a legislative compromise. They split the bill. It will be one vote on whether or not the telecommunications can be exempt for disobeying the law and invading our privacy and becoming a criminal element, listening to the government orders — that's the way I see it — and separating that vote from the renewal of the FISA courts. So to me there's no compromise. I haven't looked in great detail, but it looks like I'll be a probably a strong no on both halves of it.

Horton: Well, I'm sure you will, and I want to thank you, Dr. Paul, first of all, for the opportunity to vote for you for president the other day. Made my day, believe it. And I want to thank you very much for your time on the show today.

Paul: Thank you, Scott.

September 26, 2008

Horton: Alright my friends. Welcome back to *Antiwar Radio*, on KAOS 92.7 FM in Austin, Texas. For the first hour all week, we're focusing on the economic crisis with the experts from the Austrian school. We're streaming from the Campaign for Liberty, Ron Paul's new website, and he is our first guest on the show today.

Y'all know Dr. Paul. As Anthony Gregory says, he makes James Madison look like Alexander Hamilton. Best congressman we've ever had — I'm not going to lie about my bias. He's a medical doctor, not a lawyer, that's probably part of the reason right there. Former presidential candidate. He's the author of *Pillars of Prosperity; Freedom Under Siege; The Case for Gold; Gold, Peace and Prosperity; Mises and Austrian Economics; A Foreign Policy of Freedom*, and the new one, and my favorite, *The Revolution: A Manifesto*. Welcome to the show, sir.

Paul: Thank you. Good to be with you.

Horton: It's good to talk to you again. So let's get right to it. Right there, on Capitol Hill, it seems that the powers that be doing everything they can to push through this bailout bill. Is it a done deal?

Paul: Well, they claim not and they're still working on it, but there's a lot of politics going on, as usual. The Democrats, of course, want welfare for their group of people. We've got welfare for the rich, so they'll have to get some welfare for the poor. I think McCain has muddied the waters because he came over here and the Democrats saw this as a good chance to play political games. So instead of allowing it to go forward, my interpretation is that they probably purposely slowed it up. And I think as soon as he leaves town, they'll probably have an agreement if he ends up going down there for the debate. So that's the kind of thing that gets involved first. It's serving as many special interests as you can and then also getting involved in partisan politics.

Horton: The special interest thing must really play into it besides just the bankers who are being bailed out. The obvious targets of this... All the news reports say that the switchboards are just lit up, that the American people — at least the ones interested enough to call Congress about it —

are as angry as they can be and are adamantly opposed. So I guess they've got to figure out a way to pay off 435 different little districts in different ways in order to get these votes lined up, huh?

Paul: Yup. That's what they'll have to do and do some arm-twisting and promises. The bill won't have everything in it. It won't be overly apparent, but it may be future promises and things like that. So it'd be a lot of activity between now and probably Sunday evening. It may well go into Sunday before they pass something.

Horton: And now, the Treasury and the Federal Reserve, from my understanding, have already given up $700 billion of American taxpayer money for this. Why are they even bothering coming to you guys in the first place? Why do they need a law passed if they can do anything?

Paul: That's a pretty good question. I don't have the absolute answer to that, because, you can go to the Fed, and they can borrow unlimited amounts, and they buy up so many assets and they did extend about $700 billon worth already. It might be just that old saying about pushing on a string; there's a limit to how much more borrowing banks want to do because they might not want to borrow any more and have borrowing on the books as much as they just want somebody flat out buying these things. And maybe they just quit even taking loans from the Federal Reserve. There are some good banks. Especially the small banks are calling in and they don't like it. They say, "Why don't you just punish the people who got us into trouble? Why should you punish everybody?" The small, solvent banks shouldn't be penalized.

Horton: I have this Bloomberg article here that says that the FDIC has a secret list and that they're afraid to release it because it'll cause more panic.

Paul: Well, I guess if your bank is on the list it would make you worry. I'm not usually one to say don't sweat things too much, but in many ways, that isn't the problem. It isn't the problem that if your bank closes for a day you're not going to get your money out. The big problem is getting money that has any value, or exactly when you want it. As this economy unwinds, Social Security beneficiaries are always going to get their checks, and the checks are going to gradually increase, but they'll never keep up with the cost of living. So it's the value of money that we're dealing with, and every time they prop up the system of bad debt, bad investments, what they're doing is diluting the value of the dollar and they just can't keep up with that.

Horton: Well, I learned watching the president's speech the other night, that the cause of this is those darn foreigners, apparently in a plot to destroy us, have invested a lot of money in our economy.

Paul: Yeah, we've got to check into that. You know, it's always the Chinese's fault or somebody else. They work hard, sell us goods, we give them paper money, and they save and then they start buying stuff up. The embarrassing thing is, is they actually are our banker and act more like capitalists than we do. I mean, we act like the aggressors and the Chinese are over there buying up assets and participating in investments in Iran, and we're over there trying to start a war with them. There's quite a difference in approach. It's hard to believe that we've gotten ourselves into this mess.

Horton: We saw the dot-com bubble in the '90s, and then, as it's been explained to me by some of your colleagues in the Austrian School, what happened was instead of letting there be a recession when the Nasdaq bubble popped, they kept inflating and they created a new bubble in housing instead. So, I just wonder, is there such a thing as a war bubble? Is it the money that is being spent on the war that is then turning around and going into the housing, or are these separate issues?

Paul: I think they're connected. I think they're all one thing. It's a dollar bubble and we increase the amount of dollars we have to pay for the welfare here at home, the military-industrial complex for all the activity we do overseas. But it's not like Osama bin Laden didn't warn us. He was pretty clear on what he wanted to do. He wanted to bleed us. He wanted to drag us out there and spread us around the world and dilute our military strength, and then, wreck our economy and bankrupt us — he even stated this. So it seems pretty silly for us to do exactly what he wants. So we continue to follow that policy, but I think our financial problems are so intertwined with our foreign policy. If you got rid of all the militarism, it wouldn't solve all our problems but it would be a big help because we probably could end up balancing our budget and a lot of that money would be spent here at home instead of overseas and maybe then we could work on domestic welfare and clean that up, too. I think the easiest thing, politically is to attack the militarism overseas.

Horton: I thought it was funny that, between the Federal Reserve and the Treasury coming up with $700 billion and then trying to get $700 billion out of you guys in the Congress, the Congress went ahead and gave the Pentagon, and I guess other agencies, a $612 billion appropriation earlier this week. Where did they get that money?

Paul: Yeah, this week. And they're yelling and screaming we have to do this to bail out Wall Street and some of the conservatives say, "Oh no, we shouldn't do this. We shouldn't do this. This is a serious problem." But they all voted for this other expenditure, the continuing resolution. A lot of them voted for that and that was huge. And then there was the military budget, over $600 billion. It goes on and on. We've had dozens of bills this week. Everybody knows I'm going to vote against them even if they have a dollar in them, because you've got to make the point that it's the spending, that's where the basic problem is. They're dealing with the symptoms and the consequences. Figuring out what to do with the failed banks is one issue — and that's important — but that's dealing with the symptom as a consequence of all this overspending and the monetary system.

Horton: You know, it's kind of throwing me for a loop: it's great to see you being interviewed on all these TV shows, because they know that you said this was going to happen and that there must be something valuable they can learn from you. Then they bring you on, and you explain that all the things that they say are the cause — rewind just one more step, you're telling them, it's the government's easy-money policy that created the bubble — and they run out of arguments against what you're saying. They don't really know what to say to that, but it seems like it's almost impossible for you to actually teach any of these people enough that then they would use that as the basis of a question for any of their other experts. Like, "Well, that's what Ron says," but…

Paul: They're very frank about it. They say, "Well, we don't want to deal with what led up to this. We want you to deal now with the problem." Of course, we can. We can talk about these mistakes they're making now, on not allowing the market to liquidate debt and argue our case, but, really, we won't get very far until they understand how the bubble came about.

Horton: I hear you say often, and usually you have such a short amount of time on these TV interviews and you've got four different people interviewing you, and they don't know what you're talking about. I think, probably, a lot of people in the audience don't quite get it either, so I wonder… Don't give us the extra-long explanation, but explain what you mean when you say that the Fed's easy-money policy creates "malinvestment." What does that mean? That everybody starts making bad investments? And why does easy money make them make bad investments instead of good ones?

Paul: That's overly simplistic but you've got to get it out as fast as you can. We also use the term "printing money," which is not actually correct, either. It's the creation of credit. People don't ask... When they talk to the Fed, they don't come and say "Hey, give us easy money. Give us more money." The term they always use is, "We want low interest rates. We want low interest rates." And how do you get low interest rates? They have to put a lot of money out there to buy debt and that lowers the rates of interest.

Now, according to Austrian economic theory, interest rates are vital to give information to the investor and the businessman — the entrepreneur — to decide what to do. This is another fallacy in the system, and I try to get after them as much as I can because people say "Well, see, this is another time capitalism just fails." That, of course, came out of the Depression. They said in the '20s the gold standard and capitalism failed.

But the real problem is that when the Fed lowers interest rates, they create money. We don't have any savings. Savings are supposed to tell you when to invest. If there are no savings, interest rates should be very high — and then the businessman backs off and the consumer backs off. The consumer says, "Oh, interest rates are high. I'm going to save more money," and there is a natural cycle there. But, when the Fed comes in, and when interest rates in the market should be 8 percent and they make them 1 percent, there's a disillusion in that everybody thinks, "Oh, there's a lot of savings out there. We have to get busy." Then the so-called malinvestment comes in, the builders say everybody can have a house and so they overbuild their houses. Then our housing programs insist that we make these bad loans. But there's enough bad loans just from the artificially low interest rate, and then it feeds on itself. Because of the inflationary impact, the prices of these houses go up and people feel very, very rich.

One time Alan Greenspan argued with me before the committee about whether we had capital or not and where this was coming from. And he said, "Well, it comes from the value of the house going up," and I told him flat out: "I think you're confused on what is debt and what is real capital." And he called that savings and capital because the nominal amount of dollars, of the house, is going up. But if that were the case, it shouldn't dissipate so quickly.

Real capital wouldn't just disappear that way. Just think of the disappearance of all this capital, and it's very important. But that's it: low interest rates cause businessmen to do the wrong thing. They over invest and they malinvest, make a lot of mistakes, then the market dictates a correction. Then everybody hesitates to allow the correction, but the correction is locked in place. Most important thing we can do is allow the correction to happen, let the bankruptcies come, let the prices come down. What's so terrible about a nice house going down in value? Somebody who maybe was frugal enough to save his money, he might get a real good deal. And those houses have to get in the hands of stronger holders.

Horton: Now there are some who are saying that this is just the beginning, that when you really start peeling the onion, and you look at all the bad debt held by American citizens, businesses, municipalities, and states, and all these different things across the country, that really we're due for a major unraveling here. That this is just the tip of the iceberg.

Paul: I think that's a good possibility and it's worldwide, too. I believe we're facing something that we've never faced in history before. Because there's generally been a few sound currencies. There are no sound currencies for 35 years, it's a paper-backed world monetary system. We have had the advantage of that and other currencies are based on the dollar, too, because they have dollars in reserve. So I think it's worldwide and I think we're only seeing the beginning of this coming apart. But by not allowing the correction, we're destined to make this much more severe and last much longer.

And this is a tough sell. I compare this to talking with a drug addict. You tell the drug addict, "Look, you don't need this anymore," and then he says, "Oh, I'm not going to feel very good." So he gets another fix and he feels pretty good, he feels better. But you keep doing that, you kill the patient. But if you put up with the withdrawal symptoms and do what you're supposed to do, you can save the patient and you can feel a lot better. Right now, we're addicted to easy money and big government spending and all these bail outs. It's not easy, politically, to argue the case for tightening your belt and suffering the consequences when you think maybe next week — you know, Sunday night we passed this $700 billion package — next week the stock market might go up a thousand points, and then, later on it's going to go down, or something like that. But the short-term fix is what they want and that's what politicians will generally always do.

Horton: Yeah. Well, strange timing, too, because they want a short-term fix, but I don't think they want it this close to the election, that short-term, because we're going to still remember their names, the people who voted for this thing.

Paul: Yeah, I think that's the case. What I think is happening is they've had a lot of control, they've had a lot of profits, they probably know pretty much what we know, but I think they're arrogant and believe they can always contain it and take care of it. I remember another debate I had with Greenspan, when I challenged him about the balance of payments and how gold was important. He says, "Well, I used to believe that. But we, as central bankers, have learned how to get paper money to act as if it's gold." You know, gold itself. So he was sort of a bit pompous in saying that "Yeah that's true, but well, this fiat currency by us smart, central bankers, we can make it work." And I think a lot of them believe that, but I'm convinced that they can't make it work. I mean, you can't make a wristwatch out of paper, so I don't think the paper standard is going to work.

Horton: I expect his new book, titled *Mea Culpa* to come out real soon here. You talked about, during your presidential campaign, Dr. Paul, about how if you were president what you would like to do is have the Congress legalize competing currencies so that banks could issue their own money backed by commodities such as gold and silver. How does that work? Or how would it work?

Paul: What you have to do is get rid of legal tender laws that prohibit us from doing it. Only the Federal Reserve Note is the technical legal tender. If we could legalize the circulation of gold and silver — preferably really one metal would be better — but if you had two metals, there shouldn't be a fixed ratio. But let's say you had gold circulate parallel to the dollar. We're very accustomed to this because worldwide you have dozens and dozens of parallel currencies that are fluctuating from minute to minute, so we could handle that, especially in the electronic age, to adjust. People who opted for getting paid in a gold standard, and buying in gold, and saving in gold, they could do it. For instance, if somebody had been on a strict gold standard in these last ten years the price of their gasoline would not have moved. It would be essentially the same.

I argue this because the system we have today is very, very complex. I don't think it would be wise to purposely turn it off in one day — even though if you have runaway inflation it is going to get turned off in one day and we would like to avoid that. But this way you can introduce it to people, and they could make their decision and if they thought they'd rather get paid in gold then they could do it. Then under that standard, I think we'd gradually just absorb the paper money.

Horton: Well, back in, I think 1981, you were on — I guess got created — the Gold Commission and wrote its minority report. Is there any chance that perhaps this would create enough new interest that you could create another gold commission, and maybe your minority report could serve as the majority report this time?

Paul: Well, that thought crossed my mind. They're not quite ready. They're not serious up here about having a monetary conference and they're not going to admit that this system is done in. They're trying to salvage it. But, we really ought to start thinking about that and laying the groundwork, which is generally what I think that I do all the time, laying the groundwork for the day when it comes that we have more people interested than ever before. Just a few minutes ago I had somebody come up to me on the House floor and they brought me an article that was on the internet, that somebody had on the internet, and they said "You know what? If John McCain would do this, he'd win the election cold." It was a pure Austrian economic article, the one that I put on CNN, and she was just bragging about this and thought it was wonderful. So we are changing minds, but they're not quite ready to have that key conference to have monetary reform.

Horton: Alright, well, we'll wait. We'll see what happens. You just keep teaching them as well as you're doing and we can't do anything but better, I think, from here.

Paul: Okay, Scott.

Horton: Alright. Thank you very much for your time today, sir.

Paul: Thank you. Bye-bye.

Horton: Alright folks, that was Dr. Ron Paul. He represents District 14. In South Texas. He's the author of *Pillars of Prosperity*, *Freedom Under Siege*, *The Case for Gold*, *Gold, Peace and Prosperity*, *Mises and Austrian Economics: A Personal View*, which I highly recommend. That's such an interesting read. *A Foreign Policy of Freedom*, which, man oh man, it's just a collection of speeches from the '70s all the way through today, and just nothing but right the entire time. The best. You'll learn so much reading that book. And, of course, my favorite: *The Revolution: A Manifesto*.

November 21, 2008

Horton: Introducing Antiwar.com's man in the House of Representatives, Dr. Ron Paul. Welcome back to the show, sir.

Paul: Thank you, Scott. It's good to be with you.

Horton: I guess I could've mentioned that you just finished running for president of the United States, too.

Paul: Yeah, I think that did happen this last year.

Horton: It sure was a big deal. Bigger than I ever dreamed it would be. Congratulations again on that whole thing.

Paul: Well, thank you. It did stir up a lot of interest and I was very pleased. Especially the young people responded very well to our message of freedom.

Horton: Now, one of the terms that you threw around in that campaign that I think most people probably weren't ready for was the term "empire." I guess it used to be, when I was a kid, no one ever took it seriously when someone called America an empire because that's what the Soviets said about us. It was the kind of thing that a communist would say, but not necessarily true. Yet you used that term quite a bit and it seemed to go without saying to you that America is not supposed to be an empire. So what exactly does that mean to you, that America is an empire? And what's wrong with America being an empire, sir?

Paul: Well, I guess it's the opposite of what many of us believe a republic ought to be all about and I think Cicero had something to say about the Roman Republic versus the Roman Empire. He, like many of us, believe that governments should be small, and they should be local, they should be representative governments and the government's authority should be minimal. But it should not be designed to tell other people what to do with their country and their lives and to invade countries and to be aggressive and protect natural resources, in the old days go and steal their gold. All of these things mean that they use force to impose on others the will that that particular country wants.

Now our empire really blossomed when the Soviet empire collapsed, because we were the sole superpower. Instead of us backing off and becoming a more dignified republic, what we did is we just filled the vacuum and said, "Aha, the responsibility is ours." And people who did this actually saw this as like a moral responsibility: "It is our obligation; we are good, and we are wonderful." You know, the philosophy of the neocons. They saw this as a mission and, of course, they never really understood the great danger of this and some, I guess, were well-intended. Others I'm sure knew exactly what they were doing because they loved to wield power and control all finances, control all natural resources. If you love liberty, you hate empire.

Horton: Well, what is that great danger? What is it about empire abroad that threatens our liberty here?

Paul: First off, there's always a cost to it and the cost is you build up enemies and then you're forever threatened. So when we go overseas and we do things we shouldn't be doing, we build up enough enemies and sometimes they want to come here and attack us and do great harm to us. The other great harm is that there's an economic burden that is a great cost. Empires end for financial reasons as the Soviet empire ended and Osama bin Laden understands this. He wanted to drag us over to the Middle East because he says, "We will destroy you, because you will eventually go bankrupt." And, of course, probably one of the most important reasons to not want empire, it's an attack on personal liberties. Because of the nature of empire where you need to use force, you need to confiscate more wealth from the individual and you are always under siege, so to speak, the people get frightened and they say "Aha, we are under threat so therefore to be safe you have to give up more of your freedom in order to be secure," and certainly that has happened wholesale since 9/11. So the loss of personal liberties is the number one, and then along with that we become a much poorer nation and then you become more vulnerable to outside military threats as well.

Horton: On the financial costs, it really is the kind of situation where without question it's a net loss to this country. We're not going and looting everybody's gold and ultimately profiting from all of this imperialism. Everything goes out and nothing comes back, like Garet Garrett said.

Paul: It goes out and no, we don't quite do it like the Romans did, because one of their goals was to go and take the gold. They brought the gold back in and then they lived beyond their means and they weren't productive, and they didn't care about their freedoms. And then their bread and circuses finally undid the empire. Morally, it's the same thing. The gold today is to have a pipeline through Afghanistan, to send a pipeline through Georgia, to control a dictator in Saudi Arabia that will be friendly to make sure that we have free flow of oil that may be below market price. So it's on and on. It's sort of a remnant of the idea of mercantilism that you can't exist as an independent nation because you have to have control of your natural resources. It's not all old colonialism, but it's new in the sense that we still want control, but we don't quite say they are our possessions. But, those who have us occupying their countries see us as almost colonialists because we go in and our troops are there. So the result is always the same: the belief that republics can't exist unless we have this control of the natural resources and have this power that is overwhelming and can deal with any threat outside.

Horton: Something else I know that you've been very concerned about over the years is the centralization of power in the presidency and it just seems so ironic to me that George Bush apparently can simply sign the Status of Forces Agreement and make a deal to keep American troops in Iraq, while Nouri al-Maliki has to submit it to the cabinet and to the parliament and to the president, and they have all these separations of power and checks and balances in the new Iraqi democracy, apparently.

Paul: Yeah, you'd wonder. And then the hypocrisy. We don't advocate democracy the way so many people talk about it, but democratic elections, we still use those. But then we send our troops and our money, and we kill people because we're going to "spread democracy" around the world. It's such a farce. I think you make a good point by saying that maybe the Iraqis want a better democratic process with the people speaking up through voting more so than the people demand here. But we're totally apathetic with this. I mean the Congress endlessly, Republicans and Democrats, are always anxious to turn more power over to the executive branch and sometimes I think they do this because they don't want the responsibility for anything. They gave Bush the authority to decide what he wanted to do with Iraq. It didn't say go to war. It didn't declare war. It didn't say don't go to war. It said, "Do whatever you want." And I think what they were thinking about then is, "Well, if this goes badly then we can criticize Bush for it." And they don't take any risk whatsoever.

Horton: And in fact, many of them have said, "Well, I didn't vote for the war. I voted only for this authorization for Bush to do the right thing, which I thought was something else."

Paul: Yeah, and that's no easy out. It's still giving up your responsibility and not reading the Constitution correctly, because this accepting the idea that the president can start a war is a serious mistake. The Constitution is very clear that troops shouldn't be sent into battle and a war shouldn't be fought without the people speaking through the Congress and having an up or down vote on war.

Horton: We have a Status of Forces Agreement with Japan, Korea, Italy, Germany and so forth, but we also have treaties with them. It seems like Bush is using the Status of Forces Agreement in place of a treaty, which he would have to submit to the U.S. Senate for ratification.

Paul: It's worse than what we have with these other countries when we have a treaty. But even that, I'm not happy with because even though we might have a treaty with Taiwan, I don't consider that, in a strict sense, a constitutional law. These treaties weren't meant to repeal law and repeal the Constitution, because under these treaties most people assume, "Wow, if Taiwan is ever attacked by China, we automatically go to war." Well, that wasn't what we were supposed to think about treaties, that you could just literally amend the Constitution in this manner. I just don't think we have the right to do that, but we don't have the moral right either. Let's say even if you could do that legally, let's say it was constitutional and it was legal to have a treaty to go to the defense of A, B, C country. But what right do I and one generation have to sign a treaty or an agreement that the next generations 40 or 50 or 60 years ahead have to automatically be committed to going to war? So I don't like those treaties whatsoever, but like you pointed out, I think this agreement is even worse. We have taken a further step because we don't even have a treaty with Iraq, because really, frankly speaking, I don't think there is a true government of Iraq. The United States government is the government of Iraq. So I guess the power speaks for itself.

Horton: There's a major development in the battle over, well frankly, the entire theory of having a rule of law in this society when yesterday as the result of a habeas corpus hearing mandated by the Boumediene decision of the Supreme Court last year, a judge declared five enemy combatants were not in fact enemy combatants and has demanded that the Bush Administration set these Algerian men free.

Paul: Well, that's encouraging, but it's sure discouraging that they've suffered for so long because we've violated some of these basic principles of human rights. I know there's no reason to be too optimistic about the new administration, but let's just hope that we have a little bit of improvement. At least just hope it doesn't get a lot worse than what we had with the Bush Administration, but so far, I'm not overly optimistic about that either.

Horton: If the American people had come to their senses and elected you this November, what would you do with the men at Guantánamo Bay and at the various black sites around the world? I guess it goes without saying that you would do your best to set the innocent ones free, but there are actual 9/11 conspirators and others like that within this mix. Do you put them on trial in New York City in federal court or what do you do?

Paul: Yeah, I'd put them in trial under our federal laws and give them right to counsel and recognize that they have a right of habeas corpus. People that there's no evidence to hold them, they should be released. The greatest threat, and this is a principle known for a long time, is that if you abuse those principles of law and you let one guy go free, that's not nearly as bad as if you institutionalize the abuse of law for all of us, for all little things, and that's essentially where we are today.

Because we are frightened and have to catch all of the terrorists, we have victimized ourselves, so we have no right of privacy. The right of habeas corpus is slipping away and so I think that that should be more important than the idea that one potential ally of a terrorist happened to be sent back to another country. I'll bet the information is available about these people in Guantánamo and that it wouldn't take too long. I would think in a month or two you ought to be able to sort that all out and decide who should be released and who has enough evidence against them to be tried. We have a pretty good precedent for that because they had good leads on the ones that participated in that bombing of the towers the first time. They were arrested and convicted and are in prison. So that's the way that it should be handled.

Horton: I saw on the news the other day — I'm sorry, this goes back to the military spending — Barney Frank apparently wants to cut the Pentagon defense budget and was being attacked by some Republicans. Do you anticipate working with him on that?

Paul: I haven't talked to him about it, but that is my argument. I don't call it "defense money," I call it "military money," because I think it doesn't help our national defense. No, I think that budget is huge and that's where we should cut. It's easier to cut there, especially overseas military expenditures a lot easier than saying, "Well, we don't like the Federal government involved in education and medical care." I don't think it makes any sense to pick on that first. But it depends on how they do it.

Let's say if they cut $10 billion and take that and add some more and spend it all on another program here at home and didn't do anything to cut back, then that's a little bit risky. But I've also taken the position that it is much better to spend that money here than overseas, even though I would prefer not to even spend it here at home. My idea of getting back to some common sense on the budget is if you can find one of these military appropriation bills that you can cut $10 to $15 billon out of it, put half of it to the deficit and the other half to a program here at home. Even if it's a program that we don't think is perfectly compatible with what our goal should be. At least politically you would move in the right direction of cutting spending, cutting the militarism, cutting the deficit, at the same time it would be tiding some of these programs over where we've taught so many people to be totally dependent on the government.

Horton: That's probably only going to increase as we head into this recession, of course. I'm sure you saw the numbers that unemployment is as high as it's been in, I think 16 years. The stock market had another massacre yesterday, I think 400 and something, 500 points lost. How bad is this recession going to be and how long do you think it's going to last, sir?

Paul: It's bad. Some days it even shocks me, which is pretty difficult to do because I've been anticipating a lot of problems. At the rate they are making mistakes, which are daily, I would assume that this is going to last for a long, long time. But I've dated the beginning of this mess in the year 2000. I don't think we just went into a bear market here a year ago. I think the bear market started in the year 2000. If you look at the Nasdaq, it's pretty good evidence, in real money, the Dow never went to new highs. But it was temporarily slowed up. The correction, with the housing bubble, and the so-called financing that came from high housing prices, but that's all ended. So we're already into this thing that's been eight years and people who have invested in the stock market twelve years ago are just barely even. So it's been going on a long time already and the unemployment statistics and all that we see now are just getting worse every day.

If we don't do the right things and allow some of these corrections and allow housing prices to get down very, very low quickly, where people will say, "Hey, this is a good deal, I couldn't afford this and I want to buy a house." That needs to happen as quickly as possible instead of artificially keeping these prices high. I am expecting that it may be another ten years or so before people say, "Aha, the correction, the recession, depression has finally ended." It may not go like the '30s, but it can be in a way insidious and longer and that is also very bad. Just think of what's happened in Japan here since 1989. They've been living with a very weak economy for almost twenty years. Their stock market, the Nikkei was 39,000 in '89 and now what is it, 12,000 or something? It's just a fraction of what it used to be because they never wanted to allow the banks to write off the value of their assets because it would look like the banks are technically bankrupt, so they never allowed the correction and they are still struggling.

So I suspect that we are going to do that and probably what will happen is we will destroy the value of the dollar. There'll be a currency crisis and then we may be forced then to revamp the system and hopefully we will come up with sound money. That could end it sooner than this insidious slowing up of the economy, where every single day you hear bad news and people keep getting poorer and poorer.

Horton: It seems like the national governments of America and Europe are getting together and, in fact… I guess at the G20, I don't know if that includes India and Brazil too or what. What are we to expect from these big meetings of all of these central bankers and finance ministers? They keep talking about a Bretton Woods 2 or 3 or whatever number Bretton Woods we're on now. What do you think is going to happen there?

Paul: Well I think that they are going to keep working on it and they will probably not be able to come up with a new plan within a week or two. The other day when I asked Bernanke about this, he totally denied it, but I just don't believe him. I think that they have been talking about a new reserve currency, because they know what we know, that the dollar reserve currency has ended. It just doesn't function anymore. Although people are still holding dollars and hoping that they can get out of the dollar in time, but I think that we are going to see the dollar get weaker and prices go up and interest rates go up and the worse it gets the more pressure will be put on them to have a new reserve currency. The trouble is that they want to come up with a new fiat international reserve currency, like under the IMF and worldwide regulations and world government. The battle is on between them and us. They want the big government. We want a small government. We want honest money. We want money that comes out of the marketplace and we want it to have real value to it such as silver and gold.

Horton: Do you think it's fair for me to try to remain optimistic that if all of these world leaders try to put together some sort of global central bank like that, that it just won't work or is there actually a danger that it will work? That they would be able to institutionalize something like that?

Paul: That's a good question. That's probably the key question, because if they are successful, that means we're all going to be a lot less free and we're all going to be a lot poorer. They always can have it work for a while, because in many ways a lot of Austrian economists in 1971 probably would've never predicted that that dollar system would work for 37 years and they got away with it. A lot of confidence is placed on the dollar and it took a long time to make us a poor nation and an indebted nation, it just didn't happen overnight. So they might be able to come up with something that would work temporarily, but ultimately history has shown that to really get a new start and to get calmness back in the system, you have to have a sound currency. They themselves may use gold, if they become desperate and say, "Hey look, this is not going to work unless we at least pretend that we are going to have some dollars held in reserve for this new currency." They still do have a lot of the gold. The central banks still do hold a lot of gold, so they have to know what we know as well.

Horton: Every time you're on the Neal Cavuto show on Fox News channel, he seems to ask you the same question, which I think is a very interesting one and I'm not sure if I really understand the answer. He seems to say, "Yeah, but Dr. Paul, everybody else's currency is made out of phony money too and there's really no reason that ours can't remain the reserve currency because everybody else's is worse, even the euro and the yen and what have you."

Paul: And I usually concede a bit to him on that, because the euro is a fiat currency and they have more socialism than we do. So there's some merit to that. I don't personally sell dollars and buy euros or yen. I guess there's some smart people that know how to trade maybe or make some money doing that, but I don't think that they are the answer. But I think the ultimate test is not so much how many euros you get for a dollar as much as how much goods and services you get from it. Even though the price of oil is down today, I don't think the amount of money we're going to have in our bank account at the end of each month is going to go up. I think really prices are going to stay high and the cost of medicine is going to be high and education will be high and food prices are going to be high and something else is going to get expensive and oil prices may come back up because we still have inflationary pressures.

So I think even though I talk about the end of this fiat dollar reserve standard because there's so many imbalances, that is one thing. The other thing is, does that mean the dollar is done? No, the dollar isn't done, but it could end quickly. Just as this emergency came up very, very rapidly — just think of all that has happened in three or four months. When a currency goes, it goes quickly once they lose confidence in it. So inflation is insidious for a long time and you say why isn't the inflation worse because there's so much new money? But then, when confidence is lost, all of a sudden you see them really dumping the currency and then the prices soaring. So I think that is what we have yet to see about the dollar, but at the same time I wouldn't bet on another currency like, "Aha, all we have to do is have the euros or yen and we're going to be protected."

Horton: Ladies and gentlemen, that's Dr. Ron Paul.

Paul: Thank you, Scott.

February 18, 2009

Horton: Introducing our guest today, Dr. Ron Paul. Of course, he writes for us at Antiwar.com. His archives are at Antiwar.com/Paul, including his new one that we ran yesterday, "Just Say No to The Draft."[3] And, of course, he ran for president last year and did a great job teaching people all about peace and liberty.

Horton: Welcome back to the show, Dr. Paul. How are you?

Paul: Thanks, Scott. I'm doing fine, thank you.

Horton: That's great. It's good to talk to you again. I guess the first thing I want to ask you about is the news that Barack Obama has approved the sending of 17,000 more troops to Afghanistan. You did originally vote for the resolution for the attack on Afghanistan, isn't that right?

Paul: Well, the resolution never said — I don't believe it had the word Afghanistan in it. It was authority to go after those individuals who were responsible for 9/11. So it was rather specific on who the target should be, but it was never for taking over. The resolution that dealt with Iraq was much more specific, the one that he used for authority to go into Iraq. This one was generalized to go after those who were responsible for 9/11. But never once was an implication, "Oh, yeah, this is the authority you need to occupy Afghanistan and go into nation-building and protect oil lines," and all that kind of stuff. That wasn't there. But that is right, I did vote for the authority to go after al Qaeda.

Horton: So, at this point, is it not — or is it? — clearly the legal case that Barack Obama does not really have the authority to expand this war without some sort of new resolution by the Congress?

Paul: Well, that's right. He never had the authority to take over this country, invade it, and occupy it. But, indirectly, he gets the authority because Congress keeps voting the money. Some of the legal people say,

---

[3] Ron Paul, "The Draft: Just Say No," Antiwar.com, February 17, 2009, https://original.antiwar.com/paul/2009/02/17/the-draft-just-say-no/.

"Well, no, it's not new authority, but Congress gives him the money so it's an implied authority." That's why we should have all been much more cautious over the years. The Congresses should have been dealing with any type of war. There should never be war unless there's a declaration of war, then it's very, very clear.

But presidents do it and the Congress goes along with it, and they don't assume responsibility that they should be doing and then we end up with this. So they don't even come back. It's true. Technically, Obama should be asking, "Am I allowed to expand the war? It's not declared. How many troops are we allowed to put in there?" It looks like "whatever the president says." That, to me, is a tragic way to run foreign policy.

Horton: What, if any, do you think is still the mission in Afghanistan?

Paul: I think it still has a lot to do with natural resources and pipelines in a strategic area of the world like that. Others would argue with me and say, "Oh, no, that's not it. It's just this neocon philosophy that we have to spread our goodness around the world." I don't think they can describe their precise goals themselves. They're not saying, "Well, if we go in there and we achieve this in 24 months, then it's going to be all over." I think, from what I can tell what they're doing, it's a permanent presence, just like in Iraq. They're not going to be leaving Iraq. There's no way they'll be leaving Iraq in 16 months.

Obama's been pretty honest about Afghanistan all along. In the campaign, he said he would put more troops in Afghanistan and the people voted for him. So it's one of those things where people aren't even on our wavelength on what type of military activity we should be engaged in around the world, and I'm just hoping that we can get some new people involved and another generation that'll wake up and say enough is enough.

But also on our side of that argument will be the fact that these kinds of interventions, policies overseas, they come to an end when the countries go broke, and we're on the verge of that, so who knows, Scott, we may have our way before we know it.

Horton: Yeah, well, there's the easy way and the hard way, it seems like. Maybe we have already chosen the latter there.

So, let me ask you, if you had been the president, if you'd been elected and you were the president, would you have any mission remaining in Afghanistan or Pakistan? Of course, it kind of goes without saying that as long as Osama bin Laden has not been brought to justice, that the mission there is open-ended, nation-building aside or oil pipelines aside.

Paul: No, I said many times in the campaign, just come home. We just marched into these countries; we can just march out. I'd come home from the whole Middle East. I'd come home from Europe, I'd come home from Korea, I'd come home from Japan, and save a lot of money.

But, you say, "Well, what about this target? What if the evidence is really there, like they claim, that al Qaeda and bin Laden are responsible? Should we totally ignore it?" Although, obviously, our foreign policy was a precipitating factor, it's pretty hard to say, "Well, he just killed three thousand Americans, we don't care about him," and let him go. But we should at least make an attempt to do it within the law. Which means that if we knew he was in Pakistan, maybe we could ask the Pakistani government, can we go in?

We don't need to go in with these armed forces. I'm sure you recall my proposal back then was not to send the Army in, but to revive the old idea of the letter of marque and reprisal. If we have an enemy of 25 people, do we declare war against the Muslim world? It makes no sense. Why don't we go after the ringleaders and target those individuals? To me, I think that's why the founders were rather wise in giving us that option, where you don't have to declare war against an entire country if you're dealing with a bunch of thugs.

Horton: Of course, that didn't get anywhere. Instead, everyone opted for the authorization which, as you said, the language you thought at the time was specific enough that it was about the individuals, not overthrowing Afghanistan's pseudo-government and replacing it with another pseudo-government. But it was narrow enough to satisfy you then. Do you regret that they've taken such advantage of something that you did vote for?

Paul: Yeah, I don't like it all. I didn't even like it then. That's why I immediately followed up trying to get people interested in saying, well, yes, I can't totally say… It's sort of like Pearl Harbor. What do you do? Our policies had a lot to do with antagonizing the Japanese. When you put an embargo on a country, in a way, it's an act of war. But you can't say, "Oh, they bombed Pearl Harbor, but it was our fault, so we don't do anything." By that time, you have to sort of defend yourself and against innocent people getting killed.

That was the reason I introduced the bill to emphasize letters of marque and reprisal. But the Congress wouldn't do that. But they could still target the enemy, but in a very, very narrow sense. I think the evidence to show that they weren't really all that interested in getting bin Laden was the fact that militarily, they probably had him about captured and they walked away at Tora Bora. So maybe they liked the idea of having him out there in the wilderness someplace because they could always use him as the enemy that we have to fear and the reason why we have to be over there. Even though they're claiming we're over there to go after him, they're really over there to deal with gas and oil pipelines and the whole Middle East situation.

Horton: Now, let me ask you about gas and oil pipelines. From the point of view of X make-believe oil company, it makes a lot of sense to me, economically speaking, to invest money in lobbying and influencing the Congress to help secure your pipeline route through some Central Asian country nobody's ever heard of in order to protect it. But I know you're an economist and you're a Texas Republican, and you know about how oil markets work. Texas City is all full of oil. That's part of your congressional district. Can you address the issue of whether that's necessary? Because a lot of people would say, "Yeah, they say it's for democracy, but really, we need that oil. We need our marines over there to secure those oil pipeline routes or else something bad will happen."

Paul: Well, I don't believe it. If that were the case, Japan would be awfully concerned and have a huge navy and a military and say, "Hey look, we don't have any oil in Japan. The only way we can have oil is we have to invade and occupy and steal the oil from somebody." They just go to Amsterdam and buy it and they get all the oil that they need. What would these people do with their oil if we weren't there trying to control their governments? What if we didn't have a puppet government in Saudi Arabia? Somebody would have the oil and it wouldn't be any good to them unless they sold it. So the motivation would be to sell it to us.

By the time you add up all the costs of the military operations and the cost in American lives in order to pursue this policy, it makes our oil very, very expensive. Let's say none of that worked and still, we didn't have easy access to a lot of Middle East oil. If you believed in freedom, you still wouldn't worry about it. You'd say, "I guess we need an alternative source." If the market were permitted to work, they'd come up with an alternative source. Maybe we'd have electric cars. Maybe we'd have more nuclear power. Something along those lines.

But instead of depending on the markets, here we have a new president saying, "Oh, what we to do is we have to invest money in alternative fuels just in case the price gets too high." They have no confidence and no faith in freedom. They do not understand how markets work. They don't want them to work, and then that's the reason they're willing to invest all this money and lives… Just think of the lives that have been lost. Not only the lives of Americans, we lost nearly 3,000 on 9/11. But since then, we've lost over 5,000 in the Middle East, plus tens of thousands who have been wounded and made sick. At the same time, millions of displaced Arabs and hundreds of thousands killed. And holy man, it just goes on and on.

And then we wonder, people still wonder, "Oh, no, they don't like us because we're free and prosperous." Maybe when we're not so free and not so prosperous. Maybe everybody will love us again or something. I don't know what their theory is.

Horton: Well, yeah, once we get rid of the Bill of Rights and completely destroy our economy, they'll leave us alone. I guess the real worry, then, is what happens when the terrorist attacks continue because the foreign policy continues?

Paul: Yeah. They don't forget. Americans have still not even learned that we overthrew the government back in '53, the government of Iran. And that they're still annoyed with that, so when we're over there meddling in that area, that brings back memories. Probably just a small percentage of Americans realize that they have been justified in turning against us when we're always meddling in their affairs.

One thing, though, Scott, that I've been encouraged by in this last year or two in talking about this and this foreign policy, has been to talk on college campuses, how many young people are starting to realize that, and we did get a lot of responses. Even today I had a lot of good responses on the article against the draft. These young people, they know they're not going to get anything out of Social Security, and they see a financial mess and they can't get jobs. And they're being threatened possibly with a draft or a national youth service. I think a lot of these young people waking up.

Horton: I spoke with William Astore, who's a retired colonel in the U.S. Air Force and a professor. He was talking about Commander David Petraeus, the head of CENTCOM, and how he likes to talk about "The Long War." And the implication being that it seems like Afghanistan may really only be the beginning. That, really, any country with a "stan" on the end of it is likely to be occupied by American troops in the coming decades on some kind of permanent basis. I wonder if you can address that and, perhaps, include in your answer something about the draft and whether you think that that's the kind of consequence of having a foreign policy so expansive, even from this point on?

Paul: Yeah, I've heard those talks about "The Long War" I think they're anticipating. But the limitation won't be from just changing party leadership, Republican or Democrat, because the policies are the same, so they're going to continue. But what might limit it, like I said before, might be the ability to finance it, just as it became difficult, if not impossible, for the Soviets to do it. That helped bring them down.

But let's say the financial crisis lingers awhile longer where the dollar isn't totally destroyed and we are able to pursue this policy for another ten or fifteen years, I think the likelihood of a draft is going to continue to grow. Obama and Rahm Emmanuel, who's an important figure in the presidency in the White House, they believe in the draft. They believe in national youth service.

Besides, another thing I'm sure you've heard recently is this talk about when you have a difficult economic situation, sometimes war gets you out of these. It's taught to us so often that "the Depression never ended until World War II." That was like, "Oh, we finally got a war going and that ended it," which is a complete fallacy.

Horton: It seems like we'd all be stinking rich right now. We've been at war nonstop for a few years here.

Paul: Of course, it's the war that has helped bring us to our knees. That whole argument, one can show it, and I can argue the case even from memory, is that World War II was not much fun. I was born in '35, so I did have a memory of the war. And, boy, there was rationing, and I was in a family of five boys. Things weren't all that robust. There were no new cars on the road. People were driving junk cars and they had a difficult time.

The Depression actually ended when the debt was finally liquidated at the end of the war and then there was a lot of consumer demand and a lot of people came home. So the war didn't end the Depression. It was ending the war that ended the Depression.

Horton: And that's something that we've talked about on this show a lot. But you're right that it really does seem to be a defining myth, particularly for these economic times. The *New York Times* wrote just the other day that — and Dr. Paul, pardon me, but really, they did it with a straight face — that World War II, one of the things that it was really good at is it brought down the unemployment rate.

Paul: Yeah. What a way.

Horton: With the draft, with conscription.

Paul: Yeah. I think I'd rather live in poor conditions than putting on a uniform and getting shot at, especially for some war that made no sense.

Horton: And what is your moral case against the draft? Obviously, you're a patriotic guy and you're all about the Declaration of Independence and all America's founding traditions and all those things. You don't think people should have to serve their country?

Paul: Well, I don't think you can serve your country if you succumb to slavery. You could say, "Well, we need you to be a slave and work in this plant to manufacture products we need." Obviously, slavery doesn't enhance your country and it can't be patriotic. That's the same way with the draft.

I start with the basic principle that our lives come to us in a natural or God-given way and we have a right to our life and to our liberty. The government should be fairly limited to protect that life and liberty. The responsibility on how this life is being used is yours alone, as long as you don't hurt other people. So it's a moral principle. And secondarily to that, I think it's so impractical, it causes people to go to war when they shouldn't go to war. It's economically a disaster. There are many other ones. But the basic argument is, each and every one of us have a right to our life and we should not be controlled by our government and told what we can do or can't do.

But I would use that same argument to the right of your income, too. I think it's a moral principle that your income is an extension of your life, your blood, your sweat and your energy. Therefore, the government doesn't have a right to your income, either. Because that is, in a way, a form of slavery, too.

Horton: Now, I'd like to ask you about Iraq. Various reports have it, at least, that President Obama means to stick by his plan to get the combat forces, although the definition of that seems a bit flexible, out of Iraq in 16 months. I'm not sure if you've been keeping up with Gareth Porter's work at IPS, but certainly the *Washington Post* and other places have covered General Odierno's and General Petraeus's pretty obvious attempt to try to spin this, that they've warned us that if we don't stay for at least 23 months, then things will go bad and it will be kind of the Vietnam "stab in the back" all over again, and it seems to be bordering on outright insubordination on behalf of Gen. Petraeus. I wonder if you can comment, sir?

Paul: Well, as a matter of fact, Gareth Porter was in my office this week and we did talk about this. I don't think there's any chance in the world that the troops will be out of Iraq in one, two, or even three years. And you implied that they might change the name, the active personnel versus somebody just sitting there. But they're not going to close that embassy down. That's an affront to the people. What about those 12 or 15 bases that they have there? We're not going to leave those. If there's more violence next week, I think more troops would be sent over there.

I think it's a whole farce to think that all of a sudden, we're going to leave after all this investment in time, of energy, to protect these oil companies' interests over there.

Horton: You think that really is the root of the policy in Iraq, is basically the same as Afghanistan, it's mostly about controlling that oil?

Paul: Yeah. Probably more so in Iraq. Afghanistan doesn't have the… It was more geography there of transportation. But I think definitely in Iraq it was involved. But I think you can't argue that Israel doesn't have something to say about this as well. There's very, very loyal dedication to whatever Israel wants in the Congress. And many members of Congress, even though they know it might be the right thing to do, wouldn't take a certain vote if they thought this was construed as being anti-Israel.

I think in terms of what's pro-American. What's best for America? And, when people say, "Well, your position doesn't sound like it's pro-Israel," I say well, "I'd take all the funds away from all those Arab nations, too." And I wouldn't be sending weapons over there to Arab nations. I wouldn't be propping up enemies of Israel, either. So I just think the noninterventionist foreign policy serves our interest best, but it serves the interests of all our friends and all our potential enemies as well. I think the world would all be much more peaceful for it.

Horton: Are you concerned at all about the seeming insubordination and the dispute between the generals and the president? Or do you buy that there even really is a legitimate dispute going on?

Paul: I think there is, and I think it's healthy. I like that, that they are doing that. It will be interesting to see how that plays out. But obviously, there is a disagreement and these military people who are arguing this from a strictly military point of view, they may be absolutely right. They might be correct in saying, "Oh, if you leave in 15 months, there's going to be a mess here and a mess there." But, I figure, yes, there could be. But it's not my fault. The mess is because we went in there in the first place. Yes, it's tough getting out of there and there may be some repercussions. But I still think long-term, it would be better that the local people there solve these problems. To say that if we walked out of there tomorrow and everybody would be hugging and kissing each other, I don't think I'd argue that. But it might be a lot better than we anticipate.

We walked out of Vietnam and it's unified. That's more than you say for Korea. Vietnam is unified and they're not exactly hostile toward us. We have American investors over there, and we have a much better rapport with Vietnam now that we're not fighting with them. So it could be better if we just walked away than some people realize. But I wouldn't laugh at what the military people say, it could be rough and tumble. But that's the fault of the people who voted and put our troops over there and stirred up all the fuss.

Horton: It seems like Gen. Petraeus wants to have it both ways, where he claims he's created peace and prosperity for Iraqis and his strategy is so much better than that of Gen. Pace and Gen. Sanchez and his other predecessors in the "surge" and buying off the Sunnis rather than fighting them and all that. But at the same time, he's basically admitting that he hasn't really solved anything at all because if the U.S. military isn't there to stand between the groups, he says they'll all start fighting again.

Paul: Right. Of course, my conclusion would be they haven't solved anything, and we've spent too much. So admit the truth and get out.

I guess it boils down to what they think our role should be in the world. I don't think we should be the policeman of the world. We shouldn't be a nation builder. We should be minding our own business and providing for the defense of this country, which we can do very adequately. Nobody's going to invade this country or bomb us or attack us. We're more likely to be hit by a few nuts with homemade bombs or razor blades by us being over there. So I see all that we do over there as a great danger to us rather than helping us in any way whatsoever.

Horton: I'd like to ask you about probably the most controversial topic of the show today. War crimes prosecutions or potential criminal investigations into the "principals," they call them, the leadership of the last administration, and perhaps, their lawyers who helped them construct the legal arguments for them to torture people and violate the FISA felony statute which forbids them to tap our phones without a judicial check.

Are you in favor of criminal investigations or any of these truth commissions or things that people are talking about?

Paul: Yeah, I'm in favor of it, but I don't expect anything to happen. Because the policymakers who stand behind either a McCain or an Obama are exactly the same. Of course, Obama's already backed off to protect the state secrets. You can't interfere with the importance of the state. The state has an interest in this. So they are not going to pursue it, but they should. People commit crimes, they should be investigated, the whole process. The whole idea of how many lies were told to us and how much were deliberate, I think there should be an investigation. But I'm very pessimistic. I don't think it will happen.

Horton: I once had a friend who joked that the whole Monica Lewinsky investigation was simply a conspiracy to get rid of the independent counsel statute.

Paul: [Laughter] I guess that's possible.

Horton: It seems like they sure are better off without it up there in D.C. right now.

Paul: Remember during that time, it was also used as an excuse, "Well, let's just drop a couple of bombs on a few people to distract us from Monica Lewinsky."

Horton: Right, right. Operation Desert Fox. Gotta get those weapons.

Paul: Oh, boy. That to me, even though Clinton dropped a lot less bombs than Bush did, it was pretty abhorrent to think that bombs could be dropped on people, and innocent people killed with the flimsy excuse that we had there. That's pretty bad.

Horton: Yeah. It seems kind of strange to name it "Desert Fox," but maybe that's just me. Wasn't he a Nazi? Anyway, one last issue here before I let you go, Dr. Paul, if that's okay. I'd like to ask you about the regime change and back again in Somalia that's taken place over the last two years, if you can just tell us what you know and what you think about that.

Paul: Well, I try to keep up on that and I have a really good staff that's good on these issues. I keep telling them, this is something we need to watch because there's not much attention given to it and I consider it very, very important because of the geographic location, as well as other oil reserves in that region. Of course, Bush was a lot smarter than Clinton was in his early years by us sending troops over there and getting trapped. But then we went and used a proxy army, used the Ethiopians to go in. But now they've had to be pushed off. So, no, I think it's chaotic there. I don't know the minutiae about that. But I don't expect anything good to come from it. I don't expect us to walk away from that, either. I think that we're either going to use proxy armies or we, ourselves, will be involved once again in that area.

Horton: It seems like the news reports are saying that basically the very same people who were overthrown two years ago by the American-backed Ethiopian invasion are the same people who've taken back over now.

Paul: Yeah. So, right now, it's a failed policy. But I'm not sure they won't have enough determination to come back with a Plan B. If I'm correct, if policies don't change, Obama will be very much involved there, as well.

Horton: I'm interested in one of the aspects of it that you mentioned there, that it goes with such little coverage, America's intervention in Somalia. Do you think the average member in Congress even knows America had a proxy war in Somalia?

Paul: I wouldn't think 10 percent. But you know the other place that they don't watch, and it stays quiet? That's in Colombia. We've spent a lot of money down there. Early on, I think you implied maybe our military serves the interests of our companies. Well, that's why we're down there in Colombia. We're protecting oil interests as well. There's a lot of money involved down there. I think some Americans have been killed and some held hostage, but that's kept very, very quiet. You hear very little about that.

Horton: But that's all in the name of protecting us from the cocaine supply.

Paul: That's right. I mean, we've got to teach the kids what to do and how to run their lives. It's the fault of the growers, it's never the fault of the people here or the fault of the stupid drug laws. They're not about to think about that.

Horton: I guess your argument is that that's basically an excuse, that that's just cover for, again, protecting oil interests.

Paul: Sure. That's why when we had the early votes, when we did have a little bit of a debate early on, it was construed as if you voted against this, you were voting for drugs. It was indicating you were weak on drugs. And no politician, they claim, can exist if you appear to be weak on drugs. But, of course, I've taken this position for a long, long time and it was used against me a whole lot. And I just think the people are a little more sophisticated than we give them credit for. I take a lot of stands that are controversial and up until now — I don't know what the future will bring — but up until now I've been able to convince my district what I'm doing and why I'm doing it, even if I do take a position that the drug war is a total failure and we shouldn't be wasting any money. I'd like to encourage others to do the same thing.

Horton: And that really has proven true in terms of the war, like in Iraq, for example. They scheduled the vote in the Congress right before the midterm elections in 2002, and so many Democrats were intimidated into voting for a war that they opposed. Meanwhile, you're a Republican from Texas who opposed the president, who nominally is also from Texas, from the same party, opposed his war in your district and walked right back into your House seat because they respect the fact that you don't sell out, that you stand by what you say and you explain what you mean very well.

Paul: That is required. I've had people come up to me after I've taken some tough roads, they say, "You know, I agree with you, but I can't go home and explain that to my people." Well, they might be just not energetic enough to do it. But that's my job, is to explain exactly what I'm doing if I'm representing them so that they understand it. Of course, it's in my interest for them to understand it, too, so that they don't just yell and scream at me. And now, though, after a few years, people expect and understand what I'm doing, and they're not surprised at all when I have to stand alone.

Horton: Alright, Dr. Paul. I've already kept you over time. I really appreciate you coming on the show today.

Paul: Okay, Scott. Bye bye.

April 22, 2009

Horton: Introducing our first guest today, it's Dr. Ron Paul. Of course, you all know, he ran for president last time, and also, he's the author of the excellent libertarian primer *The Revolution: A Manifesto*, which I highly recommend you go out and get, and share with everybody you care about. Welcome back to the show Ron. How are you, sir?

Paul: Thank you, Scott. Good, thank you.

Horton: It's very good to have you here on the show today. Let's talk about warfare. What's going on in Afghanistan? Looks like they went from — I forget how many troops were there in the first place. They said they were going to add 17,000 more, then they made that 20,000. Then I think they added another 10,000 on top of that. Is America starting that war all over again? And how long do you think we're going to stay in Afghanistan?

Paul: Well, it's a continuation. I guess there's nothing brand new. The expansion of the war into Pakistan has already started with the last administration. Proves our point that foreign policy stays the same. Interestingly enough, I just recently, within the last hour or two, came from a foreign affairs committee where Hillary Clinton was testifying about foreign policy.

Horton: Oh yeah?

Paul: I got my five minutes in and brought up the subject, and actually told her I was pleased I heard that the rhetoric and the tone of foreign policy was changing, and that they were reaching out a little bit. I said, "But words are one thing, but actions are even more important." So I tried to get her to tell me where have we seen any significant change? Have you brought any troops home? Have you done anything? And emphasized the fact that Obama immediately increased the military budget by 9 percent and expanded the number of troops in Afghanistan. And I said, "Is there any place where you can give me a little encouragement that we've actually had a change in policy?" And the only thing that she could offer was not that she brought any troops home, or they cut back in any way, because they haven't. She was saying, "Yes, we will be out of Iraq."
But I think that's a pipe dream quite frankly. I think there's chaos there,

and I think it's stirring, and I think if it gets a little worse, there's no way they're going to walk away from Iraq, and the troops will stay there. Of course, they're expanding in Afghanistan, and she testified of the importance of not dealing with Pakistan because it was the rogue nation and they had nuclear power. And I mentioned that in my statement to her. I said, "You know, the Soviets had tens of thousands of nuclear weapons and intercontinental ballistic missiles, and we talked to Khrushchev, we talked to the Chinese, and we didn't have to fight the Russians and the Soviets." So I urged her to maybe be a little cautious. You don't have to get too excited about the fact that the Pakistanis have this. It's serious, but there might be other ways of handling this rather than saying that we have to go back in there and do nation-building. But I'm afraid, as you are well aware, foreign policy doesn't seem to change no matter what they tell us.

Horton: Well, it even seems from the point of view of a pragmatic imperialist that messing around in Pakistan is really dangerous because they have nuclear weapons. Here's a country that is basically a country because they have one military, but other than that, it's sort of a pseudo-state drawn by the British. And here we are messing around bombing in there, and this is how the Khmer Rouge came to power in Cambodia. We disrupted the society so much by bombing the country during the previous government.

Paul: I think that's a good point because they don't have the intercontinental ballistic missiles. They are not a threat to the United States *per se*, but locally, we have large bases, or troops marching in, are getting involved inside of Pakistan more than just drones. They might just want to test one of their weapons and cause chaos there. So you're right, the disruption is the most important problem. Just think of how things finally got settled in Vietnam once the French and Americans left.

Horton: Well now, Dr. Paul, I think some people might be surprised to hear you say that you don't think anything really is going to change in Iraq, even though they're escalating in Afghanistan. They have promised by the end of 2011 they're going to have all the combat forces — in fact, I think they even say all forces — out, as per the Status of Forces Agreement. What indications do you see that lead you to believe that that is so much smoke and mirrors?

Paul: Well, because they never said they would close down the bases. They never said they would back away from a billion-dollar embassy. They never have changed their policy of maintaining stability, they're just hoping that they can do it without American troops. They wanted to rename them. They won't be combat troops, but they would keep them there, and they're expecting the puppet government, the local forces that we've trained. The tragedy is, is that the instability exists, and we've trained both sides. We've trained Sunnis and Shi'ites. I don't think all of a sudden, the Sunnis who have been kicked out of power all of a sudden love the Shi'ites who are more likely to be allied with the Iranians. I think it's unstable, and therefore, with the weapons that we have provided, that violence is going to break out and if we do back away. Let's say they bring half of the troops home and are sincere in what they tell us, and by the time they remove 50 percent, what if the violence is multiplied three times? There's no way they're going to leave. Then there's the possibility then that one of our bases would be hit.

What I fear most is something like that, some big weapon getting in and some problem comes, or some bomb goes off that literally kills hundreds of Americans as it did in Beirut when the marines were killed. Fortunately, I think, for us and our country is, although Reagan made a mistake by putting those troops there, he at least said, "I'm coming out there. I didn't realize how dangerous and how irrational these people were." So he left and admitted that he made a mistake by going in.

That's not going to happen today. If a ship is sunk or an American plane goes down and they want to blame Pakistanis, or the Iranians, or something, I'm afraid that the American people would overwhelmingly support massive escalation and even make it a bigger deal than the Gulf of Tonkin Resolution or going into Iraq. That's what we have to really worry about.

Horton: Yeah, in fact looking back on that, it's almost like "only Nixon can go to China." It took somebody with Ronald Reagan's cold warrior stature to be tough enough to withdraw troops and still stand up tall, and then I guess go take it out on the people of Grenada or whatever later. But if it had been Jimmy Carter, he would not have been able to get the troops out of there. The pressure would've been much tougher on him to stay longer don't you think?

Paul: Oh yeah, I think so. It seems like when a Democrat gets in power, they have to prove that they're appealing to conservative militants. So they go overboard in trying to emulate Republicans. But what do the Republicans do when they get in? They want to neutralize Democrat big spenders on welfare. So, we as Republicans then come in, like the Bush administration did, and expand welfare domestic spending. Then since both sides are supported, that's why in the midst of a financial crisis, the deficits explode. The significant figure that I've looked at just recently is that 12 months ago, our national debt was $2 trillion less than it is now. We went up $2 trillion in 12 months. That's the rate of indebtedness that we're incurring.

That's very dangerous, and I even pointed this out to Hillary today that great nations end not because they get defeated militarily. We didn't have to defeat the Soviets. They end for economic reasons. And I think that's what's going to happen here, and I even brought up the subject of the American empire. She was very, very friendly, and matter of fact, she even made some very positive comments about the Ron Paul supporters, which really was a shock. It was very pleasant. She went out of her way to be friendly toward us and complimented our supporters on how energetic they were and how determined they were.

Horton: Well, I'm trying to find reasons to like her better than Condoleezza Rice, but I haven't come up with any yet. I'll let you know if I find some.

Paul: Yeah, well yeah. It's hard to make those choices.

Horton: Well now, on the Iraq thing, basically what you're saying, I think, if I can boil it down, the difference between Barack Obama's Iraq withdrawal policy, and the policy that you would've had, had you been the president, is that he's accepted, basically, the Bush premise that we have to win. We can't leave if there's a problem left behind. We have to be able to say the "surge" worked all the way up until the last troop leaves from Kuwait and maybe for a few months after that. Whereas your position is, "We're leaving. And if the Sunnis and the Shi'ites go back to war, we need to recognize that as a consequence of our invasion in the first place, and we've just got to go." But I guess you're saying under the way it is in the Obama Administration, as long as there's violence there, we're never leaving.

Paul: Yeah, and I think his definition of leaving is different than my definition. My definition is leaving is not having military personnel there and turning the bases over to whatever government is there. I would even, because symbolically it's so bad, I would not get involved in that embassy because I think that is a real affront. We could have a small office over there. That ought to be turned over to the Red Cross or something like that, but I would start leaving. I don't know why physically you couldn't accomplish that in six months.

Who knows, maybe it could be very violent and that wouldn't surprise anybody, but who knows? It might be a lot less violence than we've seen in the last five years. A lot of people have been killed and a lot of people displaced. I think there would be a struggle for the balance of power, but maybe there would be a continuation of the northern part for Kurdistan where that would be maintained. Who knows what would happen in the south? But all I know is that this is not going to last. There are just too many reasons for these people to get fighting and killing each other again.

Horton: On the larger issue of the cost of empire, as you were discussing with Hillary Clinton — of course, I'm madly refreshing Lew Rockwell's blog here looking for the YouTube — but as far as the cost of all that, you mentioned the outrage over the so-called, or I don't know if you mentioned outrage. You mentioned the increase in the budget. I'm going to mention the outrage that they call this a "cut," when they increase the defense budget by 9 percent, as they said a few weeks ago. On the right wing, this was denounced as a "cut," as apparently, they were shuffling some budget items around inside the Pentagon. But I guess I'd just like to give you an opportunity to really drive home to people the cost of maintaining a world empire, where on the balance sheet are we in the sense of how much money we make off of empire and how much better off we might be without one?

Paul: Yeah, the special interests are still in charge, whether it's Republicans or Democrats. The bottom line is the increase in the amount, and then, of course, he severely criticized going back with these supplementals. Now he did put 130 billion in the budget, which is different and that's for next year, but this year is continuing the policy, although his argument there is, "Well, this year is still Bush's year, so we have to continue the maintenance." But even though he won the votes of those who wanted to end the war, and bring troops home, and have a different foreign policy, out of fairness to Obama, he was pretty truthful about Afghanistan. Remember during the campaign he actually came across sometimes more hawkish than even McCain did. McCain ended up saying, "Yeah, me too. I'm for that." But Obama was the first one to start talking about expanding the war in Afghanistan, which makes no sense whatsoever.

But no, they shift things around. They'll cut the one program and save a couple million dollars, but then they'll give billions more to something else. I'll bet you most of the people in this country believe he has cut military spending, which is not true. This is one advantage I have on the committee and being a Republican, is that I can criticize the administration for a foreign policy where they haven't done what they said. But even the Democrats don't want to criticize her for a couple reasons. First Israel, and the second reason is, is they don't want to offend their president. They want to be unified, just like so many Republicans didn't want to offend Bush. They figured, "Well, he used to be conservative, so we don't want to take him on. We don't want to fight him." So they went and voted with him all the time. The Democrats are doing a bit of that too.

Horton: Now as they spend us into bankruptcy, it seems like everybody forgets all the stimulus and all the war spending from the last eight years. And now stimulus and war spending apparently is the solution to our crisis. Honestly, as I guess you know, I spend most of my time paying attention to all this foreign policy stuff and I can't really keep up with the Austrian economics about all the developments in the financial crisis, but at least a few times in reading and watching the coverage of the financial crisis on TV, I'm reminded of Garet Garrett's book, *The People's Pottage*, where he talked about the 1930s and what he called the "revolution within the form," where they didn't really throw the Constitution out, they still kept it there in the window, or whathaveyou. But basically, they changed the entire nature of the way the federal government interacts with the society. The revolutionaries weren't on the outside of the gates, he said, they were on the inside.

I just wonder whether you think that really compares to what's happening now with the power grabs by the Treasury Department, the executive branch. It's almost like after 9/11, it seems like, where they just get carte blanche. I wonder whether you think that to call what's happening now, something that came to a "revolution within the form" is going too far. Or if that is what you think is going on, can you give us the basic outlines of what are the major changes that we're dealing with here that are going to bear consequences for us in the future?

Paul: I think it is a continuation of that revolution that Garrett talked about. Even though it wasn't a steady progress, what they were doing in the '30s, they backed off a little bit, especially after the war. But they never changed total policy, it just meant that they slowed it up a little bit. Right now, I think we're much further along. I think what he talked about is absolutely coming to bear, and it's a form of fascism. There's less respect than ever for the law. There's no hint that they're ever going to return to sound money unless we do have some philosophic revolution to offer our solutions to the problems. So hopefully we can do this, but I think their side is still winning. Like you say, we got into this mess by spending, and borrowing, and printing money, and they think we can get out of this problem by just doing more of the same thing. It doesn't make any sense at all.

April 22, 2009

Horton: What changes have really happened? I mean we already had a Federal Reserve, and an SEC, and a Treasury, and Commerce departments, and all these things. What's really changed other than the raw numbers of dollars that they've taken from us for all their various bailouts and so forth? Is the structure of the government really different now?

Paul: Yeah, I think there's been some major changes, because they're getting much closer to control. There's ownership in banks and insurance companies, they own stock. It's much closer to a fascist system where there are a lot of benefits to big business, and there was a military-industrial complex and all these things. Now it's much, much closer. They're deeply embedded together, so I think we've made a big step moving in the wrong direction, but also think it's unstable. The big question is what we're going to replace it with.

Horton: I know you're aware of the Red Cross report, the Office of Legal Counsel memos, and now this new report from the Armed Services Committee about the torture regime that ruled during the Bush-Cheney years. I wonder if you're calling for, or have you called for, an independent investigation, a special prosecutor, or congressional hearings, or anything along those lines? What do you think should be done, sir?

Paul: I haven't been that specific, and I may well get that far because it's just in the last couple days where I've been asked about this and whether or not I would support further investigation and prosecution of those who are guilty of those crimes. And I say, absolutely yes. We impeached the president not too long ago for infractions that were less serious than some of these charges that have been levied against our leaders of the last administration. So I think Obama is very much involved in protecting state power and state secrecy, and his first announcement sounded pretty bland that he wasn't going to pursue it. Not he's saying at least he's going to look at those people who wrote up the legal documents, but the people who participated ought to be looked at. If you were an honest American trying to do your job in the CIA and you were asked to waterboard somebody a couple of hundred times, you'd think, "Well maybe this is torture. Maybe we shouldn't be doing this." So I think everybody has responsibility, and I think they should be investigated and prosecuted if the evidence is there.

Horton: Alright, everybody. That's Dr. Ron Paul. Thanks very much for your time on the show today sir.

Paul: Thank you very much.

May 29, 2009

Horton: Our next guest on the show is Dr. Ron Paul, Republican congressman representing District 14 in South Texas. He's the author of the books *The Case for Gold*, with Lewis Lehrman; *Gold, Peace and Prosperity*; *Mises and Austrian Economics: A Personal View*; *A Foreign Policy of Freedom;* and *Pillars of Prosperity*.

Horton: Welcome back to the show sir, how are you doing?

Paul: Thank you, good to be with you.

Horton: *The Case for Gold*, that was the minority report of the Gold Commission, right?

Paul: Right.

Horton: So obviously you have the background in economics and more and more of those of us who watch cable TV news can see other people in the media finally picking up on this fact and asking you about your view. I'd like to ask you, principally, about some of the things you said on CNN yesterday. I think they basically started off the interview the same way I'd like to today with the question actually suggested by a caller earlier. Barack Obama says that the worst is over, that the economic recovery has begun. Yesterday you didn't seem to buy that. I was wondering if you could explain why not?

Paul: All they're going by is a blip upward in the stock market. A lot of people are losing a lot of money not just in the last couple of years, but they've been losing a lot of money for the past ten years. If you go back to the Nasdaq bubble collapse, a lot of people lost a lot then and they never got back in. Then with all the new credit in the last ten years, there were enough speculators going in and people wanting to spend money and they bid these markets up again, all at the encouragement of the government and the Federal Reserve. But now, with this bust, it's gone down again and I think it's in bad shape. Besides, everything we've done so far has been completely wrong. We've created more spending, more debt and more inflation, created a lot more money out of thin air.

So for them to think this is over, it would mean that we, as Americans, would never have to work again because the foreign governments and the foreign people just love us, they trust us, they trust our military and they trust our economy. And therefore, all we're obligated to do is create money and then they'll sell us whatever we want. That's just a dream, so the fact that the market's up a little bit, I don't think that's indicating in any way that this recovery is on its way up.

Horton: But now the Nasdaq bubble popped back in 2000 and they succeeded in at least making it seem like we had a recovery all the way up through last year. So could it be that we're… even if it's a pseudo-recovery that we're going to have it and basically things will look good, at least for the next few years?

Paul: It's always possible. It might be six months, it might be a year or so because even in the '30s, they got some recovery periods of time, unemployment went down a little bit. As long as the Roosevelt and Hoover policies continued, the real rebuilding of the economy couldn't occur. So even by 1939, there was very, very high unemployment rate, 18 or 19 percent, and we're doing the same thing. So the fact that there is some correction, people feel good about what's happening or at least they have this wishful thinking, I just don't think it's going to be real growth. We haven't gotten rid of the bad debt. We haven't gotten rid of the malinvestment. We haven't restored sound money. We haven't got the government's role defined the way it should be in a free market. So, no, I don't see any way that we're going to come out of this as of now even though you might see, maybe even a year of some improvement which I doubt.

Horton: We've talked before in terms of foreign policy about how difficult it can be to come up with a libertarian solution to a problem caused by a gigantic empire. It's the kind of problem that your policy or mine wouldn't have got us into and yet here we are, so how do we have a libertarian solution to a war, for example? It's sort of the same question here, isn't it? The boom and bust cycle, I know as a subscriber to the Austrian theory of economics, you blame on the fractional reserve central banking system that we have. But now that we're in this mess… Take the hangover analogy: everybody felt really, really good last night because they were drunk, but now they've got a hangover. Is there an argument to made at all, sir, for a little bit of the hair of the dog to get you through? Maybe your headache is so bad in the morning, a little bit of beer would help to dull you out until lunchtime?

Paul: Yeah, I sometimes use analogy of drug addiction. The drug addict might want to get off drugs, but he doesn't like the consequences of not having the drug. He's always needing the drugs to feel better, but to get off there are consequences. So the addiction is big government, we're addicted to big government spending, we're dependent to the government and all it guarantees, which doesn't do much more than give us a lot of moral hazard, makes us do the wrong thing. This is a lot bigger problem than it was with the correction that we've had over the last 35 years. We have a much bigger bubble. It's worldwide. It's never been this way where one single currency could inflate, like we have since 1971.

So that's the reason I'm not a bit optimistic about what's going to happen. I think what we're doing is we're leading to a dollar crisis and the end will come and we'll have to change our ways. But we don't have to do that if we all of a sudden had more libertarian, constitutional policymakers. We could easily come to our senses and say, "Look, it's going to be a bad year, but we're not going to bail out anybody, we're not going to print any more money, we're not going to have any more deficit financing, we're going to lower taxes, we're going to get rid of the income tax, and we're going have a backing to our currency." And then they say, "Oh, it sounds fine but how are you going to cut the spending?" That would be the biggest challenge because nobody wants their programs cut.

But I would — and I've said this many times — I would cut overseas because I think politically you could do that. Right now, the people might accept cutting overseas, but the people in charge will not, those who love the military-industrial complex. This last week it really bothered me to no end and see what Obama did with the Senate when they were dealing with the supplemental. Obama goes and makes these rash promises overseas of giving the IMF $100 billion. Where is he going to get $100 billion? And now they're working on gimmicks to put that into the budget where it doesn't show up and they call this that we're going to trade assets. We're going to give them $100 billion and they're going to give us scraps of paper and say, "Oh yeah, we have something like an IMF bond," It's a trading of the assets or we then have a line of credit. It's actually crazy, it's unbelievable that they're doing that. In the midst of all this, all the spending and everything now, we're going to give four international organizations like this another $100 billion.

Horton: It's all just a bookkeeping trick at our expense, right?

Paul: Right, that's it but the consequences will come.

Horton: I'm not very good at playing devil's advocate cause I'm a pretty anti-interventionist kind of guy myself, but I want to try to see if I can poke holes in your theory here a little bit about, what ought to be done here. If unemployment gets up to 30 percent, or worse, we could have a civil war. Take the 1930s, if unemployment was 25 — almost 30 — percent and Roosevelt, by inflation and by do-nothing work programs was able to bring that unemployment rate down to only 15 percent, isn't that important? Couldn't it be that America would've become a fascist or a communist dictatorship in the 1930s if something hadn't been done about that unemployment?

Paul: Looks like they did a lot of big government programs back then and they've continued, and look at what they're doing now, even with the bailouts. They're using it as an opportunity to become fascistic, they're taking over ownership, or becoming very socialistic. But the question is, nobody wants civil war, 30 percent unemployment rates? But I'm convinced that the policies that we have now are much more likely to give us than if we do the right thing. If we did the right thing and we had a bad year, and you had a 30 percent unemployment rate, yes, the government's responsibility would be to quell the violence.

But the whole idea is that if we don't do anything differently and we continue to spend and you have a collapse of the dollar, you're going to have this. That's the whole reason why we don't want them to follow these policies. If we did have it under today's circumstances or if we try to improve things and it got worse for a year, you have to still blame the people who created the mess, created the bubble, made the mess. They have to be blamed for it, not those of us who are getting the drug addict off his drug. If we take them off the drug and give them some medication and they're getting better, but they don't feel very good, the doctor shouldn't be blamed for that, the person who got sick and got addicted could be blamed. The most important thing we do is blame the right people for the crisis we're in. If we blame free markets and capitalism and sound money like we did in the '30s for our problems, we can't have a recovery. I mean we're going to lose even more freedom.

The only advantage we have today — that I think is a big advantage — is in the '30s they didn't blame the Federal Reserve system. They blamed the gold standard and they blamed capitalism. Well, today, we have to prove to them that we haven't had capitalism for a long time and we certainly haven't had the gold standard, so we have to blame the paper standard, we have to blame the Federal Reserve, and we have to come down hard on them and they have to be the culprits. I think we can come out of here with a victory, but it will be touch and go on what happens if we end up with violence and, of course, that's what I worry about the most.

Horton: If we can stay on that drug analogy, when I say we could have this terrible high level of unemployment that could lead to disaster — that's the "kick." That's getting off of opium and it's really uncomfortable. But when I'm saying, maybe it would be better to inflate, have make-work programs, etc., to keep that unemployment rate down, you're saying that is the equivalent of more drugs and we're running a risk of overdose. We're running a risk of inflating so much to try to keep people employed that everybody ends up unemployed, the patient dies on the table of too much paper money.

Paul: Yes, and your argument has some credibility because that's essentially what they do — what they have done in the past 35 years — every time a recession came along. They didn't want to really have the true correction; they say, "let's keep inflating." The Nasdaq bubble breaks, then Greenspan comes along and he gives us the housing bubble. That's why people are tempted to believe your argument, and yet this is different. Finally, it doesn't work anymore. Finally, the money doesn't work anymore, and that's why the value of the dollar is so crucial. Like today, the dollar was down over a percent and that's a lot for one day. Even that isn't the best measurement of the dollar being down against other currencies. The other currencies aren't worth anything. They're all paper currencies. Ultimately, the only thing you have to watch is the value of the purchasing power of money throughout the world, in particular with the dollar, and I think the purchasing power of the dollar will go down.

Horton: One of the things that's argued is that if we followed your approach and do nothing, we could go into a deflationary spiral — which I guess the analogy would be coming off of a heroin addiction so harshly that they end up having a heart attack and die anyway from kicking the drugs — that you would have good businesses that ought to survive, all things being equal, that will be brought down by everybody else being brought down, and the whole economy will end up — because of systemic risk and so forth — being destroyed, including the parts of the economy that on any given day, ought to be sustainable projects.

Paul: I think people ought to concentrate on the word "correction." We talked about recessions and depressions and deflation, but what we are looking for is a correction. That's a good word because there's been a lot of mistakes made, there's been too many houses built so we have to correct that. So what does the government do? They come in and say, "Oh, the prices of houses are going down, we have to prop the prices up and at the same time we better stimulate housing because that will create jobs." No, you don't want that, you want it to correct. You want the housing prices to go down so poor people who did happen to save some money can buy a house again. Then when all these corrections are made, then we'll have real growth again. We can't patch it up just like we did for all these recessions that we've had for 35 years, because this one is quite different.

Horton: And now to wrap up this conversation, Dr. Paul: How much money do we really spend on our military forces around the world and how much of that realistically could be cut? If, for example, you were the president, instead of Barack Obama, what kind of military budget would we be looking at for, say, next year?

Paul: Some have done some studies and they add up the total amount per year that we spend maintaining our empire and it comes up to over a trillion dollars. But you can't cut all that because what they work into that is some interest, and taking care of veterans, and whatever. But you could cut a lot — How many hundreds of billions of dollars could you cut if you didn't have troops in Korea, or Japan, or Germany, or the Middle East? I would say that you could very quickly — first year or two — you could probably save a couple hundred billion dollars and then the next year, even more per year. The big thing would be the shift of attitude, the change. People would know the direction we're going in.

The whole world would change if they all of a sudden realized that we weren't going to be the bully of the world, telling everybody what to do and if they don't do it our way we either bomb them and say do it our way then we give them more foreign aid. A lot of money could be saved, so just the perception would be very good. Matter of fact, if we didn't have our navy over threatening Iran, who knows — and we had a different policy — maybe oil prices would come down, especially if we quit printing so much money and didn't run up so much debt.

Horton: Then again, that would be terrible, right, for any price to come down according to all the experts running this thing.

Paul: Yeah, they want it to go up.

Horton: Maybe we should just threaten them some more to stimulate the economy.

Horton: Alright I really appreciate your time on the show today, Dr. Paul. Thank you.

Paul: Thank you, Scott.

September 23, 2009

Horton: I hold here in my hand a book called *End the Fed*. It's by Representative Ron Paul, and he's also the author of a great many other books. He writes for us at Antiwar.com. You can find his archives there, at Antiwar.com/Paul. I'm happy to welcome him back to the show. How are you doing there, today, Dr. Paul?

Paul: Good. Thanks for having me on.

Horton: You're welcome. I'm happy to have you here. Let's talk about war. In this book, *End the Fed*, about the central bank, you bring up foreign policy, and America's relationship with the rest of the world over and over again. What's the connection, sir?

Paul: It's almost hard for me to talk about one subject without talking about the other. I remember during the campaign it was announced that the debate tonight would be on economic issues, and not foreign policy.

I don't know how to separate the two, because there's always an economic consequence, rather serious, on domestic policy, because you spend a lot of money, you run up the debt, it causes monetization of the debt. It causes inflation. It takes funds away from domestic spending. So I keep harping on this.

The Fed facilitates excessive spending, whether you want it for domestic reasons or for international reasons. It tends to be that liberals want to spend it here at home and conservatives tend to want to militarize it. So it makes it easy. If we had to pay for every penny we ever spent overseas and collect it as we needed it, it wouldn't happen. Can you imagine what the people would say if their taxes went up in order to pay for this? But the sinister tax of inflation, where they just print the money, and then you suffer the consequences later, that, to me, is one of the most horrible parts about the monetary system that we have.

Horton: You really make a very strong case about that in the book, that we could not have an empire, we could not have our troops stationed overseas, except for the fact of inflation. Because really, it's kind of a hidden tax, right? It's like picking the corners off the dollars in your pocket. You don't really realize that you're being pickpocketed, because it's just a little at a time, kind of right out from under you.

Paul: Then the consequences always come later, and you never know exactly who the victims are. Right now, some of the victims of past inflation have been… Some prices are high, cost of government, the cost of education, the cost of medical care. That's related to inflation, but nobody wants to relate it. If that were the case, the liberals would be the biggest champions of sound money. In the past, and even today we do have some that recognize this, that running up debts and printing money is not beneficial. But we still have a long way to go to educate enough people to realize that we are only looking around for the victims. But it would be very difficult to run these wars.

I once read an article that made the case that, never has there been a war without debasing the currency. In the old days it might have been diluting the coins, or clipping the edges of the coins, or printing paper money. Today it's a mere computer that creates credit out of thin air. Nevertheless, it's still sinister, and as a good rule to remember, if you have inflation and debasing of the currency, you eventually wipe out the middle class. At the same time — for a long time — in the process, the wealthy just get wealthier.

Horton: Yeah. It's really incredible. You began the last chapter, *The Way Out*, Chapter 15, with this quote from 400 B.C., about the debasing of the currency.

Paul: That was from *The Frogs*, I believe, wasn't it?

Horton: Yeah. Aristophanes.

Paul: Yeah, that's it. They've been doing it for a long time. In the book, I mention a couple of biblical passages. The Bible has something to say about honesty of weights and measures, and yet we continue to do it.

Even most people know recent history. They know about German runaway inflation, and Zimbabwe, and Mexico. Yet they don't want to accept the responsibility of saying, "Oh, is that what it means? That means we have to balance our budget?"

It was unfortunate they didn't put it in the Constitution that we couldn't borrow money. Borrowing, though, isn't the full consequence, but it just sets the stage to encourage the politicians to borrow and get re-elected. But boy, when they can borrow, and then if they come up short, they can send the bills over to the Federal Reserve. That's a different story. They always take advantage of it.

September 23, 2009

Horton: I hear a lot of people who are really free market types say, "Well, we've got to have a central bank. I'm completely against the scandalous bailouts, and these trillions of dollars, and they need a real audit, and they need to be put in check, but at the end of the day, we have to have a central bank, right?"

I was just wondering if you could really address that. Because it always seems to me like they were kind of going back and looking at the situation we're in, and what the bank does, how it operates. But it's almost like they failed to go that one more step: "Why exactly do we need the bank?" It's got to be the backstop, because the entire banking system is built on fraud. If the entire banking system wasn't built on fraud, then we wouldn't need a central bank that would be the lender of last resort to make sure that the thing doesn't come unzipped — just like what happened a year ago.

Paul: I think they fail to look at history. They fail to look at our Constitution. They fail to understand free market economics, and therefore, out of convenience, they go along with the conventional wisdom of 50 or 60 years of government schools, because they do teach you that very early on, that it's perfectly alright, and the Federal Reserve is there to get us out of trouble.

But they ought to look at it differently. They ought to look and see the relationship of the Federal Reserve and all the problems we've had. If the Federal Reserve does as I argue, that they create the bubble, and the bubble causes the need for the recession — or the correction — then they're looking at the wrong thing. They can hardly expect the Federal Reserve to solve the problems they created by doing exactly the same thing. It just won't happen.

Horton: It goes to the age-old question of "stupidity or the plan?" too. I think I've read quotes from around 400 B.C., these people back then, wondering the same thing. Whether Ben Bernanke really just believes the Milton Friedman, rather than the Murray Rothbard explanation for the Great Depression, and no matter how many times you explain it to him correctly, he just is not smart enough to understand, or has too much prestige at stake to go back on his opinion, or if he knows good and well that what he's doing is actually very destructive, but he's pretending to play dumb, basically, to you. Which do you think it is there?

Paul: I think it's the prestige issue. He's argued this case for a long time. He's staked out his reputation on it. He did his thesis on this, and he has to make it work in order to prove that he's correct. I think it's more that, I don't think he does it deliberately. I think that he's just intellectually confused. He certainly isn't an Austrian free market economist, and he certainly isn't one that thinks we should follow the Constitution in a strict manner, because it's rather clear on what we can do and can't do.

So, he's written about it, and he agreed with Milton Friedman, and he said that, "Yep. Our only problem in the Depression was, we didn't print enough fast enough." So he's doing another test, and he's going to print faster than they did in the Depression.

But they followed this policy to some degree in the Depression. It prolonged it. They propped up bad debt and bought bad debt. Now we're doing it even more so. So, in that case, since he's doing it more than they did in the '30s, it means that the very, very weak economy — regardless of what the government calls it — the very weak economy is going to last longer than the Great Depression.

Horton: You talk about the threat of massive price inflation as a result of the massive inflation, the actual inflation: the creation of new currency. But I talked with Bob Murphy on the show last week, and he said that the Federal Reserve was paying the banks to basically keep all their money at the Fed. They created these trillions of dollars, and they gave them to all the banks. And then they said, "But don't spend it. Don't lend it out. Leave it, in fact, in our vault."

I wonder exactly how that works, and is that dictionary definition inflation? Will it necessarily lead to mass price inflation if the banks, in fact, don't circulate the currency around, they just keep it to keep themselves from going out of business during the hard time?

Paul: That's right. This is propping up the banks. The banks you can borrow the money endlessly, and they get money injected into it. Then, if they leave it at the Fed, they get paid interest on this, so that discourages the need to loan the money out. But there is a condition where the Fed does inflate the currency and pumps the money out. And yet, the banks themselves get skittish, because they've been burned, and they're not anxious to loan. But then, the people aren't anxious to borrow.

Who's going to go out right now and build a house? Because there were too many houses built. So it's a condition called "pushing on a string." The question is, does that mean there will be no inflation? Currently, I think there's still a lot of inflation. The big question is: Will it get so bad the government will have to admit to it? I say it will.

Eventually this money will circulate. We have a vehicle for distributing money to be spent that is more available to us than it was in the Depression, because everybody's getting a check from the government, practically. Whether it's a welfare check, unemployment checks, social security checks. For that reason, we *will* see the inflation. It might, for a while, just be inflation of the cost of government. Taxes aren't really going down. They're going to have to keep paying for the government. So we just don't know which prices are going to go up.

But the value of the dollar is not going up. People, even though the government says there's only one or two percent inflation, people at the end of the month aren't saying, "Oh, that's pretty good. I have more money left over here before, so prices must be going down. Food doesn't cost me as much anymore." That's not happening. In the Depression, that did. There was a lot more deflationary pressure in the Depression than there is now.

Horton: Do you feel like you're making progress? It seems like, from this end of the TV that, when you go on these shows, there's really nobody prepared to try to refute you, even. So you get up there and you say, "Well, look, the recession is the result of this big, artificial good time that we had, that was a result of the Fed dumping too much credit into circulation. So now we're suffering the consequence of that." Your quick TV news oversimplified explanation of the Austrian theory of the business cycle, there. But it seems like the news people just go, "Oh, yeah. That makes sense." And it seems to me like you're actually kind of winning. There's nobody up there prepared to even try to argue with you about this stuff.

Paul: Yeah, and I don't think it's me alone. I think it's the fact that there are many radio programs like yours, and others, and, I think, the internet. I was actually pleasantly surprised and shocked at how many people have been introduced to these views as the campaign was going on. I didn't convert these people all of a sudden. I maybe helped and invited more people in. But a lot of people have heard about this. During the campaign I was excluded by certain channels explicitly because they didn't like my antiwar position, and they didn't like me being as objective as I was.

But since then, some of those same channels have had me on thirty-something times, because it's strictly on economic policy, and they are willing to listen because there's a greater demand now to explain what's going on.

I think this has been very helpful in the fact that 75 percent of the American people now support H.R. 1207, to audit the Fed. Two years ago, probably nobody would have even known. If you asked them about auditing the Fed, they would look at you: "What are you guys talking about?"

So I think we are making progress, but it means the intellectual community, and the people who circulate these ideas, have been very helpful in doing this.

Horton: And this book, *End the Fed*, it's certainly going to be helpful as well. If I can ask you one more question?

Paul: Okay.

Horton: Last I checked, you were on the Foreign Relations Committee in the House of Representatives, right?

Paul: Right.

Horton: Is there anything that you can do to stop this war in Afghanistan before it gets worse? Can you introduce a new resolution? Can you start a new fight in the Foreign Relations committee, Dr. Paul?

Paul: It'll be continuous, and I think that we've made some inroads, because some of the Democratic leadership, Pelosi and others, have talked and questioned about more troops, and Obama has actually put a relative hold on this. I don't think he's going to change policies, though. I think it's going to continue. We have a coalition of some Democrats and Republicans that just put a letter together to send to the president to urge no more troops in Afghanistan and give us a plan on bringing them home.

But you know the truth. They really aren't winding down the war in Iraq. They just bring a few home, send more over there, and then send a whole lot of contractors — and more violence — over. But he's not going to walk away from Afghanistan. That's the only true option that we have. To do half a job might be the worst thing. No, the worst thing is sending more over there to get killed.

But even if you don't send more troops, and you try to do it with a smaller number of troops, it just prolongs the agony. And they don't even talk about our option of saying, "Bring them home." They're talking about, "Should we send 5,000 or 40,000? Should we have this and that?"

I think the debate ought to be "Why did we ever go? And why not just bring them home?" You argue the case for sending more, while I'll argue the case for bringing them home. That's where the debate ought to be.

Horton: Well, I have a ton more questions here, but I know that you're in a hurry today. I really appreciate all that you do, Dr. Paul, and your time on the show today.

Paul: Thank you, Scott.

September 23, 2009

Horton: Alright, everybody. That's Antiwar.com's man in the House of Representatives, Dr. Ron Paul, representing District 14 on the Texas Gulf Coast.

January 21, 2010

Horton: I'm happy to welcome our next guest, Dr. Ron Paul, the only decent congressman in American history, and, of course, you all know him from the run for president in 2007 and 2008. Welcome back to the show, Ron. How are you doing?

Paul: Thank you. Doing well.

Horton: I really appreciate you joining us on the show today.

Paul: Good. Good to be with you.

Horton: Alright. So, the most important thing here to start with I think, is a story in *Harper's* magazine by the other Scott Horton, renowned international human rights lawyer and anti-torture hero, about three men who quite apparently were murdered on the night of June 9, 2006 at Guantánamo Bay. Apparently, there's a massive coverup involved involving the Navy Criminal Investigative Service, the Justice Department, the FBI, and perhaps even parts of the Congress in trying to kill this story. I just wonder whether there's anything that you can do about this as a member of the Foreign Relations Committee. Would you have any jurisdiction to hold some kind of hearings or do anything to further investigate this?

Paul: Well, it's probably Judiciary. I don't think I would touch it. Probably even the committees that are responsible, they're not likely to touch it, but it's just another tragedy. There are so many of those tragedies around, so I'm not predicting that much will happen, but I know International Relations wouldn't touch it.

Horton: How troubling is that? Did you have a chance to read the article?

Paul: I read it. It was a rather long article. I did not get the whole thing read. I just got the gist of it. It just got me so upset, because of just another coverup, another atrocious act by our government, so it's a real shame.

Horton: I learned when I was a kid that what brought Nixon down wasn't

January 21, 2010

the crime, it was the coverup. That's really the big deal in Washington. A few CIA agents torture a guy to death, we're used to that, that happens all the time. But the problem here is, the FBI and the Justice Department and all these other people are making sure that the investigation doesn't go anywhere.

Paul: Yeah, and I think that principle must be the same thing that helped me on getting the Audit the Fed bill along, because we were often talking about transparency. We weren't talking about exactly what the Fed was doing, but it's the transparency, the hidden activities that they have, or the coverups. So I think good people, left or right or center, always say, "That's wrong. That is wrong." The coverup is bad and the hiding of government is so bad. I've always argued that we have things turned upside down here. If the government is to have a function, they ought to be protecting and guaranteeing our privacy. But what do they do? They protect their secrecy and they go, and they do tricks like this to hide what they do. At the same time, they undermine our privacy. So I think our government is absolutely on the wrong track.

Horton: If you were the president after September 11th how would you have set this up? Because it seems like now that Obama has come into power, not too much has changed. They say they're going to give trials to some of these men, but then they say, "Well, if they're acquitted, we'll go ahead and hold them anyway." Some of these people are going to get military trials, others aren't going to get trials at all. They'll just be held by the military indefinitely. I'm not sure how much of a change Obama's making to the Bush policy, but what should be done with Khalid Sheikh Mohammed and the rest of these guys? Just put them on trial in New York, Dr. Paul?

Paul: Long-term what you have to change is the foreign policy, so we get ourselves out of this business. But yes, I would try them in our courts. The individuals that committed the bombing, I believe it was 1993, they were arrested, brought to trial. They committed the crime in this country and they're in prison for life. What is so horrible about that? It's this whole idea of secret rendition and secret prisons and torture, the assumption that if somebody declares you an enemy combatant, one individual, that that is equal to being a terrorist. They're suspects. That means you can be tried by one individual and held forever, and American citizens are subject to that as well if you're declared an enemy combatant? I think the conditions are just horrible. If we have a breakdown of law and order here, if our economy really tanks and there's more violence, you could see where they can declare martial law and start holding people like this, so I think these are key issues, although for the average guy on the street this is rather esoteric, "They haven't come after me," this sort of thing, and they pass it off.

But what I think they are doing is setting the precedent for being able to handle domestic violence here, because what happens if they get careless with the definition of enemy combatant. Almost anybody who talks sympathetically, or even not sympathetically, but just trying to explain the situation, and it sounds like, "Ah, you're one of those guys that blame America first," and you could be declared an enemy combatant, so I consider it very dangerous.

Horton: Well in fact, at least in one case, José Padilla was arrested on American soil by FBI agents and then ended up being turned over to the military and the CIA to be tortured. In fact, the FBI agent who arrested him said he didn't think he was dangerous. He was trying to flip him and make him an informant. Because he wouldn't go along with becoming an informant, that was why they declared him an enemy combatant.

Paul: Yeah, and then they beat them to death. They might not have any information and they pretend they know information just to stop the beating. It just goes on and on. How many people have been arrested, picked up over in these foreign countries just because they've been squealed on by somebody else? We pay them money to turn somebody over, then we assume, "Yeah, they said he was a bad guy. He's an enemy combatant," so we throw him in prison. I think there are examples of teenagers being put down in Guantánamo — like 14 and 15 years old — and they've still been there. So yes, something has to be done. The whole process has to change, but to change the whole process you have to change the foreign policy.

You have to release the ones you have absolutely no evidence on and try the rest. There will always be one example of one guy who got out and committed another crime. But once again, what should you do? Endorse a system where they can arrest a hundred people and one guy might know something and you torture all hundred because there's some vital information in there? What have we turned ourselves into? It's just really, really a dangerous situation.

Horton: And this goes to my next topic here, which is your really great interview on *The Rachel Maddow Show*, about two weeks ago now. One of the things that she said to you there was — from her position, of course, being a liberal progressive, she has an interest in faction fights on the right and that kind of thing — but still I think there was a lot of truth when she said that the Republican Party has a severe lack of intellectual leadership here, and it's really come down to you on one side and Dick Cheney on the other, as far as who's leading the philosophy of the Republican Party. And like you, I kind of have a problem with that. I'm sure you kind of have a problem with that. You didn't just run for president and give all those great speeches about liberty and you don't go on all these TV shows and teach people about Austrian economics and all the peace mongering you do and the rest of this in order that all your Ron Paulian fans might all line up and vote for the Republican Party, right?

Paul: No. As a matter of fact, it came up yesterday on CNN, Rick Sanchez's show, he was asking me about that. I'm essentially totally uninterested in parties. Libertarians get upset with me because I'm not interested in setting my goal as building the Libertarian Party, but it certainly isn't the goal of mine to build the Republican Party. I live in the real world and the real world is that if you want a political soapbox you have to participate in one of the two parties. But I have no criticism about people doing it other ways.

But the last thing I'm interested in is promoting a party, but it is true that I want to influence the party. But I've frequently said that if we have a true revolution, the revolution is pervasive, and it affects both parties. I refer to the old statement of Nixon back in the '70s when he declared we were "all Keynesians now," which means that the Keynesian revolution infiltrated both parties. Norman Thomas said he didn't run the last time for president as a Socialist because the major parties have accepted their platform.

So if we are successful in promoting once again the cause of liberty, it's not going to be a single party. It's not going to be the Libertarian Party or the Republican Party, it will be in an acceptance by the majority of the American people who say, "Yeah, they bankrupt us, they ruin us. They can't help us and they fight too many wars, and we only want people in Washington that will fight for those values, Republican or Democrat, and certainly on economic terms we would want to have both sides have an understanding of Austrian free market economics."

Horton: On the Cheney side of that debate, the *National Review* published a thing by Andrew McCarthy the other day saying that the reason this guy Brown won in Massachusetts was because the American people know that we have to torture people, and this is what the American people demand. Never mind — because I agree with you and I'm completely uninterested in the party politics as well — but in terms of the philosophical debate, this is a major rift on the right, whether we are warmongers and torture-mongers or peace-mongers and Constitution-mongers. If it's fair to call the libertarian movement part of the right at all, which I think is actually not true.

Paul: But still, in spite of all the shortcomings and the problems we've had over the last several decades, the individual of the top two — because they always figure, "We don't want to waste our vote for anybody else, so we have to pick one of the top two" — of the top two, the one that offers the strongest case for peace usually wins. Bush represented that position because he was critical of Clinton, all his activities. Then Obama, of course, criticized Bush and McCain for this, so the people seemed to lean in our direction for this issue, as well as back when Nixon was elected. He was supposed to stop the Vietnam War. But the problem is, the people might lean in that direction and then we put somebody in and nothing changes, but right now the people are catching on and I think that's why, not only are they catching on that you can't trust the politicians, but they're also aware of the fact that the economic system is so friable and the jobs are disappearing that the status quo cannot be maintained.

Horton: And this is not a Banana Republic, not completely yet anyway, and it is possible, and we've seen examples of the American people actually getting their way on some things when they really demand it. I'm thinking of a great article I read at Glenn Greenwald's blog, I guess about a month back or so or maybe a little more than that, where he talked about how the reason that your Audit the Fed bill with Alan Grayson was able to get out of committee was because liberal bloggers had — obviously you had already gotten all the Republicans in Congress on board, they're in the minority, they're not risking much — but liberal bloggers had set up a campaign over there at Firedoglake, which is one of the prominent liberal blogs, where they said, "Look, here's all their names and here's all their phone numbers. Call your Democrats and tell them that you support this." And apparently Alan Grayson actually had printouts and showed these other Democratic politicians, "Look, it's safe. Your base is telling you, 'Please do this.'" And so it was this coalition of us versus them rather than left versus right that really came together to be able to get that Audit the Fed bill out of committee and then eventually attached to a bill that passed. I wonder whether you think that we can follow that model and really bring together a left-right, us versus them coalition to defund these wars. Isn't that the next step?

Paul: Let's hope so, but immediately after Obama was in, our left-right coalition against the war — there were a few Republicans with a bunch of Democrats. As soon as it was Obama's war, most of them faded except for a person like Dennis Kucinich and a few others, and Jim McGovern. They stuck with us, but the Democrats are just like the Republicans, they have this obedience to the king, and they have to abide, and they won't buck them.

I think what example you described there is relatively close to the truth, because the person that introduced my bill over in Senate was Bernie Sanders, and he calls himself a progressive socialist, and Grayson would be in that camp, too. But if you look at all of the Democratic supporters of the bill, there were a lot who were in swing districts and they were first- and second-termers and they were worried about reelection, and they were influenced by the people back at home. I don't want to diminish this idea of a right-to-left coalition on some of these issues, because that's what I work for all the time, but it's not like some of these Democrats that supported it are conservatives, though we can still call that a coalition. But it is true that people like Grayson and Bernie Sanders are certainly very solidly in that camp.

Horton: Speaking of the wars here, we have an occupation of Iraq, a state, which, we'll be talking to Michael Hastings later in the show about how the so-called success of the "surge" is all unraveling in front of us. We have an escalation in Afghanistan, the CIA bombing in Pakistan, and now to some degree or another we have the Joint Special Operations Command and the CIA at work in Yemen and Somalia, major calls from movie stars and other important people calling for the spreading of the war into Sunni Arab Darfur in Sudan. Something's got to be done to put an end to this, or we're going to be in real big trouble here. This is too many fronts for even America to fight on. Wouldn't you agree Dr. Paul?

Paul: Yes, but we're not going to wise up. You'd think with this election that just happened up in Massachusetts that all of a sudden, they'd be maybe backing off from spending bills — they're not going to do it. But that doesn't mean it's not going to end. I just don't believe it's going to end by us coming to our senses, from my experience here, but it's going to end with the economic crisis. Right now, we're in an economic financial crisis, but we're not in a dollar crisis. We're still printing money and the world's still taking our dollars, but one of these days they're going to quit.

I just came up with a figure today that we have to borrow — or to roll over and borrow — new money of $67 billion every week of this fiscal year. One of these days one of those auctions won't go so well, and that's when, if there's a panic, that's when the empire falls apart. That's what happened to the Soviets. It was as much of an economic issue as anything. They just run out of steam. I think that is what is going to happen to us, and it can't be all that bad.

Horton: I guess what you're referring to is there's so much debt that they'll just have to print money to pay it down, and then our $50 bills will be like nickels in our pocket.

Paul: That's right, and the debt gets liquidated, but only because they pay off the debt with money that has no value and you have runaway inflation. I think that is coming. You just can't keep printing money like this. As the productivity goes down, the good jobs are leaving us. Unemployment rates stay up. Even those who claim there's a recovery say, "Well, this is a jobless recovery." What kind of a recovery is that if somebody can't get a job? Are they supposed to feel better because there's a recovery going on and they're unable to feed their family?

Horton: I guess it's a recovery for people with lots of stock.

Paul: Or Goldman Sachs.

Horton: Yeah.

Paul: They had a good recovery; their bonus was gigantic, and their profits are huge today.

Horton: Right. Yeah, I just saw a line graph about that, where their bonuses are more than ever before. It's okay for rich people to be on the dole, just not poor people.

Paul: And the people who were fiscally prudent are the ones who will be taxed, one way or the other, to take care of the people who got the bailout.

Horton: To stick with the terror war concept here for a minute. There was a video of you from a speech that you gave, I guess over the weekend, that's gone kind of viral, where you talk about the CIA and their war in Pakistan. You really, I think, go so far as to say that the CIA runs American foreign policy basically from top to bottom. I wondered exactly what you were talking about, if you meant something that's happened just in the Obama administration that the CIA has risen in power compared to the Pentagon, or whether you were just talking about the national security state in general since World War II, or what exactly did you mean there?

Paul: More generally what's been happening and increasing and they're in the driver's seat. I'm doing a little more writing on this issue. I'm working on another book and I was doing some reviewing of the CIA, it was on my mind. When I was giving my speeches, I generally don't have notes or anything, and I was just really talking about the issues that I thought were important and that came up and I came up with a rather strong statement against the CIA. The real shocker...

Horton: Yeah, you said "take 'em out," which is what they call killing people.

Paul: Yeah. Of course, everybody knows that I'm nonviolent, and if I want to take somebody out, I deny them all their funds and revealing what they're doing, like remove them from office. But the surprise to me... to me it wasn't a surprise that those were my views because they've been my views all along. It wasn't anything brand new, but my shocker was, it drew the loudest applause. They stood up and I thought, "Wow, somebody else has been thinking about this, the FBI and the CIA and all these security agencies, a lot more than I have." I never anticipated that type of reaction, but it got some people's attention.

Horton: Of course, the Fox News guys would say, "That's just not realistic. Do you want the American government to be blind to everything that's going on in the world?"

Paul: Well, we're acting blindly now. We spent $75 billion on 16 agencies, then they get a hot lead by the phone call of the attempted Detroit underpants bomber's father and they can't handle it. That's the blindness. I think we've become blind because there are too many trees and we can't even see anything, even when it's laid on a platter. I think that's the real problem. I believe in intelligence gathering. I think good common sense and just reading the news and talking to people and looking at people who want to give you information is a good way to go, but all that money spent, the $75 billion, is spent to try to compensate for the anger we create by a flawed foreign policy. You could spend $150 billion, if your foreign policy is flawed and invites this type of hatred toward us, that money's not going to save us. It just won't work.

The more money you spend and the more agencies you have the more complex it gets, and the more information is lost. I think that is a lot of what happened before 9/11. They probably had a ton of information in there. Some people think it was deliberately ignored, but it's easy for me to understand how they could have so much information in so many agencies. The government is just so inept. I think it's not serving us well. I don't think the CIA is necessary. I think they are a culprit. I think they're the ones involved in the bombing right now. I think they're involved with torture, rendition, assassinations and rigging of elections. There's no reason for us to have an organization like that in a free society. But then again, you still could have a collection of information by people who claim they're your enemies and deal with it, and I think you'd probably have every bit as much information and maybe be able to react more sensibly with it, but nothing will improve our chances of avoiding these crises unless we change foreign policy.

Horton: I'm always impressed Dr. Paul, by the fact that when you're on these cable news shows, regardless of what they ask you, you really know all about it. You don't just have a talking point to go over, you really know all about it. So when they ask you about Iran, you can explain to them. Sometimes I wish Peter Schiff was watching when you explain that the Iranians, at least as far as anyone knows, are not even making nuclear weapons, the entire basis, the entire premise of our policy against them. Could you please explain to the people what it is that you know about Iran? I see here at Original.Antiwar.com/Paul, your last article that we published here is called "Iran Sanctions Are Precursor to War,"[4] so this is not just an academic issue. This is something very important.

Paul: If we go by our CIA, the CIA in their reports say they have no evidence they worked on a bomb since 2003. That doesn't mean that I believe that they don't have a secret desire or incentive, but we don't have any evidence. What we do is we violate the Non-Proliferation Treaty by telling them they're not allowed to have any enrichment, but they're permitted under the NPT to enrich for peaceful purposes and for nuclear energy. But we violate it by saying, "You can't even do that." So we are the violators of international law, and then we close our eyes to other countries. There are other countries in that region that don't belong to the international community for nuclear power, nuclear bombs.

Israel, Pakistan, and India, they all have them. We cozy up to them and they become our allies and we give them money. It's the fact that we can't control a few independent thugs, and that makes us furious, so therefore we have to concoct these stories that they're going to have nuclear weapons. I was in the service during the Cold War. The Soviets always had like 30,000 nuclear weapons, and intercontinental ballistic missiles capable

---

[4] Ron Paul, "Iran Sanctions Are Precursor to War," Antiwar.com, December 21, 2009, https://original.antiwar.com/paul/2009/12/21/iran-sanctions-are-precursor-to-war/.

of hitting us if they really wanted to, and we dealt with them, talked to them. We remained strong, and we won that without a nuclear war.

But here we have these Third World countries. They don't have an army or a navy or an air force or intercontinental ballistic missiles, and no nuclear weapons, and we're generating all of this hysteria. But it serves the interest of the military-industrial complex. It serves the interest of saying that, "Our national security requires it, we have to invade another country." That, hopefully, some day will change. The only thing I could tell you as an encouragement is when I go to the college campuses, they don't boo me for those kind of statements as they did at the Republican debates.

Horton: I read an interesting quote the other day from Dick Cheney, former vice president, only this was when he was the CEO of Halliburton. He had taken a trip to Australia in 1998 and he was criticizing Bill Clinton's administration and all the sanctions on Iran and was saying, "I think we could do a lot better if we were to expand and grow these relationships so that we could end up normalizing our relations and doing business." Isn't that strange, that Dick Cheney would be the one to sound like you saying something like that?

Paul: Yeah, I guess they have to pretend there's partisanship and they fight and fume — and there is a partisanship over who controls the power — but ultimately the policies don't ever seem to change.

Horton: But it seems like Halliburton actually really just preferred to make money doing business with Iran rather than waiting and just making all their money off of the Iraq war like they were going to do anyway.

Paul: Yeah, and now I'm sure they're lining up for some contracts at the present. They did get some contracts in the invasion process and the contractor monies that were spent over there.

Horton: I just saw a YouTube of you introducing legislation to legalize competing currencies, and this is sort of your other way around, rather than just outright repealing the Federal Reserve Act of 1913. This is how to make the Federal Reserve obsolete, isn't it?

Paul: That's right. I've always tried to figure out a transition. Some people say, "No, you just close the doors and bomb them and open it up." But you ought to have a transition. Like for instance, in postal services, you have a FedEx and a UPS, and hopefully they're allowed to deliver first-class mail someday. You don't have to close the post office down in one day. Fortunately, we still have competition in schooling. You can still homeschool and private school, so that helps neutralize a little bit the public school system. Also, in medicine, if they would just legalize a private option is what I would like, where you could just get out of the system and get a tax credit for everything you spend. That would be a private option.

But then in money, you can have a competing currency. Hayek actually wrote about this, and it's not so extreme, it's just legalizing the Constitution, because it was never repealed that gold and silver had to be legal tender. So you have to repeal the legal tender law so that the Fed does not have a monopoly. You should legalize the right of a private company to mint a gold coin. They would be held in check by the fraud laws and counterfeit laws. Today there are no fraud and counterfeit laws that apply to the Federal Reserve.

And then the last thing you would have to do is make sure you have no taxes on money, you don't tax dollars when you buy dollars or pay capital gains tax because the value of the dollar goes up. But if gold goes up in value and you pay sales tax when you buy a coin, and then you pay a capital gains tax when you spend the coin, it would be ridiculous, it can't be money. So you'd have to do these three things to allow people to use a currency different than the paper money.

Horton: Well some opponent of yours on MSNBC would say, "Yeah, but that would be inflationary, to have every bank and every private company introducing their own currency."

Paul: No, I didn't say that.

Horton: No, I'm saying that that's what they would say to you.

Paul: And I would say they misunderstand because all I'm doing is legalizing the Constitution that says gold and silver can be legal tender. I'm not doing anything else.

Horton: So it wouldn't be inflationary unless you could turn lead into gold.

Paul: Yeah, that's it. There would be no inflation, and the value of the gold currency goes up as the value of the paper currency goes down. Sometimes the populists who are sympathetic with what I say like the idea of everybody printing their own money, even the states, but that's prohibited. They're not allowed to emit bills of credit. We're not allowed to print money, because they did have horrendous inflation in colonial times, so I don't think that would be a good idea, at least to take that on now, but this would be strictly the gold and silver, which you can't inflate with. You get gold and silver by hard work and effort and that's why it maintains its value.

Horton: Right on. Well we're all out of time, but I really appreciate your time on the show today.

Paul: Okay, Scott, good to be with you.

March 4, 2010

Horton: ["Jack of Spades" by Boogie Down Productions plays in background.] Every hero has got to have his theme music. That one goes out to my hero, Dr. Ron Paul. Welcome back to the show, Ron, how are you doing?

Paul: Thank you, Scott, good to be with you.

Horton: I really mean that, too. I've got to tell you, at least over here at the Hate the State Estate we cheer out loud watching the YouTubes of all your TV news appearances.

Paul: Thank you.

Horton: It's just great seeing you get up there and teach these people. Especially how no matter what the question is, you always bring up war. They'll say, "Ron, what do you think about Social Security?" and you'll say, "Well, we have to end this empire."

Paul: Well you know they try to separate them into two factions. One is the foreign policy and one is domestic policy. I argue that you can't separate the two. So if you want more money in our economy and the retired people to take care of themselves, and you have a free market, you want less war and less spending overseas. But even in the transitional period, I'm willing to vote against all that operation overseas, and hopefully work our way out of our domestic problems, which means that even the transition you might be able to get a few converts to come out against the war. The big frustration is that Obama was supposed to help us out on that, and I'm sure the progressive Democrats aren't very happy with him on that issue either.

Horton: Yeah, well, they certainly don't have reason to be happy with him at all. So basically what's happening here with all these TV appearances that you've been doing… It's so cool for those of us who were big fans back in the day, when you were sort of underground and went around telling people, "Hey, did you know that there's one good congressman?" and all that. Now it's totally different, now you're a household name for everyone in the whole society. Everybody knows you now and you've been doing, since the beginning of your run for president, the world's greatest speaking tour on behalf of individual liberty and peace, I think, probably, ever. Which has got to feel great knowing that you're getting away with continuing to accomplish this on a daily basis. The people on the news keep calling you back, because you have an answer for everything that they have to ask, and it really is great.

And it seems like — I say all that to set up for a question here — it seems like it's working, at least on the young. I'm joined here actually in the studio by my friend Nick Hankoff, and he's from the Young Americans for Liberty and the Year of Youth, and he was there at CPAC, and was part of, I believe, the voting population there that helped put you over the top a couple weekends ago. So, welcome Nick, and did you have a question for Dr. Paul about CPAC and the peace movement here?

Nick Hankoff: Yeah. Hey Dr. Paul, I have had the pleasure of meeting you a couple times. Once in Los Angeles and then once in D.C. for CPAC. And, real quick, I just want to say the youth movement is, if anyone has any doubts, there are real connections being made. These are real people with their hearts really in the movement. We came together with close bonds and a lot of great memories out of CPAC, and you and just the issues of the world today, I guess, are bringing us together in this perfect storm.

But the one thing that's dividing the youth movement a little bit is how to react or what the commentary is on the relationships with names like Michael Steele or Glenn Beck or the types of names that came out before, who aren't friendly to a lot of our viewpoints. But then, somehow magically they change their opinion or come around in for a photo op and swing in and all that. So there's one side of the movement that is yelling, "heads on a stick, heads on a stick." And then the other side of the movement is saying, "No, people realize they make mistakes and they're growing up or they're changing their minds, whatever you want to call it." How do you address those issues, and how do you know when someone is being genuine or just trying to use your influence, your movement?

Paul: I try to ignore the discussion of the personalities. I don't want it to be over personalities and too often that becomes emotional. So I don't go out of my way. If they mention somebody's name and say, "do you think they're trying to come in and take over?" They may well be, but I don't want that to be the issue. I think the only issue should be what we believe in, and I see my responsibility as setting a record. Not only saying the right things but voting the right way. I purposely avoided, the best I could, from ever mentioning George Bush's name when he was president, although I was opposed to his foreign policy and his, of course, domestic policy when it came to the PATRIOT Act and other surveillance activities that he was participating in. But I didn't want to have to deal with people's emotional attachment to George Bush, especially since he was from Texas, and I didn't want to make it a personality issue.

You can win more battles if you stay in the realm of the ideas. The only problem with it is, in the media, they always want confrontation, they're always stirring it up. I do get some of these interviews mainly because I will oppose the conventional wisdom of both Democrats and Republicans, but especially the Republicans. If it's a progressive program, they might want to use it just to say, "See, these Republicans don't know what they're talking about. Ron Paul says this." And I know what they're trying to do, but I really try to stay away from it. I don't want to have the job of not only promoting the ideas I believe in, and then I have to discredit the people who are in opposition when there's an emotional attachment. I try to avoid that the best I can.

Horton: Well it seems, Dr. Paul, like the real split on the right is over war, and the positions are really being solidified. It's funny, because I know that you're almost alone in the House of Representatives, but ideologically out here in the world, where you have this whole Tea Party movement going on and, as you said, progressives who already are getting over Barack Obama after his expansion of the wars, and so forth. I wonder, do you think it's possible that Nick and the Year of Youth types, can actually help you? Is it an attainable goal really to get the right wing to be anti-interventionist? I mean, it is Obama's war now, right? What's to like about that?

Paul: Well, I think one of the reasons why I did well in the election was it was no longer me confronting George Bush, and it was Obama's war, so this should soften the position of the conservatives. The conservative Republicans were positively opposed to Clinton's war in Bosnia, which was an interventionist's war. So I think there's reason to hope they'll do better, not maybe for a perfect reason, only because they're out of power right now.

But next week is a very good chance that... There's a group of us have gotten together, along with Dennis Kucinich and some other Democrats, and we've introduced a resolution challenging the war in Afghanistan based on the War Powers Resolution. Dennis has been promised, by the leadership, that we're going to have a three-hour debate on Afghanistan. We should've had it ten years ago, and five years ago — it should be constant — but we're finally going to have a debate because funding and the promotion of the Afghan war is more likely coming from the Republicans than the Democrats, so I'll be interested in seeing how this comes down there. There will be a vote on this, and I'm hoping that we can pick up some more Republican support on this, as well as some more Democrats, for that matter. The antiwar coalition that we worked with against Bush, that has softened on the Democratic side, because of the partisan issue. That becomes pretty frustrating. But next week might be an interesting week to see what happens.

Horton: Yeah, it's too bad. I know foreign policy is not everybody's first issue, but I wish it could be Ron Paul and Dennis Kucinich in the Peace Party, and let the Cheneys and the Obamas have each other, you know?

Paul: Yeah, that's about right.

Horton: At least that way, you know, because we have somewhat of an antiwar movement on the left and the right, but it's kind of hard to bring us together. It's good to see you working with Dennis Kucinich on that. I was actually just going to ask you about that, whether you were going to be or not, so that's great to hear that.

Let me ask you about money really quick here, Dr. Paul. Well, I'll put it this way, I've got some Austrian economists in my left ear saying that the damage is done, the seeds have been sown, the dollar will be destroyed, it's only a matter of time. And then I have a word of caution that comes from a few different places, but most importantly to me, from the great Robert Higgs at the Independent Institute, who says, "Well, they know that they're between a rock and a hard place, and they will jack up interest rates through the roof before they let the dollar be completely destroyed, and they will find a way out of this. Or at least they know that they need to." So do you think that it's possible that we actually have time to maybe actually roll back the empire, and cut some spending and avoid a total dollar meltdown, and the kind of crisis that will come with that?

Paul: No, but there may be a position in between. They won't do it deliberately and calmly and more smoothly by just cutting back. But if they allow it to continue there will be a major crisis. Something will have to happen. It's not because they want to, but because they'll have to. They may save the dollar in name, but they'll have to change the monetary policy. They'll have to say, well, in picking up the pieces. But I don't think it's going to happen without a much greater financial crisis, which I think is going to come in the next several years. Nobody knows exactly when the panic hits, and everybody panics and dumps dollars, but then not only will the Fed raise interest rates, but the market will raise interest rates.

But you know, in the early 1980s, in '79, '80 when Paul Volcker came in, he took interest rates up to 21 percent and got a lot of heat for it, but in a way, if he hadn't done that, the confidence would've been further lost and who knows what might have happened. Right now, they're not on the verge of doing that because the conditions are worse and if they do that the economy would weaken so much, that they're going to wait until the market demands that something be done.

Horton: Do you think we're risking a real crackup boom, where, I think the worst case scenario as I've read it would be all the central bankers in the world panicking and saying, "Oh no, today's the day," and just dumping their debt and all of a sudden trillions and trillions of dollars will be coming back to the United States, and all of us will be the last ones holding the bag there. Is that really the kind of danger we're messing with here?

Paul: It sure is, and right now though, it's in everybody's interest to keep this game going. Whether you're holding dollars or printing dollars, and I'm sure what we do is, we agree that if you can help prop up our dollar, we're going to help maintain order in the system, so if somebody gets behind — like Greece — we will, behind the scenes, help them out. Certainly, if we can help countries like that around the world, and bail them out, we'll bail out the states like California and others, because for a state like California to default on payments just wouldn't be tolerated. But the market is what regulates this. When it gets absolutely out of control, then there will be dumping no matter how hard they worked to hold it together.

Horton: Alright everybody, that's Dr. Ron Paul, he represents District 14 on the Texas Gulf Coast there, and he represents me in the House of Representatives. Thank you very much.

Paul: Thank you, it's good to be with you, Scott. Bye bye.

Horton: Alright, also everybody go out and get *End the Fed*, and most especially, *The Revolution: A Manifesto*. That book will change your view.

May 12, 2010

Horton: Our next guest is Dr. Ron Paul from District 14 on Texas's Gulf Coast. Welcome back to the show Ron.

Paul: Good afternoon. Good to be with you.

Horton: Well, I'm happy to talk to you again. Sort of bad news with the watered-down version of the audit amendment passing the Senate, but I thought I would start this interview off with a little bit of positivity which is that well, six months ago, in the House of Representatives, Mel Watt and others were more than happy to carry Ben Bernanke's water and oppose your real audit amendment. Yet, in the Senate, not one senator dared to really come out against this audit. You get all the credit. You did it. You have the whole country against the Federal Reserve now, and you have the Senate and the entire government running scared, Ron. Congratulations and thank you.

Paul: Well, let's hope so.

Horton: This watered-down version of the amendment, the audit amendment, what exactly does it mandate? Could you explain to us the difference between what your amendment had and what this does?

Paul: Well, I guess the best way to describe it, this does require disclosure of what they did in the last two years in the bailout. It's not a true full audit, and it's not ongoing. It won't last into the next year. It's just to disclose which companies and where the money went during that scramble to bailout our economy. So it's a minor victory. The biggest victory is a PR victory in that we have the American people now very much more knowledgeable about the Federal Reserve than ever before. They know the Federal Reserve is powerful. They create money, and they bailout their friends. I think that's the most important thing. This whole story about having a real audit is not quite over because it looks like it will not be put in the Senate bill. It is in the House bill, the financial reform bill. They might have to have a conference. If they do, then they'll be an argument over which version to use, the watered-down version.

 Actually, they could use both because what was passed in the Senate although it wasn't a true audit, it was worthwhile. I wouldn't have been able to vote against it. I just didn't like the process because some of the Senators are already saying when supporters call in and ask the senator, "Why didn't you vote for Vitter's amendment?" Vitter introduced 1207, our bill. They said, "Oh well, we voted for Sanders' bill." It sort of gave them political cover, and it made people feel better about it, and it confused the public. You don't have to get rid of what Sanders did, but it would be nice if in the conference we could get the House side of the full audit. We still have a ways to go on that because they can avoid a conference if they want, and that raises other questions.

Horton: Well, I'm happy to hear you say that. I guess I would have thought that if both Houses had passed your version, then they would have ruined it in the conference. You're saying there's actually a possibility that the Senate version could be improved in the conference committee?

Paul: Yeah, theoretically it is. If Vitter's amendment, which is our bill, would have passed, it would have been harder, much harder. They could, but it would have been harder to start messing around in the conference because it has such a high profile. Everybody knows what's going on. Sometimes what they'll do in a conference is they will change things or add things that nobody knows about until a year later or something. This is being well watched. I think, right now, let's say the conference was going on right now, we could raise a lot of fuss and get a lot of attention. I think we wouldn't do any better than we did in the Senate and probably couldn't win the vote. Once again, the important issue is putting the blame where it's deserved, and that is on the Federal Reserve, for all the mischief they cause.

Horton: Well, in your TV appearances lately, and your House floor speeches, you've been really emphasizing the currency crisis as you call it. You're saying we're already in one. This is not we're in danger of having one. Am I reading that right? What does that really mean?

Paul: Yeah. Well, I say the dollar is being devalued rather rapidly. The only long-term traditional way of measuring the value of the currency is by gold. We had the Fed come in in 1913. The dollar/gold ratio was 20 to one — twenty dollars could buy an ounce of gold. Now it takes almost 1,250 dollars to buy one ounce of gold. It's been devalued. It's been devalued over 98 percent. A devaluation means each dollar is worth less. Actually, they're not dollars anymore. They're Federal Reserve Notes. It means a promise to pay nothing. Dollars have long been lost because dollars mean actually the weight in silver. I draw the analogy to the early 1970s when the Bretton Woods agreement broke down. We devalued against gold. At that time, it wasn't done on a daily basis. It was done deliberately by governments because they had to fix the exchange rate. They devalued in '71 and '73 twice for a total of 18 percent devaluation. That ushered in a horrendous inflation of the late '70s where prices were going up 15 percent a year. Interest rates had to go up to 21 percent to really save the dollar.

My argument now is just in the last ten years we've devalued the dollar by 80 percent. That, to me, means that people — in terms of the real measurement of the gold — they're rejecting the dollar, which if history proves is correct, history says this will translate into much higher prices in the not-too-distant future.

Horton: Is it brilliant of Ben Bernanke to create all this money, to give it to the banks, to fill up their bad debts, and cover all their losses, but then pay them to keep the money and not loan it out? It seems like there's a little Ron Paul on his shoulder screaming about inflation, and he's kind of taking it seriously, and he's going along this policy of creating all this money, but he's really not letting it all get out into circulation if I understand right.

Paul: Well, I don't think he has a policy that says to the banks, "Do not let it go out." I think the conditions are such that it doesn't go out. Some people don't want to borrow money under these conditions. Bankers have lost a lot of money, so they are much more cautious. Regulators, especially in housing and other things where the government is involved, they've been stung too because they were very, very loose. All these things add up that it's much better for the banks to just take the money, which is practically free from the Federal Reserve, then they go, and they make money just by buying treasury bills or doing other things and make just a couple of percentage points, but you can make billions and billions of dollars. These banks are making a lot of money. They're paying these debts. Even General Motors is paying back their debts by us giving them more money. We buy their stocks and give them money, and then they pay back the loans.

Horton: It's like German war debt.

Paul: It's all a gimmick, but it benefits the banks to run this program.

Horton: It's funny. The way you talk about the way the money is going around, GM getting bailed out, it sounds like America, giving all that money to the Germans to repay the French and the British after World

War I. Then, they ended up hyperinflating trying to pay everybody back.

Paul: Well, what about what we're doing right now? We're bailing out Europe. The market, and the reason I've been talking more about the currency is we did the bailout for two years, now we're embarking on the bailout of Europe. Usually, the dollar price of gold would just move with the stock market or the dollar, but now it moves totally independently. It moves like it's a currency in itself. It's always been a currency, but it was in limbo for the last several decades. It was only moving as strictly a commodity. Gold is both money and a commodity. Now it's proving itself. It's not moving up just because the dollar is going down. As a matter of fact, the dollar is going up. Ordinarily that should make the price of gold go down. The people are buying gold because it's the ultimate currency, and people are getting frightened enough. It doesn't take very much because there are trillions and trillions of fiat dollars and other currencies around the world.

If you had just three, or four, or five percent of that and saying, "Hey, we're getting a little bit nervous. Why don't we buy a hard asset?" it would be trouble. That's why I expect all the currencies of the world to depreciate against gold in the very near future, which means it's going to usher in a panic situation where prices are going to start to soar.

Horton: Alright. One last question. I know you're in a hurry. How would the U.S. government pay for its endless warfare without the Federal Reserve?

Paul: They can't do it. They monetize that debt. Next week we have a supplemental coming up. I don't know if you recall, but when Bush was fighting those wars, the Democrats condemned them because it was always emergency funding. It was never through the budget resolution. But Obama's doing the same thing. It's going to be as a supplemental emergency and then we'll pay for it. But there's no money in the bank. Even if we raise taxes, there are no revenues to collect. Revenues are actually going down because the economy is so weak. It has to be paid for by the Federal Reserve. The Federal Reserve directly or indirectly will create money and credit and pay these bills which just puts more pressure on the dollar. We've gotten away with it for a long, long time, and the dollar is still better than the other paper currencies, but we're entering the stage now where all the currencies, especially the dollar now, is being devalued on a daily basis.

May 12, 2010

Horton: Alright. Thank you very much for your time on the show today.

Paul: Thank you very much.

June 18, 2010

Horton: Welcome to the show, Ron. How are you doing?

Paul: Good, Scott. Good to be with you.

Horton: I'm really happy to have you here. Let me tell you real quick, here, if I can try to sum it up. I got a dream going on here where there's a real realignment in American political thought. I learned in junior college that in the 1930s, Roosevelt realigned everything. He got all the conservatives and almost all the liberals, town and country and black and white and East Coast, West Coast, and everybody together in this giant, new New Deal coalition. Kept him in power through four elections, and this was a giant sea change in the way American politics was from then on, as we all know. This is what we need right now, sure seems to me. And it also seems to me that the three most important issues, as you consistently identify — the preservation of the Constitution and the Bill of Rights, an end to corporate welfare and bailouts for the richest and most powerful among us, and peace in our relationship with the rest of the world — are three issues that ought to, and in many ways do, completely transcend the left/right spectrum as it exists today.

My question for you is, what do you see as the future of this realignment? What do you see in terms of the possibility of alliances left, right, Tea Party, and progressive, and libertarian, and otherwise, in order to really get these most important problems solved?

Paul: I hope your dream is coming about, because the liberal media has already written off the whole movement. They said, "Oh, it looks like the Tea Party movement, the disgruntled people of America who've been speaking out…" I think they're claiming they peaked last August, and it's been downhill. They've had a few victories, but nobody cares about it anymore and their crowds are smaller. They went on and on, and they're trying to bury the whole notion that the American people are upset with the status quo of the Republican and the Democratic leadership. I can't make the prediction, but I'm very sympathetic to the idea that something like that is going on. Because I do talk to a lot of people, and why I am most enthusiastic is because the young people are thinking this way. Young people who are inheriting this mess know that it's not a very good deal for them, and they don't like the war. They believe that we should follow the rules in the Constitution. They're principled people, and they don't like special interests. They don't like corporate interests taking over.

The overriding issue of all this is that of finding out what the government is doing. I think that was why Audit the Fed became so popular with young people. They're sick and tired of the government being secretive. At the same time, the government works very hard to invade our privacy and what we do and how we spend our money, so it's ripe for a change. I think, in many ways, the intellectual revolution is ongoing. It's probably at its early stages, but let's just hope we can keep this momentum going.

Horton: Everybody knows about your work with progressive congressman from Florida Alan Grayson on the Audit the Fed amendment, but you're also working with him on the War Is Making You Poor Act. I was wondering if you could explain a little bit about what that is.

Paul: Yeah. He sort of grabbed an idea that I've been talking about because he knows I would not support a bill that would expand the welfare state back here at home. He is a progressive, so he's for the medical bill and these other things, but he knew how to write a bill that would get me interested. Of course, it was to save money from overseas and take that money and pay down the deficit. It's pretty hard to turn that down, because that's pretty good. This is where I think we should start. I think it's easier to start cutting the militaristic budget that we have, and the idea that we have to police the world. More people are starting to wake up to this. At the same time, offer tax cuts. That's pretty good for a liberal Democrat to go along with us on that. I do get criticized, at times: Why do I even talk to Barney Frank, and why do I talk to Grayson because they're so bad on economic policies.

But in other things, hopefully the progressives, their eyes will open up and say, "Hey, if they're right on civil liberties and they're right on the war, maybe we should pay more attention to the Federal Reserve and the gold standard and limited printing of money and deficits." I think we're making some inroads. A lot of people that will support us will say, "I used to be a liberal." Or they'll say, "I used to be a supply sider. I used to be a neocon." And once they see the whole picture, they'll come and say, "I think you guys have it right."

Horton: Right. I know I've been getting emails lately. One of my most radical new listeners is a former military recruiter. They're listening to

Antiwar Radio, including a couple military officers listen. So, you're right. You never know who you're going to win over. It does seem to me like this War Is Making You Poor Act is the perfect left/right issue, really.

Paul: Yeah. That's true.

Horton: We'll cut your income taxes.

Paul: And also, because there's no leadership on the left on this. It used to be that it would all come from progressive Democrats and a few Republican conservatives, but now they're so much quieter with Obama in. That's why I think if we can bring them together with a coalition led by libertarian types, I think that we may make some progress.

Horton: What about the Tea Party right? These were the people who pretty much supported the worst of the Bush policies that you always opposed. And yet, the right is out of power now, and there's a lot of talk about the Constitution from the other side of the Tea Party movement. Do you think that you could show them that the Bill of Rights is part of the Constitution, too, maybe?

Paul: Yeah.

Horton: Is there hope there?

Paul: It'd be nice. Sometimes, I think that might be every bit as tough, if not tougher, than getting a liberal Democrat to say, "Cut down on the war spending and cut taxes." That looks like it might be easier than converting some of these people into believing that we're still patriots if we say we ought to defend this country and not pretend that we can police the world. That one is tough, but we do have some coming that way. If you take somebody like Jimmy Duncan. He is strictly Old Right Republican, and he's a fiscal conservative and he doesn't believe that we should be involved — and, of course, Walter Jones has come over this way. There are a few, but the really, really hardcore neocons, that's a real job for us.

Horton: Indeed. You've had a lot of great moments, but it seems like one of the very greatest was, I think, in 2007 when you introduced this American Freedom Agenda Act that said, "Everything wrong is hereby repealed. We're going to start getting it right." You think you might could try that again for 2010?

Paul: Yeah. We might just do that. Who knows, 2010? It would be nice if we did this amendment that I've introduced in the past, I haven't done recently. It was the Liberty Amendment. That just eliminates everything that's unconstitutional within three years and repeal the 16th Amendment — no income tax.

Horton: Wow. So then, that would be the PATRIOT Act and the Military Commissions Act of 2009, and all of those things, too?

Paul: Oh, yeah.

Paul: Everything that is not explicitly authorized in Article 1, Section 8.

Horton: Oh, so we're talking about repealing the 20th century and the 21st, too?

Paul: Yeah. At least, it's great symbolism for us. But you know, most of this stuff is going to fail. How do you get rid of Keynesian economic intervention? They take our country into bankruptcy, and everybody starts ignoring what the federal government's telling us to do. And I think it's already starting. I don't believe that laws are going to permit nullification, but just the failure of government will permit nullification. The liberals don't like the feds telling them about marijuana, and the conservatives don't like them telling them about some of the conservative issues and school issues and things like this. So, if the government is flat-out broke, they might just be unable to stop the states from acting on their own.

Horton: You told the *Washington Post* back when you were running for president — and I know you were half-joking, or maybe you weren't — you told them that, "Ah, we could protect this country with a couple of good submarines." You really think we need only that small of a military force to keep this country safe, sir?

Paul: I really do, but I would still allow the militia sentiment to exist so that if anybody ever tried to march on our shores, that everybody would be ready for them. But no, nobody's going to attack us. Why are we building tanks and bomber aircraft? Those are, today, ancient weapons. I think we could do with a very small military.

Horton: Alright, well thank you very much for your time on the show today, sir. I sure appreciate it.

Paul: Thank you. Very good. Thank you.

August 27, 2010

Horton: Welcome to the show, Ron. How are you doing?

Paul: Thank you, Scott. Good to be with you.

Horton: I'm very happy to have you here and I was so happy to see your statement on the mosque issue. You know, before I ever learned, I think even about George Washington and the cherry tree or Davey Crockett or anything, I learned from my dad that the highest value in America, the most important thing about America as a place, is freedom of religion, and that's what we all value the most and is the most special thing about this land. And it's just amazing to see the demagoguery and it was just great to — of course, you never do disappoint — but it was really great to see the stand that you took on this and everybody can read your article. "Mosque Demagoguery Is Bipartisan"[5] is the title that it goes under at Original.Antiwar.com/Paul. Thanks for that and can we start I guess with what you think of that? Religious freedom as the highest American value.

Paul: In that statement I make the point that conservatives who brag about being big property rights people are the ones who demagoguing the most about why they shouldn't build this, Newt Gingrich in particular. To me it was an opportunity to defend property rights in the pure sense of the word because it is closely related to First Amendment rights. If we protected property rights, we would protect a lot of the amendments. You'd protect the Second Amendment, you'd protect the First Amendment because it would be your property that is being used whether you are running a newspaper, whether you have a church or whatever you are doing. It's the property that should be protected and then I think the conservatives wimp out on this, but the liberals are never good on it.

The liberals came along and they say, we've got to protect freedom of religion and expression — and they're right about that — but they're so weak on property rights and they always want to regulate property. This would have been a time that it should have been pointed out that the conservatives have sort of sold out and that liberals who don't understand

---

[5] Ron Paul, "Mosque Demagoguery Is Bipartisan," Antiwar.com, August 22, 2010, https://original.antiwar.com/paul/2010/08/22/mosque-demagoguery-is-bipartisan/.

the property rights very well ought to learn a lesson. I just thought I would give them my two cents' worth. And I find it interesting and fascinating and sometimes entertaining when I read a blog by someone who is a very, very liberal person that say, "This is very great, but it really is confusing what's happening to the world. The world has turned upside down when I agree with Ron Paul and he is speaking more what I believe in than our own president."

But I think the most I can expect — or any of us can expect — coming from a libertarian viewpoint is that we stimulate people's thinking. So those who give me some support and say, "Yes, I agree with Ron Paul in foreign policy or civil liberties, but…" I keep saying the but always means, of course, the economic liberty, but maybe they'll think about it. Of course, you know Scott that you've met people that will come to our side from the liberal side as well as the conservative side and say, "Yes it finally makes sense." I see it's a tremendous opportunity now to increase our ranks because the liberals — the Keynesians, the interventionists — have failed so miserably with the economy. This, I just saw as an opportunity. I hope I made a few points.

Horton: Well, an important point you made was that Islam was not the motivation for the September 11th attack and that's really the subtext of this entire thing is that it's us versus them and them is 1.3 billion people in the world.

Paul: Yeah, and this was, of course, the big motivation for writing this as well. I didn't take the same position of everybody who said that were giving advice. Some supported the people's property rights, but they were giving strong advice: "Well, perceptions are so bad. Just don't open the mosque there. We don't want you to do it." There is a lot like that. But the people who were really beating the drums, they need to continue to blame Islam for 9/11. They don't want to blame a small number who belong to al Qaeda who committed the violence. They want to blame all of Islam. You know, "It's a hate religion," and, "It's a religion of the devil," and these kinds of things. I have met and known and are friends with too many Muslims in the medical profession for me to even think, let alone let them challenge, the principle that you stated, that this country was built on an understanding of tolerance of all religious beliefs.

Horton: On the foreign policy thing too, you always make the comparison to medicine and say, "You know, if you diagnose the illness wrong, you're going to get the treatment wrong." And here we are still operating on the false premise that they attacked us only for how nihilistic they are and how good we are and I guess perhaps we are still operating somewhat along the premise that we still have to invade them and occupy them and give them democracy so that they won't be oppressed and won't want to be terrorists anymore and I'm thinking if we got the diagnosis wrong and we continue to act the way we are acting, we're going to end up having a lot more terrorism in the future.

Paul: I think that analogy works both on the economic mistakes — if you continue to make the mistakes and not change your course of action — and foreign policy. It's the same thing. If the Global War on Terrorism is a good idea and we have to continue to do it and not realizing that we increase our danger to us — the national security — and we increase the odds and the chances of our national bankruptcy, it's foolhardy, it's insane. It's almost national suicide to do this. But people don't like to admit they made a mistake. Can you imagine George Bush analyzing this: "Well, you know, now that I look back, we made this mistake?" No matter how bad it gets, they are not going to admit it.

What are the expectations that Bernanke is going to say, "Well, my whole life was wasted. My monetary theory is completely wrong. It's made things much worse"? There's no chance of that. Somebody else has to come in and offer a different alternative and we have to convince people philosophically in order to persuade and we can't do it by out-demagoguing them. We have to educate people to come around saying there is another way to look at this.

Horton: Well, now, one of the most important issues going on right now is the expansion of the War on Terrorism under the special operations forces. I'm sure you have seen these *New York Times* and *Washington Post* articles about this and I'm sure you know from your experience on Capitol Hill about what's going on in Yemen and the drone strikes and expansion and that kind of thing. I believe that Dennis Kucinich has sponsored a bill to, at the very least, ban the assassination of Anwar al-Awlaki, the American citizen who is said to be hiding out in Yemen. Are you a co-sponsor of that and could you take it further to ban this global assassination program in general?

Paul: Well, I think somebody did this. This might have been one of the better executive orders. I think one of our presidents actually said that the law was supposed to be that. But you shouldn't even have to have a law, just common sense and common decency should mean that you don't assassinate people. But no, it could be done more explicitly. It could be done on the House floor and the Senate and do resolutions. The whole problem is presidents especially don't necessarily follow the law. There are a lot of laws on the books, laws that violate the Constitution. The Constitution is the real law. We don't live in a lawful society. They generally do what they want. The Congress does what they want. The executive branch, the courts do what they want. But any legislation that would suggest that we ban and not participate in assassination, obviously I would be strongly supportive of it.

Horton: Now you brought up Ben Bernanke and the complete failure of his economic theory. Well I just heard on the top-of-the-hour news that he gave his speech in Jackson Hole, Wyoming — which is I think where Dick Cheney lives, part of the time — and in that speech he said he wants to reduce the interest rate that they are paying the banks to keep their reserves at the Fed to nothing and to force the banks to go ahead and lend out all the new money he has created. Are we facing an inflationary depression or is there still so many bad debts left to be repaid that we are still going to have deflation anyway?

Paul: Well, there's a strong contest going on. Markets always want to deflate; governments always want to inflate. Now, he thinks that he has been — You know they talk about "pushing on a string" and not having it work. Well, he's been hammering on a string and hasn't worked. Now what he is trying to do is force the banks to loan this money rather than just putting it back in reserves. If they make less, maybe they will take a little more gamble. But there are a lot of people who are skittish about borrowing money right now and banks are going to be held accountable. Keeping reserves making zero interest may, from their viewpoint, be a better deal than going out and making loans in an economy that nobody knows what is going to be like. And there is now a growing consensus that the economy is going to continue to get weaker. No matter who is running the bank, they might think it's more prudent to keep the reserves in reserve without interest. That's almost like putting it in a shoebox.

But I think what's going to happen is the inflationary impact is going to come. This money will eventually filter out there and as things go on when you are not earning any interest, you're going to find more and more people putting their money in gold and silver and I think that will be done by foreign countries as well and there are going to be alternative currencies, as difficult as it is for people to deal in euros. I think people will start using euros and other currencies and I don't look forward to any economic expansion here anytime soon.

Horton: We are looking at more or less as a model the 1970s where they call it the "stagflation," right? The high unemployment but all the stimulus and all the inflation in the world doesn't solve the employment problem. Now we just have high prices, too.

Paul: Yeah, but I think it's going to be a lot worse than the '70s. There was always a little bit of growth and things seem to move along but the inflation was the main thing. But I think the economy is going to be much, much weaker, and then when the dollar's rejected you're going to have a lot more inflation. Probably it's going to be an inflationary depression rather than just stagflation.

Horton: You're talking about once the world gives up on the dollar reserve standard and all those dollars come back.

Paul: Right, and they are going to come back. What's China going to do with a trillion dollars if this market starts to slip? They will try to moderate their dumping of dollars for a while but if it moves rapidly, they are going to have to invest those dollars rather… And I think they are already doing this. We are wasting lives and money trying to protect our oil in the Middle East while they are over there actually being able to bid on some contracts in Iraq to drill oil. And, of course, they're friends with Iran and they'll have inroads to that country's oil. But it just seems like they are a little more capitalistic than we are. They make stuff for us and we give them money and now they are starting to invest around the world. I think we live in very dangerous times where things could change rather quickly. Something breaks out in Iran, which a lot of neocons would like to see happen, this could be devastating to the markets.

Horton: Well, I'll tell you what, I'll make you a deal, Dr. Paul. You run for office again, I'll vote one more time.

Paul: You will? One more time, okay. Well, we'll see what happens. It's a little bit premature to talk about it, I guess.

Horton: Well, here's waiting for February. Thank you very much for your time on this show, as always.

Paul: Thank you, Scott. Good to be with you.

November 23, 2010

Horton: I'm Scott Horton and our next guest on the show today is Dr. Ron Paul. Very happy to welcome him back to the show. Hey Ron, how're you doing?

Paul: Doing well, Scott. Thank you.

Horton: Very happy to have you here. So, first things first, big news today, there was a skirmish in Korea, apparently started by the North. The South retaliated. Two are dead, sixteen wounded and I think the world wants to know if Ron Paul had won the presidency in 2008, what would your Korea policy be? And how different might this situation be this morning?

Paul: Well, I'd pretty much ignore the whole thing and I'd continue to work on bringing our troops home by this time, though. If a good president had been elected, he'd have had the troops out of Korea, and we wouldn't have been involved. This assumption that we're automatically going to go to war if there's a war over there is ridiculous. War is supposed be very, very cautiously done and only done with a declaration, but we sign treaties, station troops, and assume that no matter what happens we're going to be in the midst of a war. This whole idea that North Korea is going to be a danger to America or South Korea is total nonsense, they're having a little border skirmish there. Compare it to the skirmishes going on between Mexico and the United States, it's rather minor. So this whole idea that we have to show our muscle and come down hard is wrong. The neighborhood should take care of it. Maybe Japan wants to have something to say about it if something flares up. South Korea's so powerful, they can handle themselves. China may have an interest in settling things down, too. But the United States has no business over there, it's not in our best interest, and the sooner we realize that and get out of there, the better off we'd be.

Horton: Alright, now if George Bush had not undone Bill Clinton's Agreed Framework deal from 1994, which basically said we'd give them light-water reactors that won't produce weapons-grade material, we'll bribe them with fuel oil and with money if they will just promise to stay within the Non-Proliferation Treaty and their Safeguards Agreement, if that deal was still on and you were the president right now, would you continue under that deal or you'd go ahead and write that off as well?

Paul: Well, that's messy too. If they do what we tell them, we're going to give them some benefits. If they don't do what we tell them, we're going to threaten with bombs. I don't like those options, but I would try to work toward normalizing things to talk to them, and trade with them and if there's something that can be done to develop peaceful use of nuclear power with guidelines, I think that's worth talking about. But to have something and say if you do this, we're going to send you this and give you some benefits, I don't think we need to do that. I think that things have been worked out in other countries around the world, so I think we should have left that open at least, but I think we should have this other option rather than just either bomb them or bribe them.

Horton: So, in other words, just promise not to go to war with them — or not promise not to start one — and drop all the sanctions, try to open up trade and just treat them like a normal country.

Paul: Yeah, and we should have done that with Cuba a long time ago. I saw some good statistics here although we haven't normalized things with Cuba, the amount of farm products we're selling into Cuba now is really doing pretty good. We need to continue in that movement. So that's been argued by many, especially the Founders of our country, that if you trade with people, you're less likely to fight with them.

Horton: We have a War on Terrorism going under the Authorization to Use Military Force, supposedly at least, from after the September 11th attack, but I was wondering with your position in the House of Representatives, is there any way that you could try to pass a Boland-type amendment that would forbid Barack Obama from spending American tax dollars, or printed dollars, waging war in Yemen or Somalia or Pakistan, since those are not official wars but we seem to be waging them anyway?

Paul: Well, it's a shame that the Boland amendment had to be passed. I don't think I was there when that was voted on, but I would have supported it, but that's the Constitution — they're not supposed to do those things. You're not supposed be involved in war unless the Congress approves it. So another Boland amendment dealing with the Middle East, that's not going to happen because the Republican leadership, and even their program that they circulated before the election, was sort of bragging that they would support Obama in almost anything that they would do, so the Republicans would never bring up a Boland type of amendment. And the Democrats aren't going to bring it up and they couldn't get it passed, so it's tragic that we even have to think along those terms, but it's based on the assumption that our presidents are going to act outside of the Constitution, that they're going to wage war secretly.

And it's so bad now that even if we denied them official funding, at times, they can raise money in banking, in the drug war, they can raise money by finagling the Federal Reserve's ability to subsidize foreign countries. There's all kinds of things that they can do. Government is out of control, but we should do our very best to try and get the control back.

Horton: Well, if you were sitting on the National Security Council right now advising Obama, what would you tell him about Yemen and Somalia? There are bad guys there, apparently.

Paul: I'd just say come home. You know maybe even if there are bad guys in Yemen, they have to deal with them. I mean there are bad guys in the United States, and they might even be foreign-born, but if somebody from Yemen here in the United States and he causes a crime, we don't call up Yemen and say, "You ought to get over here and take care of this guy." We arrest them and we try them. We don't expect them to come over here and pick them up and take them back home. So, if there are bad people over there, they should take care of it and, of course, the hostility directed towards the United States would be greatly reduced if we realized and understood what blowback is all about and why people do want to harm us.

Horton: Well, that's a very important point, something we talked about at length with Tom Engelhardt about Chalmers Johnson — his book *Blowback* — on the show yesterday.

Paul: Aha.

Horton: And, of course, people remembered you confronting Rudy Giuliani about that with the simple truth right that history began before September 11th. That wasn't the start of this war, that was just one step in it.

Paul: I think we're in a 20-year war, now. It's up next year. I think we embarked on this after we sort of encouraged, or at least said we wouldn't be concerned if Saddam Hussein went into Kuwait and settled their border dispute on who owned some oil wells down there. So when we invaded Kuwait and went up into Iraq and continued bombing for ten years and starved so many of their people, that was the beginning. It's been going on for 20 years now. I'm in the process right now of trying to label exactly how much that cost was, which is hard, whether it's a financial cost, lost jobs, debt that we have, lives of our American soldiers that have been lost. It's been long, going on for a long time and I think it's expanding.

Obama hasn't slowed us up one bit. He's taken into Pakistan, he's into Yemen, and they want to go in Iran, and they don't hesitate to threaten North Korea — so it's ongoing. The real tragedy is I'd never believed our leaders would actually be so bold as to say war sometimes can help you get out of a bad economic situation. We knew those ideas floated around, but they're a little bit more blunt than I'd like, that a war is actually helpful — which is insanity, because it really isn't. War always hurts the economy.

Horton: David Broder, the dean of the Washington press corps, ran an article in the *Washington Post* like that recently and apparently George Bush had made a comment like that to the president of Argentina or something. But you've pointed out many times that Osama bin Laden said his plan was to bleed us to bankruptcy, he understands real economics apparently. That's what he said, right? That he was trying to get a reaction out of us, to bog us down and break our empire in Afghanistan just like they did with our help against the Soviet Union in the 1980s.

Paul: Yeah and he…

Horton: Which you opposed at the time, by the way.

Paul: He even implied they weren't going to concentrate on coming to our shores, he said "Fine, you come, and we'll fight you on our sand." And I think he also made the statement if I'm correct…

Horton: I'm sorry, I'm sorry Dr. Paul, hold on right there. [*Commercial break.*] I'm talking with my hero Dr. Ron Paul. You might remember him back in 2008, he gave the greatest speaking tour on behalf of individual liberty and peace in the history of mankind. And we're crossing our fingers and hoping he reprises that role in the next presidential election. I won't make you answer me now though, Dr. Paul. I'm sorry, so when the break kicked in, you were in the middle of a point about Osama bin Laden trying to lure us into Afghanistan, to bankrupt our empire.

Paul: Yeah, I think he was rather clear on that, at least to me he was implying that maybe they don't have to plan another attack in this country because we're right over there. Just think, after we went over there — To his surprise we went into those countries wholesale, so there were a lot of targets. He's killed 6,000 of our people. There were no al Qaeda in Iraq before we got there. We pretended we were going in there for that, but Saddam Hussein didn't permit al Qaeda there. Now there is al Qaeda in Iraq.

Horton: Yeah, there's still a problem there.

Paul: Yeah, and, of course, the country is a mess, they say, "Oh yeah, we're on the verge, one of these days we're going to have a government," but we continue to build bases there. The resentment is strong. There were no weapons of mass destruction. They're now a close ally of Iran. As bad as Saddam Hussein was, his balance of power said that he had to tolerate and protect Christians, so there were a million Christians that lived there peacefully. Now, more than half have been routed, and they expect the rest will be routed. Our going in along with the help of the British actually de-Christianized a place where Christians had lived for one of the longest times in all of history. So, the achievement is a disaster — and they're bragging about how wonderful it is — in the expense in terms of dollars and lives lost and, of course, collateral damage over there is unbelievable.

So I think Osama bin Laden sits back and looks and says, "Well" — he's still achieving bringing on our bankruptcy — "the Americans are stupid enough that they're destroying their own liberties." It's almost like Osama bin Laden is enjoying what the TSA is doing to us. But it's our fault, but also there's a rising outcry right now, so I think the American people are beginning to wake up. I think that's something about what's going on with the Tea Party movement. There is a healthy resistance to what's happening right now.

Horton: After all they're Democrat wars now, what's to believe in there for a Republican, right?

Paul: Yeah, for sure.

Horton: Well, I'm not sure if you saw this, but *Rolling Stone* published an interview with one of Osama bin Laden's sons just a couple of months back where he says in plain English that, "This was my father's dream, to lure the United States into Afghanistan to bleed them to bankruptcy and destroy them like the Soviet Union."

Paul: You'd wonder why the American people wouldn't pay attention to those kind of statements and think that maybe our foreign policy is flawed. But no, there's too much control on what the people see. Actually, as far as foreign policy goes, most Americans probably don't even care. They don't pay that much attention to it. That's why I sort of like the TSA issue because the pictures of this groping and the abuse are front and center. It's on our TVs today and everybody's heard about it and it's so abusive that I think the American people are saying, "Boy, maybe things are as bad as some of us have been saying." So I think this helps wake up more people.

Horton: Yeah, I think that's probably true and it's a great entryway to talk about foreign policy, too. I remember especially when you were running for president before, they would ask, "What departments would you abolish?" And you would surprise everybody by saying "Well, how about we abolish the Department of Homeland Security?" But, of course, if al Qaeda's going to attack us all day, every day without the Department of Homeland Security then we need that thing and you must be crazy. But then you can make your point: Now all we have to do is change our foreign policy, we won't need a national police force at all.

Paul: Well, I mean that they were supposed to be protecting us. We were spending $40 billion before 9/11 for gathering intelligence, and there was a lot of information there that could have helped prevent 9/11. But now we're spending $80 billion and they think, "Oh, we must be a lot safer." Of course, there's more that would like to kill us than ever before and we're bankrupt and we're undermining our liberties, so I would say, to the famous question of all politicians on the Hill, "Is the country going in the right direction or wrong direction?" I would firmly answer, "So far, we're going in the wrong direction." I'd sure like to help turn the direction around and go a different direction.

Horton: Yeah, and the Department of Homeland Security — just even the name of that thing — plus all the Fusion Centers and the policy of really kind of consolidating police power in this country, it seems like, if we can't get that thing repealed sometime soon, and Homeland Security is a permanent fixture of American society, then we're going to have a lot of lost liberty.

Paul: Yeah.

Horton: More even than we've been anticipating perhaps.

Paul: And that's not going to be on the agenda, you know. I think there were three of us who voted against it when they were establishing it, but we might be able to get them to back off on a couple of things, but you know how bad the PATRIOT Act was and people start complaining and campaigning against it and the Democrats didn't like it. So as soon as they had a chance to obviously lead the charge for renewing it and making it more permanent, so it's hard to cancel things out. That's why it will not be easy to get rid of Obama's medical care system, too. Although that was a big issue in the last campaign, I just hope we can do some good on that, but the idea that in six months from now that's going to be repealed, it's just not going to happen because, first off, he'd veto it anyway.

Horton: Alright, well Dr. Paul, I have a dream, not that it'll work out or anything but here's what I'd like to see. I'd like to see you run for president again, but with Russ Feingold or Dennis Kucinich, a good progressive who's good on peace and the Bill of Rights and the most important things, who is for accountability for criminals in government, and on Wall Street, etc., then we could redo the two-party system in America and we could have us versus them. Peace and Freedom versus the War Party, and then you could just make your major talking point that Sarah Palin and Barack Obama ought to run together — it's the war and inflation party. Then we can just get rid of all this silly old left/right and have a real realignment and keep our Bill of Rights.

Paul: Good point. I think that people ought to contemplate what you have said.

Horton: I sure would like to see that. You know, your son has made such great inroads with, as you say, the Tea Party right, the new kind of populist Republicans, the out-of-power right wing, and it just seems like you're the perfect one to finish that realignment with this upcoming campaign and get somebody like Feingold or somebody who's really good and see — You know a lot of people on the left are really disappointed in Barack Obama for filling out George Bush's third term. And it seems like if it really is the kind of crisis and emergency that you and I — I think — agree that it is, maybe now is the time for a real shakeup, for a real realignment of American politics.

Paul: Well, we certainly need it and there's more people talking about it, but unfortunately, the base becomes pretty loyal. I think you're right, I think there are a number of progressives that are breaking away but in Washington, I run into the people who are partisans before they believe even in their progressive ideas — they're not basically principled. But the people outside of Washington can see that Obama has come up short even in those areas.

Horton: Yeah, well 'fraid so. Well thank you very much for your time on the show, I know you have to go Doc, but I really appreciate you staying on with us here.

Paul: Good, Scott. Good talking to you.

Horton: Appreciate it. That is the heroic Dr. Ron Paul.

February 24, 2011

Horton: Our first guest on the show today is Dr. Ron Paul, my hero. He is the new chairman of the House Financial Services committee's subcommittee on domestic monetary policy. Welcome back to the show, Ron.

Paul: Thank you, Scott, good to be with you.

Horton: Very good to have you here, and very good to see you with the gavel in your hand on C-SPAN, that's a big change, huh?

Paul: Yeah, that's for sure.

Horton: Man, that was a big thrill, watching that. Alright, so, let's start with first things first here. Obama says the U.S. is considering full range of options on Libya, and CNN is reporting, "Official U.S. military options for Libya being planned now." So I guess there's a question whether they're going to try to go through the UN or not, but doesn't seem like there's a question whether the Obama administration is going to intervene militarily somehow in the uprising in Libya. Dr. Paul, what do you think?

Paul: I can't say that I'm surprised, I'm surprised they haven't done something sooner, because that's their nature. They think that no matter where there's a problem, we're supposed to send in troops and pick the next dictator — and that's basically the problem with the Middle East. There's been a lot of dictators over there, most of them have gotten support from us and even though Gaddafi hasn't gotten as much as others, in a way, he's been sanctioned. We have learned to invest in their country and make deals with them, so we more or less have been types of partners with him. But since he's on his way out, I think, whether it's Egypt or Libya or wherever, our CIA, our State Department and now maybe the military will be very much involved in maintaining our special control over some of these countries.

Horton: It's funny, in Egypt it was so obvious that Mubarak's regime was backed by the United States and that the United States was why he had been the dictator of Egypt for so long. In Libya, we've only been sending military aid to Libya and so forth for the last five or seven years or something since Bush Jr. let them back in the fold there in 2003. And so it's not so clear that he's an American-backed military dictator like we had in Egypt, so apparently the Democrats, or the White House, they think that they can get away with taking the side of the people against their own U.S.-backed military dictator there in Libya.

Paul: Yeah, it is certainly a more mixed bag than it is in some of those other countries. But I think overall, the neoconservatives who tend to have a lot of influence on our government, they always have the same goal, and that is to have influence. In some places they have more control. Look at Saudi Arabia: It's been total control and support for a dictatorship even before we even knew much about the term neoconservative. That's been going on since World War II. But Libya's not so clear-cut. I think the goals are always the same, and sometimes they're patient and they'll wait, and this might be seen as an opportunity for them. If they're talking about using the military, this means that the military would be used not only for defending some innocent people, but I'm sure it will be used to prop up the next guy that's going to take over.

Horton: A lot of people are saying that the reason Libya's so important in this case is not just for the rights of the people that live in that country, but the precedent set if Egypt and then Libya are able to be overthrown by their own people, then Saudi Arabia could be next, and that's the one that everybody seems to be worried about. So, let me ask you, if one group of people or another somehow successfully overthrow the government of Saudi Arabia, would we need to intervene there? That's where the bulk of the oil supplies are, and all that, right?

Paul: Well, I would never consider it a need, I would consider that a detriment to us. But there's a lot of others who will feel compelled to be involved. It may be just to protect our naval bases, and they're not even principally in Saudi Arabia. The whole Persian Gulf is, quote-unquote, "owned" by us. It's our navy that stays there. Can you imagine if another country had that much presence in the Gulf of Mexico, what we would think? So yes, I think if the government of Saudi Arabia was threatened, we'd be very much involved.

Horton: But if you were in charge when something like that happened, you wouldn't be involved at all?

Paul: No, I'd be less involved before it even got started. We would bring our navy home. There is a potential for disruption because it's not a good situation. It's all artificial. The people have been abused, we've had dictatorships over there that we propped up, and so it's unstable. Yet the people, in a lot of ways, these uprisings are very, very healthy. This means that the people are rebelling, and they want some changes. The real problem is, and the question is, what's going to come of this? We love to see the overthrow of Mubarak, but what's going to come of it? The military's in charge. The guy that runs the military was a good friend of Mubarak and he's an authoritarian, so they essentially have martial law there and nobody knows what the consequences will be. But I think we should stay out of that. I think they should settle their own problems, but if we'd been out of there forty years ago, I think there'd be more stability right now. But the instability comes from the fact that we have been propping up people who have not been fully endorsed by the people.

Horton: A lot has been made about the rising food prices around the world, and in many cases these North African and Middle Eastern countries have extremely poor populations who live pretty much right at the edge — a few dollars a day anyway — and then apparently the price of food is getting so much that that's really behind a lot of this anti-government sentiment and these protests around the region. And I've heard it said, but I'm not sure I could prove it, that America's monetary policy has something to do with the price of food in North Africa. Could you make that connection?

Paul: Oh yeah, I think so, because we've been allowed to export our inflation. We print up the money, it's the reserve currency of the world. We don't have to absorb all that new money, it goes overseas. I think countries like even China, especially since they take so many of our dollars, and they send us goods, that they're going to have an inflationary bubble. But all the world is going to be inflated. The prices aren't set by individual states. So food prices are going up, not because of food shortages — in places that may be true to a degree — but they're going up because of the debasement of the currency. In many ways, you can say central banking, ours in particular and others, caused these problems.

And people are rebelling because prices are going up. That's essentially what the problem here in this country is: The debt is overwhelming, and we can't afford the things that we own and the things that we want. There's not enough money to go around. So they're printing like crazy, but it's still not satisfying the people. In the past, we would tolerate the unions, and they'd demand wages that get wages way over the market value and since we were so wealthy it was okay. But now the price of labor is so high that we can't afford it any longer, and the people who are paying it, the Tea Party-type people, they're rebelling.

So, in many ways, the disruption that we're starting to see in this country is related to central banking, and I don't think we can ignore the central banking. But let me tell you, Bernanke's coming to the committee next week, and I may well bring this up. But he will deny wholeheartedly that the central bank has anything to do with rising prices — of anything. I don't know whether he's just in denial or whether he has to say those things to try to protect the central bank, but he will not accept the notion that central banks are responsible for even contributing significantly to these uprisings.

Horton: A wise man used to always say, up to and including this week, that all empires eventually fall, and usually for financial reasons. And that's really what we're talking about with all these uprisings in the Middle East, these are almost entirely against American-backed dictators there, American protectorates there — and there you have it. You inflate to prop up your empire, and that ends up being the cause of its dissolution.

Paul: That's right. And they're going to say, now that the oil prices are going to go up, the Federal Reserve will come back and say, "Well, it's the disruption over there, it's the rebellion, it's causing the price of oil to go up, that's where the inflation is coming from." In the '70s, when we had inflation of 15 or 20 percent, that's when they put an oil embargo on and oil was a couple bucks a barrel, and it soared up four, five times as much. So it was always "the Arabs" that caused the inflation. But it was the fact that there had already been a lot of printed money circulated, and the dollar was buying less for other commodities. The embargo was part of it, but there was also the inflation and the debasement of the currency.

This is the same way again. It is the disruption over there and the uncertainty about the leaders of these countries — that's the precipitating thing. But it's also the fact that people want to get more for their dollar. This is what the price of gold has been telling us, that the value of the dollar is way down, and prices are going to go up, and they're going to go up in food and commodities and energy. But believe me, they will use this as an excuse for the high prices, and they will be in total denial, and they'll never admit anything to do with the fact that we print money like crazy and doubled the money supply in the last couple of years.

Horton: To be realistic, none of us have too high of hopes that from your new position as chair of that subcommittee, you'd be able to actually repeal the Federal Reserve Act of 1913 and get rid of this institution, but I wonder if you think that it's possible if not likely that you actually could push through some legislation to legalize competing currencies, as you so often talk about.

Paul: I don't think yet. I don't think they're going to buy into that. Matter of fact, last year we had a lot of co-sponsors on the transparency bill — the Audit the Fed — and that's still going to be popular, and we got token audits of the Fed. We are getting a little bit more information. But we tested that among other members, and they seemed to be very, very vague on having any idea what we're talking about. So I don't think it's going to happen, but that doesn't stop me from talking about it, because whether it's legalized or not, there will always be competing currencies. The black market always exists when the economy breaks down, and it happened in the Soviet system, and it happens to some degree here already, and it's happened around the world.

I just want to talk about it because if we have total breakdown, people reject and say, "This guy's right, the dollar is collapsing, prices are too high, what are we going to do?" Then that is when we have to start saying, "Well, what we ought to do is obey the law and have alternative currencies, and if you don't want to close down the other system entirely, just allow us to use silver and gold as legal tender," like is still the law of the land. We're supposed to be doing that.

Horton: I know you're out of time and I'll let you go, Dr. Paul, but I really appreciate all your efforts, all your great interviews on TV and all the great speeches you give on the House floor. And all the great Youtubes that these things provide us, and all your efforts on behalf of liberty.

Paul: Thank you, Scott, and keep up the good work.

Horton: And if I can just say one last thing, on behalf of civil liberties, I'd like to ask you to try to reintroduce that American Freedom Agenda Act of 2007, that was my very favorite.

Paul: Okay, we'll certainly be able to do that.

Horton: Alright, excellent. Thank you, sir, appreciate it.

Paul: Okay.

Horton: Alright everybody, that's my hero, Dr. Ron Paul. He represents District 14 in the U.S. House of Representatives, where he writes articles, gives speeches, and votes no.

April 1, 2011

Horton: Our next guest on the show is Dr. Ron Paul. He is the chairman of the Monetary Policy Committee, a subcommittee of the Financial Services Committee in the House of Representatives. He's been writing a bunch of great articles and giving a lot of great speeches lately concerning the war in Libya. Welcome back to the show, Ron. How are you?

Paul: Thanks, Scott. Good to be with you.

Horton: I'm very happy to have you here. What do you predict for the short-term in the American war in Libya?

Paul: I think in the short-term, it's just going to continue to escalate. I don't think they'll be walking away. I don't think they're going to stop. We'll continue to spend money and send weapons. The marines are not too far away. The CIA's already involved. The only question is, who's in charge? They'd like to be responsible for everything — that is our American leaders — and at the same time put the management on NATO and then claim that it's NATO and not the United States. I think we're already deeply embedded there. It's probably going to continue for a long time and just contribute to the mess that we're already involved in.

Horton: I guess knowing how it is in Washington, D.C. when there's a blunder like this, a pretty obvious blunder where they have no long-term exit strategy, it seems like default back to the State Department system of doing things. Like in Afghanistan and Iraq, we'll have to create a democracy and train up an army to protect it and all this now, right? How can they back out short of that?

Paul: Yeah, it'll get so messy that they'll figure to salvage anything, that we have to establish the government. Already they've sent the CIA agents over there, an ex-Libyan, to go over there and be in charge. Our government's already picked the person they want to run the country. They're going to pretend they're not going to use military force to kill Gaddafi. It's just a mess. They're in a war, but they won't call it a war, and they won't fight it like a war, and they shouldn't be in the war, and yet they think something good will come of this. I cannot conceive of anything beneficial coming from it.

April 1, 2011

Horton: Your colleague, Representative Dennis Kucinich, has gone on the record saying that this is impeachable. Do you agree with him about that?

Paul: I think it's impeachable in the sense that it disobeys the Constitution. But so many presidents have done that in the last hundred years or so. It's an offense that is unconstitutional. The Congress should take it upon themselves... I don't imagine it's likely to lead to somebody introducing a resolution to impeach him, because I think it would distract from something we can do more immediate, like denying all funding for the war or making the Congress vote on this one way or the other.

Horton: That certainly would be something to see, the Congress at least attempt to deny funding. But Hillary Clinton made the statement yesterday, or the day before, that even if Congress did refuse to provide funding for it, that they would just ignore it under the plenary and inherent powers of the presidency.

Paul: When you think about it, how secret funding can occur through the Federal Reserve system, what does it matter? What does it matter when Congress is totally irrelevant? Just released figures said the Federal Reserve had loaned money to banks and other governments of $3.3 trillion. If you need funding and the Fed to create it, why don't you set up a central bank? The rebels in Libya have already set up a central bank, so maybe we've loaned them... I wonder if they've come to the discount window yet. That whole thing is absolutely out of control.
    And yes, they can ignore what the Congress does. If they don't have enough money, they have ways of just printing the money. That's why this thing will continue until they just ruin the value of the dollar completely.

Horton: John V. Walsh was on the show and was saying we really should pursue impeachment here. He was saying this would be really a great end to the empire. Instead of waiting for the dollar to break and for total catastrophe, if we could just say, "No. That's it. This is the final straw. We're going to remove this guy from power, and we're going to mandate and end to these things." If you guys were to suspend the payments, and Hillary Clinton and Barack Obama and Robert Gates were to just continue anyway, there's your grounds for impeachment, and perhaps a real beginning to the end of the empire short of that economic catastrophe that you talk about.

Paul: Well, that's theoretically a possibility. It's not likely to happen. If two or three of us introduce a resolution of impeachment right now, it wouldn't go to the floor. But let's say it did go to the floor, just to prove that the support isn't there, you might get eight or ten votes under today's circumstances. Then that can be construed as a vote of endorsement. "Oh. Nobody cares. It must be legal if the Congress won't vote for the impeachment."

So it's not an easy problem to solve, but Congress I don't think right now has the backbone to do anything about it. Even though I'd have to admit there's better talk now than there was with the Republicans when Bush was doing it. There were hardly any Republicans saying anything. But I think a much larger number today of people I talk to on the Republican side are willing to take the president on and declare this unconstitutional and illegal. Not that they'd be looking to impeach, but at least there's more resistance.

But that's pretty traditional. The Republicans were pretty much opposed to Clinton when he was bombing in Bosnia and Serbia and that area. Republicans said, "Oh, this is horrible. This is horrible." But then when Bush did it, it was "wonderful, wonderful." Now some of those Democrats that were with some of us, a few Republicans who opposed Bush's wars, they're now supporting Obama's wars. So we need a little bit more consistency. It's just a shame that Congress, especially the House, is so willing to give up its responsibilities and deliver all this power to the executive branch.

Horton: Back to the situation actually in Libya. You cite Michael Scheuer in one of your recent pieces here — I'm not sure if it was a speech or an article you wrote — about the dangers of the unintended consequences of intervening there. I wonder whether that part of it is really being discussed on Capitol Hill at all, about the effect this could have for the broader threat of terrorist attacks on the United States.

Paul: They talk about the CIA going in, and they've asked some public questions about that. Sometimes the administration just ducks it, or most of the time they will. The issue of blowback, I don't hear that brought up too often, because I still get a little bit of grief over that when I bring it up. Matter of fact, I was in a station just a little while ago, and the host was saying, "Well, wasn't it true that you got booed and all this because you brought the subject up? That's going too far." He goes, "If you say there's a possibility of blowback, that means you're blaming America."

Well, we don't blame America. You and I are Americans. We don't get the blame. But we can blame bad political judgment and bad policy that may have a ramification that actually hurts America rather than helps —

that's quite a bit of difference. But unfortunately, that discussion isn't going well up here. They're not quite willing to get to this point. But there will be a lot of Republicans now speaking out against what Obama's doing.

Horton: I've always thought that some of the most important things I ever see, say on TV, which you do talk about often, is the reality of how we got into this mess and what it's all about. As you say, not just for foreign policy reasons, but for domestic reasons as well. I was actually just talking with my previous guest about "Islamophobia" in America, because Islam is said to be the motive for the terrorists to do what they do against us. It seems like in this time more than ever, we really need anti-demagogues like yourself who can just say, "No, no, no. This is not about Islam. It's about the consequences of intervention."

Paul: It's very important for them to broaden the enemy in order to justify what they're doing. If they admitted the truth and said, "Yeah, there are radicals in all religions, and maybe they were motivated on it from their point of view by reason and saying, 'Look, this is what's happening to us and we're going to do such-and-such. We're going to commit these acts of terror.' And they're a small number," that's not enough. Then you only have to attack and get the people who did the harm. But if you can build up Islamophobia, then you can justify going into all these countries. Then you not only go and try to get the bad guys that might've attacked us, which was a very narrow target since there weren't that many. I bet you there were less than 100 that even knew what was going on. But now what Obama has done is further endorsed the principle of preventative war, which is initiating force, which is aggression.

Horton: Alright. Well, I sure hope you run for president again, Dr. Paul. Last time was the greatest speaking tour on behalf of peace and individual liberty ever. I know at least here in Los Angeles, the Ron Paul kids are just raring to go. So get to it. (Laughs)

Paul: Thank you, Scott.

April 22, 2011

Horton: I'm Scott Horton. Anthony Gregory says our next guest makes Thomas Jefferson look like Alexander Hamilton. It's Ron Paul. He represents Texas District 14 in the U.S. House of Representatives. He's the chairman of the House Subcommittee on Domestic Monetary Policy, and he's the author of the brand-new *Liberty Defined: 50 Essential Issues that Affect our Freedom*.

Welcome back to the show. Ron, how are you doing?

Paul: Thank you, Scott. Good to be with you.

Horton: I'm very happy to have you here, and I just love this book. Part of what I love about it is, of course, just all of the substance. But also, it's imagining all the people who are going to read this thing. And especially, like I was telling the audience earlier, I have this fantasy that some of these cable TV news personalities will even be able to get through it, the way you have it so encyclopedic like that. I think this is really going to do a lot to change the conversation. You didn't really have a campaign book last time.

Paul: Right. I hope you're right about it. I tried to make it — A lot of times I've written about the theoretical parts of monetary policy and foreign policy, but this deals with individual issues and problems that we face. I'm sure people might just look through the contents and pick something and say, "I've been wondering about that. How do you answer this question?" I'm hoping it will help others to answer these questions from the libertarian freedom movement viewpoint.

Horton: Another thing about this book is it just shows, first of all, that you're a very smart guy, that you're very interested in all these things and have been for a long time. But it also shows the silence of the rest of the Republican Party. I don't know if anyone else in the Republican Party has this kind of intellectual firepower to bring to bear. They say Newt Gingrich has a pretty high IQ, but it seems to me like you are the only intellectual leadership in the Republican Party right now. They're pretty much at sea.

Paul: I guess they have intellect and they're smart people and have high IQs, and I've always wondered about that. I've never figured I had the highest IQ, but there's something that some people have. It's sort of a motivation to look for truth. If you have a high IQ but you're using it to promote welfarism and militarism, that's one thing.

It's our motivations. It's our values that really count on what we want. If you accept the basic principle that it's better to live in a free society than a totalitarian society, it's pretty easy to start defending our position without claiming that "I'm smarter than you are and that's why you have to listen to me." I think you have to have some moral authority behind what we argue. To understand the monetary issues, sometimes you think you have to understand every detail about the Fed. It gets very complex. But if you look at it from a moral viewpoint, why should a government be allowed to counterfeit? All of a sudden, it's simplified, and we can bring in a lot of people into our area of thinking and to understand that issue.

Horton: Speaking of which, of course, the question that everybody wants to know the answer to is whether or not you're running. I don't guess I'm lucky enough that you would make that announcement on this show, huh?

Paul: Can't quite do that, but I've been getting a lot of encouragement. This week, I was over at Mississippi State and then Florida State last night. The receptions are pretty good, so I think there's at least more young people who are enthusiastic about what I've been trying to do in the last several years, or all these years. The support has grown in the last couple years. I think it looks like it's continuing to grow. I've been encouraged.

Horton: I'm very happy to hear that. I saw in the Daily Paul that Jesse Benton said he's got the paperwork all filled out for the exploratory committee, he just hadn't submitted them yet. At Lew Rockwell's new Political Theater blog, he says that you're all signed up for the Republican debate, the first Republican debate coming up. So I'm going to go ahead and accept the premise that you're running, even if you're not saying so yet.

Then that's going to lead into this topic, which is a special favor actually that I want to ask of you, which is, please let the kids, the YouTube kids, make the TV ads. Because last time, the TV ads ran to the right like typical Republican primary; "you want to run to the right in the primary, to the center in the general," that kind of thing. But you're changing the game all the way around. You don't need to do that. All of the very best Ron Paul ads from 2007 and 2008 were made by your fans, and they were just clips of your speeches and TV appearances, put together with a little bit of music. Why not just hold YouTube contests and let the kids make the ads? What do you think?

Paul: You get an A+ for that suggestion. I agree with you 100 percent. There's been some discussion, if there's a campaign, that that is the direction I want to go in. Resorting to some of the conventional people because they've been experts, that doesn't fit us. We don't have a conventional campaign, and therefore I think what you suggest is very good.

Horton: Right on. I'm so glad you see that my way. Some of the YouTubes, they're so good. All we need is a couple of clips of you at a podium and sold. You've got my vote, Mr. President, I'll tell you that.

Alright, now, here's the thing. The *New York Times* today is saying that the nation's mood is as low as it's ever been. The *Times* does this poll I think every year or so. "Do you think America's headed the right direction or not?" Kind of a general question. Mostly, I think it reflects how people feel about the economy. But I wonder how you would address that. What is it that's wrong with America? What track are we on that we're not supposed to be on here, Dr. Paul?

Paul: I think the sentiment is a healthy sentiment, because they're facing the truth. When there's a bit of prosperity still existing, and they can still borrow money and print money, and the world accepts it, people say, "Oh, I guess we're not too bad off," or, "We're improving," or something like that. Now, they're starting to realize that we're getting close to the bottom and something has to give. I see it like when the drug addict gets to the point where, he says, "I'm at the bottom and I have to change my life, and I'm going to quit," and that individual changes his or her way, and then they do something. I think that's what's happening now. People are realizing how bad it is. But it also means there's an opportunity. This is what I'm sensing with the young people, they know they're getting a bad deal. They know the foreign policy is lousy, the monetary policy is lousy, and you can't take care of people from cradle to grave and think you can do it forever.

So that's why I think we're at the point where they're going to be open to our suggestions, and that gives people optimism. In spite of all the pessimism, you can say, "Well, we're facing up to reality and now we can start improving and offering our solutions." I think our biggest job, even though I look at this in a positive way, I think our biggest job and our biggest threat is to head off the guy on a white horse. You know, somebody coming and saying, "I am going to take care of you. This is a mess that you need an iron fist authoritarian approach to our answers." Of course, authoritarianism is what created our problem, so it's sort of like the deficit. What do you do when you get a bad deficit? You spend more money. Well, if authoritarianism brought us to our knees, why would we resort to somebody that comes in and wants more authoritarianism? That, to me, is the biggest challenge.

Horton: Absolutely. In the book, under D, you have a great section there on demagoguery, and I could not agree with you more about that. Especially when you Austrian economist guys are talking about... I interviewed Charles Goyette yesterday, and it was sad. If we're really looking at a major inflation here, double digits for an extended period, savings wiped out, that really is when people start to look for answers from demagogues.

It seems to me that you're just the most important anti-demagogue in the whole society, saying that, "Look, we don't need more of what we've done wrong to get us into this crisis. We don't need to pick on the weak here." We need to recognize our problems are the world empire and all the spending there, the paper money. All we need is to believe in the Declaration of Independence and the Constitution. All we need is to just act right, like we're supposed to in the first place.

It's that we've gone wrong. It's not the American way that's failed; it's our abandonment of the American way that's failed. You're absolutely the most important voice in this society making that case, especially when it comes to the solution. Competing currencies, things like that, people really need to know, what's the alternative to doing it the way that the rest of the Republicans and the Democrats would have us do it?

Paul: I think the people are getting ready. The opposite of being a demagogue is telling the truth. I guess a demagogue is a slightly more polite way of saying people just are lying through their teeth and distorting issues in order to promote their cause. I think more and more people now are seeing through all that, so the promises are falling on deaf ears, and that's why our message is going to become more popular than ever, and that is what I'm sensing.

Horton: I gotta tell you, again, I'm just going with the unsaid premise here that you are running, and I'm just so excited about it. I read that *Esquire* article yesterday which was written by a liberal and had a couple of things wrong. But absolutely got it right, that you are the most powerful force on the right in America right now. Even if they exclude you from the Pew poll and don't ask people what they think, it's an unavoidable fact that you're the most important libertarian in the world. You're carrying this message forward.

When you announced last time on *Washington Journal* back in 2007, you were the best-kept secret of libertarians like me: "Hey, did you know there's this one good congressman?" That kind of thing. Now, you're world famous like a movie star or something. You're starting from a much higher place. All the guys on TV like you. It's going to be incredible. I'm so stoked.

Paul: You're overly generous. You're overly generous. You have embellished a bit, but I appreciate it.

Horton: You deserve every bit of it, Dr. Paul. I know I speak for a lot of people, too. Thank you for always putting war first. No matter what they ask you on TV, you always put the cost of the world empire first. And, of course, I think, like you do, that that's the most important issue.

Paul: That's really big.

Horton: I'm sorry for just talking at you during your interview when I should've been asking you questions this whole time. I'm just so glad that we've had this chance to meet again, sir.

Paul: Thank you. Bye bye.

Horton: Thank you. Alright, everybody, that's the heroic Dr. Ron Paul.

June 3, 2011

Horton: I'm Scott Horton and introducing Antiwar.com's man in the House of Representatives. Congressman Ron Paul represents the 14th District of Texas. He's the chair of the Banking Committee's subcommittee on domestic monetary policy. He's also on the Foreign Affairs committee and did I mention already he's running for president of the United States? Welcome back to the show, Ron. How are you doing?

Paul: Thank you, Scott. Good to be with you.

Horton: I'm very happy to have you here. Big doings in the House of Representatives this morning. I have to tell you I'm beside myself. I can't believe the debate about war going on in the Congress right now. Give us an update.

Paul: Well, there are two resolutions on the floor. We'll be voting shortly. Of course, Kucinich has a good resolution that said the president should buckle down, obey the law, and tell us what he's doing and get the troops out of Libya… dealing with Libya. But the speaker took it and he wanted to take that away from Kucinich so he introduced his own, and believe me he can pass it. It's very much watered down and has no force of law and allows the president to continue to do what he's actually doing.

Horton: So it's not even the kind of authorization they had, say, for the Iraq war?

Paul: Yes, so Obama — I and you and everybody else complained about the Iraq war, and the lack of necessity to go into that, and the way that they did it and it wasn't a declaration of war, but at least the president did come and got some type of authority. Where, under these circumstances in Libya, he has just gone in. He's flaunted it. He said he got the authority from the United Nations. It's very, very bad. If the House doesn't do anything, and the Senate, of course, should too, it's a very, very bad precedent. It's an unusual coalition that we've built here. Some very, very conservative hawkish Republicans are supporting us and saying, "Look. Enough is enough. The presidents are going too far, and we should exert our authority and our responsibility," so it's a healthy redirection for the Congress instead of just sitting back, and hopefully the Kucinich amendment would pass but it's going to be close.

Horton: Well, if I understand it right, when they pulled the Kucinich bill because they thought it might pass, and then Brad Sherman succeeded in proposing — or didn't succeed — but he proposed an amendment to the Homeland Security bill that basically said more or less the same thing. I think it wasn't as strong language as the Kucinich bill and that amendment only failed by five votes. I was talking to Eric Garris about it, and he said the parties were pretty much split 50/50.

Paul: Yeah, oh yeah.

Horton: The Republicans and the Democrats.

Paul: There's a big shift in sentiment. Your website must be catching on. A lot of people must be reading it.

Horton: I sure hope that's right. Antiwar.com/Paul, everybody.

Paul: The Senate is changing and that resolution that was put into the DOD budget, may or may not survive but it wouldn't be as strong as what we're doing today. Boehner pooled what Kucinich was doing. We should have had an hour debate yesterday just on that, but Boehner he decided to bring Kucinich's resolution up along with his own. What he's doing is giving cover to the Republicans so they're going to vote for this very, very weak resolution that has no force of law, and then they can vote against Kucinich and say, "Oh well, we really care but we don't want to go quite so fast. We don't really want to really undermine the president." So it's a political stunt to have the two. The only thing that really counts will be the Kucinich vote. I'll probably vote for the other one because even though it's so weak and token, it doesn't make things worse. It just doesn't do much good.

Horton: Now, I interviewed Seymour Hersh the other day about his new piece in *The New Yorker* magazine where he reveals that the 2011 update to the National Intelligence Estimate on Iran's nuclear program confirms after four more years of intelligence the conclusion of the NIE from 2007, and that is that there is not a nuclear weapons program in Iran and that they have not made the decision to start one. The last they even were looking at paperwork along the lines was in 2003, and the White House said they're "rolling their eyes" about it. That was the best debunking they'd had. But I wonder if there's any way… When they came out with the NIE in 2007, Bush and Cheney ordered the declassification of the summary — It turned out to be against their best interest to do so at the time — but I wonder if there's any anything you can do on the Foreign Affairs committee to push for the release of at least a declassified summary of the new 2011 NIE on Iran's nuclear program?

Paul: Well, at least the effort should be made. Whether or not they're going to respond is another question. I see they're trying as usual to blast Seymour Hersh and make sure he loses credibility, but no, I think getting some concrete document officially like that would be very good, and we should do that.

Horton: Yeah, it's funny they try to attack Hersh but they don't attack the central premise of the article, which is: the NIE is done, and all 17 now, apparently, intelligence agencies agreed unanimously on its conclusion and that it's the same one as before. No one's really ever attacked that assertion. They just attack him personally.

Paul: Yeah, but I guess the various countries involved probably haven't endorsed it yet. And our neocons haven't endorsed it so whether or not they're as powerful as they were in the Bush administration where they could do like Cheney did and just squelch those things, I don't know. I just hope we can get that information out. I think at least we can start quoting that and saying, "Well, why don't we? That's in the public domain now."

Horton: Well, I don't know exactly how it works with the Intelligence Committee and Oversight Committee and the Foreign Affairs Committee, but would that be within your jurisdiction to subpoena that document somehow?

Paul: Yes, but it's not going to happen because the speaker and the chairman of the committee controls the subpoenas. Unless you had a truly, truly antiwar coalition in the Congress where they really were determined, then a subpoena might be issued. Then they would have to, of course, say that it was — They would say, "Well, too much top secret in there." And they go through all those shenanigans. The sentiment here in the Congress to demand that is not that strong.

Horton: All right. Let's stick with foreign policy for a second. There was a vote about a week ago on Afghanistan that also came very close. I wonder if you think there's a real sea change going on where this antiwar sentiment in the country is finally getting through to the House of Representatives? Is it just political games or what is it?

Paul: It isn't that the House of Representatives are all of a sudden enlightened, but the people become enlightened and they send this message, so they're reflecting what they're hearing in their districts. And I would say that this may change the whole nature of this presidential primary race now, not only in the foreign policy but in the monetary policy and the huge debt. There are problems that the discussions are completely different. I think the views that so many of us have expressed for so long are much more credible now than they ever were. I don't think they'll be able to dismiss the contentions that we have about the stupidity of our foreign policy and how dangerous our monetary policy is.

Horton: And it's just next month that Obama said would be the beginning of the end of the "surge" in Afghanistan, the beginning of the drawdown, and I guess probably a lot depends politically on whether that happens on the ground?

Paul: Yeah, and I don't have much faith in that. It's sort of like it's all over in Iraq and we're just about ready to come home, and then all of a sudden you hear how many more people have been killed and what's happening to the Christians and why it's a haven now for al Qaeda when it wasn't under Saddam Hussein. They wouldn't build those embassies and those bases if they actually want to go home or plan to go home. They're planning to stay. There's just no doubt about it. They might try to fool the people for a while, but in this age of communications that we have even from over there that the information gets out and they won't be able to get away with it.

Horton: Well, they've actually been pretty public about trying to get Prime Minister Nouri al-Maliki to so-called "invite" us to stay too. They haven't made much of a secret about it: "Please, please, invite us."

Paul: "And if you don't, we'll take all your money away from you."

Horton: Right. Exactly. And now this is extremely important, but, you know, on this show foreign policy first, but I was amazed to see this clip from your hearing on the Monetary Policy committee where I believe the bureaucrat from the Fed confirmed to you that 88 percent of the Fed's bailout money went to foreign banks. Is that right, Congressman?

Paul: Well, not the whole thing. But there was one particular… At the height of the bailout, there was several weeks it was really going. And in one of the programs that they had, 88 percent did, in a short period of time, but it was a lot. Overall, it was more like $3 trillion that went.

Horton: Amazing.

Paul: But the other thing is the one section that I dealt with was 370 pages. Of course, there's 29,000 pages, it's called "the dump." But out of those 327 pages, 80 percent of everything was blacked out, it's redacted, and we couldn't even read it, so we got after him with that a little bit. He claimed that if we were specific and made those requests that they'd send it to us. I said, "Well, why don't you just send the whole thing? Let us read the whole program."

Horton: Yeah, well, don't hold your breath for that one, I guess.

Paul: Yeah.

Horton: All right. Well, listen. I know you've got to go and vote for peace, so I want to thank you very much for your time on the show as always.

Paul: Okay, Scott. Good to talk to you.

November 23, 2011

Horton: Our next guest on the show today is Dr. Ron Paul. He represents District 14 down on Texas's Gulf Coast and he's running for president of the United States. Tied for first in Iowa. Doing a really strong second place in New Hampshire, at least last I saw. He's got a great archive of articles and speeches at LewRockwell.com and at Original.Antiwar.com/Paul, a lot of great foreign policy pieces there going back to at least 2002, maybe before that, and his latest book is called *Liberty Defined*, which is excellent and I highly recommend it.

Horton: Welcome back to the show, Dr. Paul. How are you?

Paul: Thank you, Scott. I'm doing well. Thank you.

Horton: I'm very happy to hear that and I really appreciate you making time for us on the show today. I'll try to make this quick, because it's more of a statement than a question, but I wanted to explain why it is that your run for president, it's so important to me and I know I speak for a lot of people about this as well.
  You may remember the Old Right author, Garet Garrett.

Paul: I sure do.

Horton: I believe it's in *The People's Pottage* where he complains that the American people have never had the opportunity to choose between republic and empire. It's always either Wilkie versus FDR, or Dewey versus Truman, or, say, McCain versus Barack Obama, and the American people never really had a choice to choose our path here. That's what you represent to me, is now for the second time, peace and liberty and a constitutional republic and a sound economy on a silver platter for the taking if the American people will just take it and I'm so appreciative of that.

Paul: Well, thank you, and, of course, that's been our goal and I know the frustration by many by not having real choices and the old cliché, "Well, we can't vote for somebody that might offer this because we have to vote for the lesser of the two evils." But I always make the comment when they ask about this is that we send troops, and money, and we lose lives, and we kill a lot of people spreading our goodness and our democracy. We want to teach people how to have fair elections, and then they have elections, then we don't like the elections, so we ignore them. But back here at home, not only philosophically is it hard to distinguish between the two and thinking that they're really different, but competition is tough in this country because third parties aren't welcomed. It's hard to get on their ballots and they write the rules. If you're in a third party or an alternative party, you don't get into the debates.

It is a shameful system that has been offered. So I've done my darnedest to work in the Republican Party, as well as outside the party, and in education to make sure as many people as possible understand this distinction — that it's either/or. You really can't maintain the status quo. Our status quo is always moving as history shows and it's always moving in the direction of empire. And if you listened to the debates and what went on last night, it seems like there's still a pretty strong consensus with Republican candidates that's the direction they want to go.

But the one thing is, Scott, I think one thing that's good news, is I do think there's a lot of people, especially the younger generation, they're certain they're sick and tired of it. Even now, I've noticed in the last month or two, talking to the audiences that have mostly Social Security people in them, and talking about how their money was taken out of Social Security and spent overseas and how these wars are detrimental to them, how inflation is detrimental to them — they're actually listening very carefully now. There are a lot less hawkish than they were five or ten years ago.

Horton: I think I figured out something about the media's bafflement about your strength in all the recent polling and your steady growth compared to all the flash in the pan competitors on the Republican side. I think I figured out this morning, reading the winners and losers analysis at the CNN website, where you're in with the winners, but in their lack of understanding, they say, "Well, but the best he could do though, even though he was really strong, would be to appeal to independents and Democrats who maybe might crossover and help support him." It's really beyond their capacity to understand or believe that actually you can lead the Republican base to peace. It's working.

Paul: Republicans in the past have campaigned on peace, like Bush did, in the year 2000. His announced platform wasn't all that bad, a "humble foreign policy" and other words that sounded pretty good. But the other thing that they're not quite recognizing, they see the Republican Party as being a fixed number of people and they all endorse these issues. But if you go to New Hampshire, the largest registration are independents. They are allowed to vote in the Republican primary, and I think that's where we're making great inroads. We're doing really well with traditional Republicans, but we're also stirring it up and with the independents that will decide the election.

Same thing in Iowa. You can even be a Democrat in Iowa and show up at a Republican caucus, and it's sort of working in our benefit this year because there's no Democratic contest. Therefore, if people want to make their vote count, they can come over and vote in the Republican primary. And because of the frustration, and because they're starting to look at what I've been saying for years, I think they're looking more carefully now, and I think that's good.

Horton: Now very quickly, at the end of the debate, you were asked a question very softly about Somalia and the al-Shabaab movement, and you went ahead and gave a great answer and embarrassed Paul Wolfowitz and everything as the result. But I want to give you the opportunity to address Somalia and the situation with al-Shabaab if you'd like.

Paul: I didn't hear the question very well and I think she was trying to draw a corollary that the reason we have problems in Somalia is because we didn't follow through, we met resistance and we lost a man so we left, and so that's why we can't leave Afghanistan.

Obviously the longer we stay, the more chaotic it gets, the more people that die, but we really never left Somalia. We just transferred the responsibility. When they had the crisis in Mogadishu, that crisis occurred with American troops, but now we just use proxy armies. There's Kenya or Ethiopia, we just buy their allegiance and send them in and stir up the trouble, but I think the real question is why are we so worried about that? Why don't we allow people to have their self-determination? Our problems just get much worse when we think that we know what all these solutions are.

So it would have been a perfect opening for me to emphasize the value of a noninterventionist foreign policy. The argument she was making, as far as I'm concerned, she just wants to perpetuate this forever. If they want to have absolute control, they've got to send hundreds of thousands of people into all these countries and obviously it would bankrupt us. I think it's that she was talking about a failed policy and there's no way that could solve the dilemmas that we face today, especially financially, in the attack of our liberties here at home.

Horton: Representative Bachman I thought made an interesting point anyway, not that I necessarily agree with her conclusion, but she talked about how some Somali Americans — I think she mentioned this — have actually traveled to Somalia to participate in the war over there, which is a very worrying development because obviously it doesn't take much imagination for them to go ahead and stay here and commit some kind of terrorist attack or that kind of thing. But her problem, of course, is she's analyzing the whole thing in a vacuum, not as you're talking about, in the context of years and years of war over there.

Paul: Right. If you do have any Americans, or American Somalis, here and they have an interest and they're not asking you to go or send your kids, that to me is a little bit different if they want to be involved. But it doesn't seem to happen that way because too often there'll be prohibitions against that; if you go as a private citizen and start getting involved, too often our State Department will frown on that. But it's a use of force, especially government force. It tells us that we have to use our money and our young people to go over and determine exactly what should evolve. Then their argument always is, "Well, if we don't do it, just think of the opposition. Who else is going to come in there? The Chinese are going to come in, the Russians will come back in there." But the whole irony of this is we're over there, in these various countries including Afghanistan and our foreign policy against Iran. This is helping China.

We're driving people toward China. China doesn't waste all their money and lives. They're over there, they're acting like capitalists. They're in there investing in these countries. So this whole idea that it's fearful that they would use their military to take over, I think they've learned a new trick and I think they learned it from us. Unfortunately, we have forgotten about how capitalism actually works.

Horton: Afraid so. Well, we're going to learn one way or another, aren't we?

Paul: Right.

Horton: Alright, well we're already a little bit over time. I want to thank you so much for giving us a little bit of time today, sir.

Paul: Great to talk to you, Scott.

April 26, 2013

Horton: Alright, our first guest is Dr. Ron Paul, M.D. Welcome back to the show, Ron, how are you doing?

Paul: Doing well, Scott. Nice to be with you.

Horton: Well, I'm very happy to have you back on the show. It's been way too long since we've spoken and I'm really sorry to do this to you but this is kind of the part of the interview where I have to ask you to sit there and squirm while I tell you about how great you are for minute here.

Paul: Oh.

Horton: The thing of it is, Dr. Paul, is that you're the greatest American hero ever, and I'm just so lucky to have a chance to tell you this directly to you.

See, what you've done in two presidential campaigns is you've taken purist libertarianism, plumb-line libertarianism, and you have made it a topic worldwide, a household term worldwide. You've increased public understanding of real economics, of peace, and of, really, enlightenment, individualist libertarian theory in a way that no one else has ever done. It's really comparable to the Declaration of Independence being published or something like that when it comes to the amount, the number of people entertaining ideas of liberty that had not before. There's just nothing comparable to it. There's no parliamentarian in the history of the world who has accomplished what you have accomplished in terms of spreading the ideas of peace and liberty the way that you've done and I'm certain you'll live in history for a thousand years if the politicians don't get us all killed before then.

Paul: Well, I think you're exaggerating a bit, but I'll still take it. It always sounds nice but no, there's a lot of people that have done a lot of good work and I'm just one of them. The only thing…

Horton: Well, you're very humble too.

Paul: The only thing that might verify this a little bit, that we've had a little bit of effectiveness, is the fact they're still attacking me. I thought when I left Congress they'd leave me alone a little bit, they'd let me just go and pursue my beliefs and convictions and try to spread a message, but the attacks came pretty vicious here in the last week or two so maybe they still are very much opposed to what we're doing and afraid that we might influence some people. But I appreciate your comments, they're very nice.

Horton: Alright, well good. I'm glad you took them in the spirit they were meant. And now, of course, what's made them all so angry and the reason they attack you is because they're afraid of you. You go throwing around this word peace like you mean it, and in Washington, D.C., that's a terrifying thing. That's what they said: "Be very afraid of Ron Paul's new peace institute." Why don't you tell us about that peace institute, Dr. Paul?

Paul: Yes, we've set this up recently and the one individual that I placed a lot of responsibility on that worked with me for quite a few years in Washington, that's Daniel McAdams who did my foreign policy. He's very, very good. I could always rely on him for analysis and advice and he came up with this idea and came to me and I thought it sounded great. We have a large number of people, advisors, and people willing to participate and I think it's pretty important. I think your point is well-taken about peace. Why should anybody be turned off with peace?

When I go to the college campuses, I start off with the subject of liberty and then want to explain what it really means from our viewpoint. And I say why it is so important is because I believe it's the only way you can have both peace and prosperity is through the understanding of liberty and that's where we have been lacking. Too many people have different definitions of what liberty is. Sometimes liberty is using somebody else's life and money, and young people especially who are inheriting this mess have to realize this. So far, I've been very pleased with the reception on the campuses and I've continued to do that since the reception was good during the campaign.

Even though there's lots of problems and lots of concerns, I still remain rather optimistic that there are enough good people paying attention now to this message. But like I said before, a lot of people are participating in this and I certainly didn't invent any of it, but I worked hard to try to spread the message.

Horton: Well, and especially in 2007–08, during that campaign, this is what you really accomplished with that. It's in the documentary *Watering the Tree of Liberty*, which is just great, I hope people will watch it. It was that fight with Giuliani that really was the turning point. What really happened there — other than how you explained that history began before September 11th and there's more to our terror war than is commonly portrayed — it was also the fact that you are a personally conservative, Christian, Texas Republican and for peace in a way that it serves I think as a permission slip for a lot of people who have been told on TV or maybe told by the culture their whole life that the only people who are antiwar are ignorant hippies singing "Kumbaya" but who don't know anything about anything, or somebody like Jane Fonda sitting on a North Vietnamese antiaircraft gun, but that "those of us who are adults and responsible and know things, we all know that something terribly violent must be done." What you did was you said, "No, that's actually not the case." You could be a conservative Christian Republican who's very well-informed and very concerned for the future of the country and know better than to have this warmongering foreign policy — and that is what turned the world upside down.

Paul: Yeah, and I'm pleased with that because that was a challenge because for so many years, the votes that I would take with either by myself or with very few others, it was always painted as being, "Well, you're un-American, you don't care about our troops." On and on. "You're not patriotic, you don't vote for the PATRIOT bill, so you're unpatriotic." Yet, two things happened: The world was rapidly changing in '08 and '09 financially, and, of course, our country was sick and tired of the war. As a matter of fact, they were sick and tired of Bush too and unfortunately, we didn't replace him with anybody any better.

The one other event that happened that really helped me on these attacks — these so-called Giuliani attacks — was the fact that when the dust settled, the military people liked our message. I wasn't totally surprised but I was very pleased. I didn't know it would be that strong, so this sort of silences those individuals who had never served in the military, not that that should be a litmus test. But I had at least the experience of being in the military and I took these positions. They knew I wasn't against the troops, and that I was for America, and I was for peace, and for strong defense, but when they defended me not only with verbal support but also financially, I have to admit, it made me feel pretty good.

Horton: Good. You changed the history of the world right there. No doubt about it whatsoever. In fact, we were so angry at Giuliani in my living room, and then we were so proud of the way you stood up to him and answered, I'll never forget that moment. It was just incredible. Of course, you'd won me over back years and years ago, but it was really something else.

Tell us quickly, can you give us a rundown on which issues the peace institute is going to tackle first and how you're going to go about your business?

Paul: It's the big issue, of course, the foreign policy and where we are. I think the most important one right now is Syria and the Middle East. Actually, things have gotten worse today because last week Defense Secretary Hagel visited Israel and he says, "Well, they never mentioned to me that they have evidence about gasses being used in Syria." Then they announced that in public and he didn't know about it but all of a sudden, he says, "Oh, the gasses spread around by the government and therefore, we have to — That's the red line we've crossed." I think we're getting very dangerous.

We put the troops in Jordan. We've been helping the rebels who are made up of al Qaeda in there, so this could deteriorate. We're going to work really hard on trying to expose the truth there in the most diplomatic fashion possible and try to avoid the demagoguing but just say these are the facts. Even Hillary and others were admitting they didn't know who were in the factions.

So here we are, supporting once again the side of the al Qaeda; while in other places we have wars against al Qaeda and the Taliban. And, of course, their argument always is, "Well, they hate our culture and they hate us for it and therefore, we have to go over there and kill them there, so they don't come over here."

We'll work really hard to try those perceptions. I've argued for so many years if that perception isn't changed, we really can't win this. But as you pointed out, we had a surprise positive reaction to the Giuliani deal, so I think there's a lot of other people out who, once they hear about it, they'll come our way.

Horton: Yeah, when they say, "red line this" and "red line that," I don't know exactly what that means, but part of me… I have to believe that somewhere in Washington, D.C. is at least the knowledge if not the wisdom from the Iraq war that this is not always as easy as it might seem at first.

Paul: It never is and there's always the unintended consequences both militarily and also financially. If you read the reasons why bin Laden encouraged 9/11 and what he thought would happen, it's pretty astute. It looks like he's laughing at us in his grave because it seems like they've won so much. A lot of people, including Michael Scheuer, argue that we have lost these wars over there, we're leaving. Even though it's not as humiliating as when we left Vietnam, in many ways it's very similar, all of that fighting and killing, and money spent and things are more chaotic, more people dying. Think of how many people have died over there at our hands.

This is the reason that noninterventionist foreign policy is a powerful argument and it's something that if we get the information out there, it's going to be hard for people to turn it down. Especially, when it's recognized how broke this country is. The Soviets weren't defeated because we had to fight them. It was an economic issue. They defeated themselves. We're on the verge of doing that. That was one of bin Laden's plans, was to drive us into bankruptcy and bog us down and evidently, we played into his hand.

Horton: I think that is going to be a very powerful argument, especially when it's so clear, as you just pointed out, that the war in Syria is blowback from the war in Iraq already. This is the Sunni insurgency from Iraq that's fighting — the al Qaeda in Iraq guys — fighting alongside in the Sunni insurgency there.

Paul: The real irony is there was no al Qaeda in Iraq before we went in. It's so bad on the surface. You wonder are they really stupid or are they doing this on purpose? Are they on the side of al Qaeda? Which I don't believe, I just think that they are absolutely inept, they have goals and they always fail at them, fortunately.

Horton: I could see how someone would think, "Hey, let's get rid of Assad," I don't know, 15 years ago, but it seems like they would have to change their opinion about that once all this new information comes in about the way the world actually works, you know?

Paul: Right.

Horton: Because Assad's no nice guy. It's easy to promote war against a dictatorship but what's to come next? This brings us to the last topic. I know you've got to go, but I wanted to ask you real quick about *Ron Paul's America* that you're doing with Charles Goyette, who is my favorite radio guy in the whole wide world, and this is… I could not overstate the importance of this. You're going to be on, you're already on twice a day on radio stations across the country doing this sort of Paul Harvey/Cactus Pryor minute kind of a thing, and this is so powerful. All of these conservative AM talk radio stations playing Ron Paul twice a day, every day from now on. Is it already a lot of fun? Are you getting a lot of response from it?

Paul: Yeah, we are. It's going very favorably and the company that actually put it together for us and find the stations has called me to try to come up with an understanding of expanding this. They want to expand it a lot more. It's two things. We do the daily thing, but they also do a podcast. I think the limitation will be my time and my energy. I like it, enjoy it. It's not that difficult to do but there's always going to be a limit.

When I'm on a trip… This week I was up at Colgate and I had a nice visit up there, so when you're gone for a day or two, you can't quite get that studio quality that they want. They want me to do this with studio quality and make it sound very professional.

I think it can get as big as I'm able to do it, which means those individuals in stations, they're not coming to me because they're philosophic allies, but they do know and understand that there's a market out there for our message. They're not doing it on purpose to spread our message, they're doing it because they know somebody wants to hear it and if somebody wants to hear it, then they can sell advertisements. It's a market phenomenon and I hope it's successful for that reason if nothing else.

Horton: I'm always excited when I see that you're on TV and you're answering anybody's questions but the fact that in this case, you're answering Charles's questions, is just huge because he really knows what the right question is. He's not going to waste his time asking CNN fluff. I've heard a couple dozen of them so far and they're just great. I'm so excited about it. I think it's just great.

Paul: Well, that's wonderful, thank you.

Horton: Alright, well, thank you very much for coming back on the show, Ron. It's great to talk to you again.

Paul: Okay, Scott. Bye.

Horton: Thanks very much. Everybody, that is Ron Paul, the greatest American hero ever. Ever.

June 10, 2013

Horton: Our next guest is Dr. Ron Paul. He's the author of *A Foreign Policy of Freedom*, and also some other accomplishments you might have heard of. He was a congressman for a while, I think, and he's got an article today at Antiwar.com that is called "Government Spying: Should We Be Shocked?"[6] Welcome back to the show, Dr. Paul. How are you doing?

Paul: Doing fine. Nice to be with you.

Horton: Very good to have you here, sir. The big news, of course, from the end of last week and now into this one, is all of Glenn Greenwald's revelations at the *Guardian* about National Security Agency spying. One of the big things to come out of it is the whistleblower has gone ahead and come forward after the first three big stories. His name is Edward Snowden, and it turns out he's a Ron Paulian of some kind, donated to your campaign in 2012. What do you make of that?

Paul: I haven't thought a whole lot about it, but I guess his concern about privacy is the same as mine. That he resents it and sees that people who do things like that are defying the Constitution and are not representing our liberties, so I guess it shouldn't shock anybody that he would be a libertarian-leaning type individual.

Horton: Do you approve of this type of whistleblowing in general? What do you think of what's going on here?

Paul: Of course, what we want is the truth. Everybody should say, "Yes, we do want the truth." But a totalitarian, an authoritarian, when they're in charge, that's the last thing they want. They want secrecy. In a free society, you're supposed to have a Constitution designed to have the government protect our privacy and our liberties, not the secrecy of government. But when the government gets too big and becomes more authoritarian, then that government wants to hide the truth. They do everything possible. That is the reason that I've made the statement that "truth is treason in an empire of lies." Here are these individuals who come along and tell us the

---

[6] Ron Paul, "Government Spying: Should We Be Shocked?" Antiwar.com, June 9, 2013, https://original.antiwar.com/paul/2013/06/09/government-spying-should-we-be-shocked/.

truth, of course, they do break the law and they're practicing civil disobedience, and it's very, very risky. Who becomes treasonous? The people who defy our Constitution, undermine our Constitution, throw it out and not protect our privacy? No. The person who's accused of treason is the one who is telling the truth. Right now, of course, we have a CIA agent that's in prison because he told us the truth about torture, about the Guantánamo torture and revealed this. But to deny that information to the people is what I think is so dangerous. I think the bigger question is not what should the penalty be for Snowden as much as what should the penalty be for people who take an oath to obey the Constitution and do the exact opposite?

Horton: Right. It's amazing, isn't it? The way that they try to conflate whistleblowing with espionage. They say, "If you say something classified to the *New York Times,* and Zawahiri can read that, hiding out in his mom's basement in Pakistan somewhere, then you're providing aid and comfort to the enemy."

Paul: That, of course, is the demagoguery of it all, because they want to paint those of us who want to protect the Constitution and protect the Fourth Amendment, we are then said to be the bad guys. So they turn around and demagogue it and say, "Oh, he's cavorting with the enemy. He's supplying information to the enemy." This is quite a bit different than what we saw in World War II when our government was filled with spies and they would take secret information about nuclear weapons and turn them over to avowed enemies like the Soviets and actually benefit materially from this. That is quite a bit different than somebody telling the truth about our own government when it gets out of control.

Horton: Just how out of control is this? I guess it's shocking but not surprising is basically the message here?

Paul: I think it keeps getting worse. I don't know if you saw that little clip somebody found the other day of a speech I gave in 1984 expressing concerns, "Hey, we better watch out. This thing could get out of control." In the same way, even in these past ten years, I don't think something dramatic has happened under Obama. In the last year or two that all of a sudden, these programs have gotten out of hand, because they were started with Republicans, and they were started under Bush. They continue. Just because we don't hear about them doesn't mean that they weren't existing. I think it's steady. I think it's steady growth and the worse things get, the more they'll do it. Whether our foreign policy deteriorates, or our monetary policy deteriorates, the greater the power goes to those individuals who want to control things. Of course, the more powerful a government, the more secrecy they want because they're afraid to be revealed. Once they reveal what's happening, they might be challenged. So they have to then play the patriot card and say, "Oh, well. You're not patriotic. You're un-American." Remember how much they said about my foreign policy, "He doesn't care about the troops. He's un-American." This is just to try to destroy that person who is giving us the information. That, of course, is what they're doing right now with Snowden, is just to say that he's the bad guy.

What I get a real charge out of, in a way, it's so weird, is the Republicans want power. Generally, they'll say and do anything for power. They want to put Obama on the ropes and they finally get something, and I think it's great that the large majority of American people say, "Hey, he's gone too far. He doesn't care about the Fourth Amendment. He's snooping on all of us. He's spying on all of us. This is over the limit." Then we have the Republican leadership come and saying, "Hey, this is good. We endorse this." They were handed a great issue and they say, "No, we started this under George Bush and this stuff is good. We have to do this. We have to have national defense, and if you don't do this, that means you're un-American and you're not patriotic."

Horton: I saw Bill Kristol saying, "Hey, we shouldn't conflate the IRS scandal with the NSA scandal," even though the NSA scandal is a million times worse.

Paul: He's one of those Republican leaders that want to… People don't refer to him as that, but he's the one that's been behind the Cheney and the Bush operation and all the foreign policy. They have a lot of influence, obviously, in both parties because foreign policy really hasn't changed. This is why this is shocking to the progressives. This is a wake-up call for progressives. I think this is good. It's sort of disgusting to see Republicans defending Obama when we finally get him on the ropes and catch him doing some of the things that are wrong, and that could be used in a political way of trying to challenge him, but, no, it becomes totally neutralized. Which makes my point that foreign policy never changes. When Obama gets into a little trouble, what happens? A lot of Republicans come to his rescue and say, "Hey no, that's okay. We believe in this. We don't want our foreign policy to be undermined because this is so necessary."

Horton: During the campaign, Obama and Romney both bragged about how they were learning foreign policy by reading Robert Kagan's new book. He's Bill Kristol's co-author of the concept of "Benevolent Global Hegemony" and all the rest of that stuff. Obama has proudly claimed him, so there you go.

Now, Snowden in his interview with Glenn Greenwald said that his biggest fear is that nothing will change of this. And yet, immediately your son Rand, Senator Rand Paul, came out and said, "Oh yeah, well I'm introducing the Fourth Amendment Restoration Act and I'm suing, too," and he wants it to be a class-action lawsuit. He wants ten thousand people to join up to help him sue the government over this.

Paul: And I wish him well. I'm not sure who's right on this, whether Snowden will be right, or Rand will achieve what he wants to achieve, because it is so difficult. For instance, before we went into Iraq, most of the Americans, 80 percent of the Americans were saying, "No. We don't need to do this. We don't need to do this." Yet, after the war propagandists were out there, and the media pounds away, all of a sudden, they can change attitudes. So people right now are riled up, and that's great, but are they going to be there? Are they going to change the congressmen and their senators because they're having supported their position? This may settle down, not much will happen. I'm hoping it does change policy. That's the thing that really counts, will the policies be changed?

Even court fights and all, most of the time they don't achieve a court victory to change things, but they're great in calling attention to the problems out there. I remember one time, I was outraged by Reagan and the Senate passing a tax bill that wasn't written in the House at all. It was written in the Senate. We went to court, and the court says, "Oh no, you have no standing. You have no gripes. Just because the Senate overrode the House, you have no standing. You can't complain about this." The case was just thrown out of court.

Horton: That's funny.

Paul: What kind of a judge is really going to give us a fair hearing? That's the big question.

Horton: Especially something like that, where that's just black and white words in the Constitution itself. Bills like that must originate in the House. Of course, you have standing.

Paul: Yeah, that's the problem. I think it's a PR fight. You've got to get a consensus. This is what I think is shifting now. In the last five, six, seven years, there's a been a shift in attitude toward monetary policy and the Federal Reserve. Now on privacy, I think this is great. The American people are more tired of the wars now. Matter of fact, I think one of the reasons the Republicans did badly in '08 was they were tired of the wars. Now, they're getting tired of Obama and his war against the American citizens and their civil liberties. People say, "Oh, this is devastating." No, they need to know the truth, and that's the most important thing. People will not act if they don't hear the truth, but it gets very tricky if you tell the truth and you end up being accused of being a traitor. That's what's going to happen to the many whistleblowers as they take great risks in doing this.

Horton: Over at the Ron Paul Institute for Peace and Prosperity, you've been doing a lot of really great work criticizing American policy toward Syria. I wonder what you make of the fight going on inside the halls of power over what to do there? When people like Henry Kissinger and Zbigniew Brzezinski and some of the most powerful I guess they'd call them graybeards of American establishment foreign policy, they're saying, "Stay out. It could be worse. Let's not make it worse." That kind of thing. Yet, there's constant pressure always to intervene, too, and, as they say, "Innocent people are dying. Somebody's got to do something, and we're somebody. We can do something." I just wonder, what do you make of it all? What side is John McCain on? What side is America on? Where do we go from here?

Paul: All I know, is if we lose this argument — and we expand, and go in there, and start bombing, and get troops involved — and we let McCain and Graham win this argument, that doesn't say much about us who are arguing the opposite. We must not be doing a very good job of presenting our case. Our tools are more available now than they used to be. It used to be that if you didn't get on the top three TV stations, you didn't have a voice. Today we do have a voice. How many people watched Snowden on his video? Millions and millions of people. So if we lose this it would be sad to think that McCain and Graham win it, and their policies are so ridiculous to go in there and help the al Qaeda.

This argument about humanitarian concerns, that's an argument only. That isn't the reason they want to do it because the record shows that every time we go in there — We send off missiles for humanitarian reasons to kill the bad guys. Yet, thousands and thousands of innocent civilians get killed and that incites more al Qaeda. It makes no sense, and yet they keep doing the same thing over and over again.

Horton: Yep. Can you tell us real quick, before I let you go, can you give us a word about the Ron Paul Institute? I know the URL is RonPaulInstute.org.

Paul: We're real happy with that. It's just early started. It's been a couple months, and it's going to expand and grow. I guess the one thing I can tell you that I am pleased with: I thought that it wouldn't be quite as easy to get people excited about it, and people actually send some money in to help us out, as it would be to talk about economics, and recessions, and the Federal Reserve, and the United Nations, and things like that. But we've had a pretty good response and we've barely started, so we're hoping that we can have a real impact. I think Daniel McAdams, who did my foreign policy in the congressional office for years — He's heading this up. I have a lot of respect for his ability. I'm really looking forward to us having an impact. Hopefully some good will come of it.

Horton: Well, I sure have got it bookmarked and Dan McAdams is great on pretty much everything that I can think of, anyway. He's been way out ahead on this so-called revolution in Syria for two and a half years now, as well. That definitely speaks well of the whole project. Listen, I'll let you go, but I want to thank you very much again for your time, Ron. It's great to talk to you.

Paul: Okay, Scott. Goodbye.

Horton: Alright everybody. That is the great Dr. Ron Paul at the Ron Paul Institute for Peace and Prosperity. RonPaulInstitute.org. What a great name for an institute, if you're going to have an institute named after you, right?

August 22, 2013

Horton: Our first guest today is Dr. Ron Paul on the phone from his office in South Texas. Welcome back to the show. How are you doing?

Paul: Thank you, Scott. Good to be with you. Doing fine.

Horton: Good deal. Hey, I'm really excited about the new Ron Paul Channel. It's just great, and especially your whole first episode there with the secret wars and the Glenn Greenwald interview and all that. Just, it's great stuff. I'm really excited about it.

Paul: Thank you. Good.

Horton: I think it's great and I think you make a great TV host. And I knew you would. And I really like your cohost. I'm sorry, I forget her name, but I think she does a great job playing Ed McMahon to your Johnny.

Paul: Great. Good.

Horton: And it's a perfect thing. I think it's really great.

Horton: Okay, so now let's talk about important things, more important. They're letting Mubarak out of jail. What do you think of that?

Paul: Well, maybe our government with their infinite wisdom will put him back in charge. You know, who knows? The silliness of that whole thing. It can't settle things. It won't be more calm, but I just don't have strong opinions on who should run Egypt, just so it isn't us. So it's not our money or our troops or our influence or our military. I want us just to be out of there and I think we should let the Egyptians decide who's going to run their country.

Horton: Well and that's what you've been saying for a long, long time while America was backing Hosni Mubarak there, and was it, what do you think, like say for example as things were breaking loose, and everything started going crazy in the Arab Spring back at the beginning of 2011, should they have gone ahead and just kept backing him at that point rather than have the country go through all of this with the phony elections and now canceled, and the massacres in the streets and everything?

Paul: No. I think we should recognize that the policy of intervention is wrong and quit it as soon as you can because it's the intervention that generates the hatred, not only against their dictator that we prop up, but us as well. And that's why Islam has the greatest incentive to be radicalized. I mean this is why a lot of people in Iran right now would like to do us harm, and we can't get along with them. We've been in their face and telling them what to do for a long time starting as far back as 1953.

So I think whether it's supporting Saddam Hussein, or working with Osama bin Laden at times, and then switching around, and right now the Global War on Terrorism, and everything that we do, and the drone warfare, it's a great recruiting tool for the radicals. The more we do, the more al Qaeda members there are, and the more determined they will become. So as soon as you quit doing it, I think it would be better. We then would save a lot of money. We would be less hated. Our national security would be a lot better. So I don't see any disadvantages from becoming more neutral in all these areas.

Horton: Something else that you've been talking about a long time regarding foreign policy is the prerogatives of the president, and what are and are not his powers. And there are times when you said, "Hey, when it comes to troop movements, Congress should back off. That really is not their responsibility. But when it comes to deciding who commits what violence, that really is up to the Congress."

And I just wonder what you think about this so-called "red line" on Syria that Obama I guess just created in a speech, will be the history textbook version of what happened. Obama used the word "red line" and then that became a thing. Now, especially, this is important because there's another claim of a chemical weapons attack in Syria.

Paul: I think we should recognize when acts of war are committed, and bombing and invading and subsidizing and sending weapons, that's all acts of war and shouldn't be done without congressional approval. The president does not have this authority arbitrarily to say, "Well, if so-and-so does this, that means I'm going to do this, which is accelerate the war." I think he's wrong in doing that.

Someday we may find out that the last person who would have an incentive to use poison gas would be Assad. He's been warned the heavy hand of all governments will come down on him if he uses it, and if he uses just a little bit, what does he gain? He doesn't gain anything other than the fact that the heavy hand will come down on him. It will be much tougher for him. But who does have an incentive? Who has a benefit? Well, the radicals. The people who are trying to take over, and there are several groups, and al Qaeda is involved, so al Qaeda might say "Boy, if we can blame an incident like this on Assad, we're going to get the weapons. And we're going to get all these governments to come in and help us."

And we, once again, will be helping the al Qaeda. Just as we put the al Qaeda into Iraq by fighting Saddam Hussein, who at one time was fighting al Qaeda, that we have a country now that we redesigned, and al Qaeda is in Iraq and we'll probably continue to do this instead of sorting this all out. I have no idea who did it, nor does our government. But logic tells me that Assad, probably he's not an idiot. He would have to be out of his mind if he thinks a little bit of gas is going to win the war for him when he knows that all the other countries in the world will come down hard on him.

Horton: If anything, I wouldn't call it wisdom, but perhaps President Obama is afraid to intervene in Syria? He keeps sending the chairman of the Joint Chiefs of Staff out to come up with reasons why not. And he's even going so far as to sound a little bit like you here in saying, "Hey, these guys that we're backing are not our friends, and they're not going to be our friends." It's not that hard to see that close into the future here, you know?

The problem with it is, they might realize the impracticality of what they're doing, and they want to back off. But they don't start their thinking about foreign policy in a principled way. The principle that they do accept is intervention, that we have this moral obligation. If we don't send troops, we send humanitarian aid, and then behind the scenes we use the CIA, we use drones. We don't need invading armies.

Paul: But they never question themselves about intervention. The kind of mess we have in Egypt is not on should we intervene or not. It's what do we get for it and what kind of a management? Do we support Mubarak, or don't we? Do we support Morsi? It's back and forth. So it's a management thing that they debate, not a principled question on whether or not we should be involved at all.

Horton: Alright, now as you know, Bradley Manning was sentenced yesterday to 35 years for the leak of the Iraq and Afghan war logs and the State Department cables. And I just wonder if it had been President You, Attorney General Jonathan Turley, and Secretary of Defense Andrew Bacevich, would you guys have gone after this case like this and put him away for 35 years?

Paul: No. I think there'd be something done. Probably discharged. He probably should have never been in the military. But he's served a lot of time already. He's served more time than William Calley did under house arrest for killing five or six hundred innocent kids and women in Vietnam — and he didn't suffer any severe consequences. So I think that some of those people who were committing the war crimes, like the people even in Iraq and Afghanistan killing innocent people, they don't even get charged with anything. What about the war crimes that we participate in? No. It's anybody who tells the truth about it.

So, no — I think he has served plenty of time. I don't think he should be sentenced. I think that he's admitted to releasing information. He should be penalized for that with the time served. But I would just discharge him from the military.

Horton: And what about Edward Snowden? Would you go ahead and give him a preemptive pardon? Invite him back home?

Paul: Yeah, I think if — Unless there's something awfully weird that came up. He's charged with aiding the enemy, but I don't think for a minute that he did. I don't think that was his purpose and there's no evidence to that. As you know, even a judge threw out this whole idea that Manning was aiding the enemy. He wasn't doing that. They're aiding the American people by telling us the truth. So those individuals who say that Snowden was giving this information to the enemy must have that perverse understanding that we're the enemy. If we get to know what they're doing, that undermines the credibility of the empire, and that's certainly something they don't want to happen, so they have to perpetuate the lies to the best of their ability.

Horton: We're about out of time here, but I guess I'll just give you a chance really quick to invite everybody to check out the Ron Paul Channel. Could you?

Paul: Yeah. All they need to do is RonPaulChannel.com and find out. Today I'll be interviewing Eric Margolis on Egypt.

Horton: Oh, great.

Paul: And we'll continue to do those kinds of interviews and do our very best to get the information and the truth out.

Horton: Right on. Well thank you so much for your time again on the show, Dr. Paul. It's great to talk to you again.

Paul: Okay, Scott.

February 12, 2015

Horton: Our first guest today is a man whose name is on most of my shirts. He's the greatest parliamentarian in world history and my hero, Dr. Ron Paul. Welcome back to the show Ron, how are you doing?

Paul: Thank you, Scott, nice to be with you again. Thank you for the exaggerations.

Horton: No, no, it's all very much deserved. I want to mention here too in your introduction, RonPaulInstitute.org is the website of the Ron Paul Institute for Peace and Prosperity, and then, of course, there's VoicesOfLiberty.com which is sort of the improved and expanded Ron Paul channel, which I'm very happy that they're running some of my archives there at VoicesOfLiberty.com, I'm very proud of that and thank you for that, whatever part you played in okaying that if you did.

Also, I want to make sure everybody knows that you're the author of great titles like, *A Foreign Policy of Freedom*, and *The Revolution: A Manifesto*. Those are my favorites of the many books that you've written that I've read.

So, there you go. Very happy to have you back on the show. I guess the big news is, like in your essay running on Antiwar.com,[7] and all around the internet today, is about the new Authorization to Use Military Force. I thought of you actually when I saw them saying that. The administration was even officially saying that they're leaving it "deliberately fuzzy," they call it, deliberately vague.

Paul: And does it really matter? Even if it's explicit. For them, it's always fuzzy. It's sort of like the Constitution. It's pretty explicit in most places, but it always ends up being interpreted in a very funny manner.

Horton: Exactly. Now the Authorization to Use Military Force from back in 2001, they still want to keep that. That's the one that you voted for in response to the September 11th attacks, after you warned against that kind

---

[7] Ron Paul, "Obama's Force Authorization Is a Blank Check for War Worldwide," Antiwar.com, February 11, 2015, https://original.antiwar.com/paul/2015/02/11/obamas-force-authorization-is-a-blank-check-for-war-worldwide/.

of thing actually, and introduced a letter of marque and reprisal instead. Can you tell the people about what a letter of marque is and what that would have been?

Paul: This was used in the early history and Jefferson used it. And sometimes, as great as a man as Jefferson was, I look back now and think that maybe he did a little bit more than I would have wanted. Anyway, he wanted to exert the notion of sovereignty in the United States so he would use this in a naval sense, and anybody who attacked an American vessel any place in the world, he wanted to even send the navy to help.

But the letter of marque and reprisal was an accepted instrument throughout the world. That if you had a letter from your government and you were sailing in a private ship, you could act as part of the government to defend yourself, and to attack those who are attacking you. So it was more than just self-defense, it was more or less getting the authority from the government to do something in a very limited fashion. Rather than saying, "Well, the only thing that we can do with the Barbary pirates is to declare war," and that was the only option, this letter of marque and reprisal, which they put in — I guess they were thinking of things like this, to limit it.

And, of course, there were a lot of hang-ups with that authorization. And in 2001, that was actually totally abused because that was directed at those people who actually participated in 9/11. But nevertheless, they went much, much further than that and that is when I started talking about a letter of marque and reprisal. Because even though we so often can talk about what led up to it, what led up to World War I and World War II, once the country is viciously attacked and it's just there's no way you can't defend oneself against it, then you don't have many choices in the matter. But I was still looking for one, and since al Qaeda, whoever did 9/11, wasn't a precise government, you really can't declare war against a government. That's sort of similar to what's going on today with ISIS, it's pretty hard to declare war against ISIS. That's why I got to thinking about the letter of marque and reprisal, maybe this could be done by a small group of people.

As a matter of fact, can't you just see the difference that might have occurred? They knew where bin Laden was. I don't think they really wanted to catch him because he was used as an excuse for us invading various countries and building up the military. So if you had a private force that was going to be paid to go over and get him, because they had pretty good knowledge of where he was and who was taking care of him early on. Just think of the benefits that would have come from a very, very narrowed approach to going after those people that were participating in 9/11.

Horton: You were probably pretty much alone on Capitol Hill of having a realistic assessment of just how big of an organization al Qaeda was and saw 9/11 as sort of the desperate Hail Mary kind of attack that it was, rather than believing in this giant caliphate that they said was coming to get us but that didn't really exist out there. They were just looking to exploit it and get away with murder. But your way, I agreed — I remember thinking back then, "Boy, if they would listen to Ron Paul, this thing would be over by Christmas."

Paul: But again, the extent of al Qaeda was one thing, but the nature of al Qaeda was something else because I still don't think it's a monolith. Yes, it looks like they're getting organized under a force in Iraq and Syria, conditions which we created, but they're still talking about 30,000. What about the millions? How many millions of people are around that area? That claim they don't like them everywhere from Israel, on to Turkey, and Syria and Iran.

Nobody likes them and yet, there's apparent success. So it's more than fighting a country because there's people who support these people, and at least go along with it and they're not willing to fight them. That's why I think it gets to be silly if they think they're ever going to declare war against ISIS. I compared this to back in the '50s and the '40s or so, declaring war against communism. Well, you can declare war against the Soviet Union, but you can't declare war against communism because it's pervasive, it's all over the place. And people who are angry at us now, and have been radicalized and feel desperate, they're anxious to do something.

And I think right now, there's a real question about the 20,000. Everybody accepts — Well, how many people are on the way to Syria? 20,000? It's going to go from 30,000 to 50,000 in one day and we're going to be in that much trouble, so that's the reason we have to vote for more authority and more weapons. It's just the biggest mess I can conceive of in foreign policy.

Horton: And it's true that when you talk about listing off all the people who are their enemies in the region who are against them, you can include everybody they've conquered too or pretty much everybody they've conquered because we've seen how these guys acted in the past where it was the Sunni-based insurgency themselves, their allies, that turned on al Qaeda and got rid of them back in 2006 and 2007. And they're such horrible guys. They obviously have no concept of... You thought America was bad at counterinsurgency? They have no concept of "hearts and minds" whatsoever, apparently. They're happy to turn everyone against them.

Paul: It really hurts us who are trying to get the people to understand what's really going on, because all you have to do is have one person burned to death, or some people beheaded, and they don't think about the 60 that were beheaded in Saudi Arabia last year, and how Saudi Arabia may well have been instrumental, especially in the financing of 9/11. These kinds of things, it just sort of distracting, and the people concentrate on this but that's all part of the war propaganda, but nobody… If we would suggest, "Well, how would you feel if you were out at a funeral and lo and behold a cruise missile was misplaced, and they killed my whole family? Or they killed my cousin, or my friends?" How many people would feel outraged about that? But nobody wants to look at it that way, no matter how many people have died at the hands of our foreign policy, and there have been many. Some estimate it could be a million Iraqis died since we went in there in 2003.

Horton: Now hold it right there Dr. Paul, we'll be right back everybody with Ron Paul after this. [*Commercial break.*]

Alright you guys, welcome back to the show, I'm Scott Horton this is my show, the Scott Horton Show. I'm on the line with the great Dr. Ron Paul, antiwar activist, and we're talking about the past and future of the War on Terrorism, really. Sorry about the hard break interrupting you there Dr. Paul, but where we left off you were talking about a little bit of that "put the shoe on the other foot" kind of thing. You know, it's so important that, as I saw in a recent interview you did with Newsmax TV where you were basically explaining, "Hey, history was already going on before September 11th happened." It reminded me of a talk you gave on C-SPAN in 1998, a warning during Operation Desert Fox, the bombing campaign against Iraq, that this is the kind of thing that could lead to terrorist attacks against us.

There were a few different examples of that before September 11th. In the Newsmax interview — I was thinking if only you said, "It was Bill Clinton's policies that led to this." Then maybe he… Because he almost understood that the 1990s existed, maybe made it a little bit partisan, maybe the Republicans can get their head around that, maybe it didn't all just start because the Quran said "Kill Whitey," or something like that, but maybe America had done something to get us into this mess. Our government had done something to get us into this mess.

Paul: It's really amazing how much partisanship there is and yet the parties are the same. They all believe in the foreign policy of intervention, and the Federal Reserve, and welfare, and spending, and deficits, and central economic planning, and all that. Yet they really do fight tooth and nail. But I think that's part of the things that they've been snowed on. I mean these, the hardcore Republicans, and hardcore Democrats give up all their beliefs when it becomes a partisan thing.

I came across that when we were fighting these wars, and Dennis Kucinich who's an honest progressive Democrat — I could work with him and other Democrats, but too often there were a bunch of the Democrats that worked real hard with us to try to stop Bush's war, but immediately wouldn't say boo to Obama. Now if I come out, and say well I sympathize, and I think I did that on Newsmax one time, that I sympathize with Obama's statement about, "Hey, why more sanctions on Iran right now? Why not let us talk a little bit about it?" And when you listen to his words, I don't know how sincere he is, but I gave him the benefit of the doubt because I'd much rather want him to talk to the Iranians rather than saying, "Well, it's time to bomb. I guess we'll put McCain in charge of all this and let him go ahead."

But then they come down hard on you, the conservatives come down hard on you. "Oh, you're a Bush lover, or you're an Obama lover," and then if you say something about why don't we have an understanding of what's going on in Ukraine, "Oh, you're just a Putin lover." You say anything which tries to explain why there's a civil war going on there and why NATO's fighting Russia, then they, of course, want to destroy your argument only by character assassination. But that's the way things have been for a long time, and the only way we can confront that is with as many facts as we can get out there, and shows like yours and what we all try to do and fortunately we have more ability to do this now than in the old days. It used to be very different for our side, and with people like Snowden around it becomes even easier for us, but there's still a lot of ignorance out there, and there's a lot of need to just go along. You can imagine how the zombies will follow Hillary once she gets rolling.

Horton: Right. Yeah we saw that with the recent *Washington Times* series on the Libya war where almost uniformly the conservatives are just as bad as her on it, the Republicans, and so they don't want to make much hay of it, even though it's in their newspaper, the *Washington Times* there, and the liberals don't want to say anything about it even though that series is just absolutely huge, the scandal behind how, even the Pentagon tried to stop her, but nobody could, in getting us into that thing.

Paul: But even the strongest critics from the Republicans aren't saying, "Well, you know this could've all been avoided, if we wouldn't have decided that we had to get rid of Gaddafi at this particular time." I mean we were in there. We mess it up and look at what's there now: total chaos. It's either going to be they didn't use enough force, or Hillary screwed up by using the force that she did have, and her policies weren't correct, but they never look at the overall policy of the downside of foreign interventionism.

Horton: Now back ten years ago when they were pushing all this stuff, they kept threatening that this "Islamo-fascist caliphate" is getting us, right? As you were talking about before, inflating al Qaeda into this almost Soviet empire-sized thing that needs to be battled. It was a fantasy of bin Laden's — it was a fantasy of George Bush's — and yet it seems like that kind of is what has replaced the old Ba'ath regime in the predominately Sunni parts of Iraq and Syria with this guy Baghdadi who is, for intents and purposes, bin Laden himself up there on the balcony like Mussolini declaring himself the Caliph, and all this kind of thing. So, just playing devil's advocate as best I can here Dr. Paul is it possible that maybe we need to fight one more real good war here against these particularly heinous guys, the guys that Bush pretended Saddam was, and only then maybe quit?

Paul: I'm not quite ready to go in and try to clean up the mess with our money and our troops, but I do think they're stronger. They seem to be more organized, but that's not so much that their philosophy is winning out, that they're getting such support, but they're getting support out of default out of our failure which sort of — How did we beat the Soviets? We didn't beat them by military might, we beat them by them beating themselves because they had a non-viable system. But the more we get involved, the more we enhance our enemies because we send — The biggest thing is the incentive, the more — We're blamed for everything that goes wrong, and everybody that dies over there, and now it'll be Ukraine and elsewhere because we are involved. And most of it's justified, but some isn't justified, but we can be the whipping boy and they can blame us.

But then even in a practical sense, I can't believe they do it on purpose, but sometimes it's so stupid it seems like it is. Like sending weapons into Syria because "we had to get rid of Assad." They didn't even... And then they listen to McCain, "Oh, I know who the good guys are we'll send them weapons." Now who would've ever guessed that there was chaos over there, and the weapons might end up in the hands of somebody that we don't like? So we incentivize them, and we give them their weapons. Look at how many weapons and energy that we ignited in Afghanistan and how the CIA supported the radicalization of Wahhabism in Saudi Arabia.

I think if one argues it looks like they're stronger than ever, and it looks bad, I think it's a mirror reflection of our stupidity and the failure of our side presenting an alternative philosophic system. That's where our downfall is. I don't think ISIS is something that you attack militarily. We didn't defeat the Soviets that way — we couldn't — and they had already killed a hundred million. And we became allies of theirs. But it was defeated philosophically, and I think that's what has to happen, but it can't be if we're going to finance them, and do enough harm that all it does is they don't… I'm sure there's still some good feeling in that part of the world for us, but I think everything we do diminishes the good feeling for America that used to exist.

Horton: Very good point. Alright, again everybody, that's Dr. Ron Paul at the Ron Paul Institute, that's RonPaulInstitute.org and also VoicesOfLiberty.com. And I'm under the impression Dr. Paul that you actually have a new project in the works coming out, do you want to talk about that at all?

Paul: Well I have several, and I'm not quite ready to… I do have a book on war that I want to get out, and I think we're going to be modifying the channel, and our broadcasting, but it's not quite ready yet.

Horton: Okay. Well, that's great to know, though, a new book coming out about the war.

Paul: It's war as an issue, rather than a war.

Horton: Oh, yeah, I understand.

Paul: It's written from a personal viewpoint from my early remembrance of World War II and all the things that — How did I become so antiwar? It wasn't that I had it in one single day. As the years went on, I became stronger. And, of course, in Washington it seems like some people become more enamored by the establishment, but the longer I was in Washington the more adamant I was against the establishment, especially of the wars, and it hasn't hurt me for my arguments that I did spend some time in the military, so it's a lot more difficult for the attacks on me than those they can put on others. But anyway, that will be out someday, as soon as I get it ready.

Horton: Okay, great, well, certainly looking forward to that. Thank you so much for coming back on the show.

Paul: Okay. Sure thing.

Horton: Good talking to you.

Paul: Good to talk to you, Scott.

Horton: Alright, so that's the great Ron Paul. The books are *The Revolution: A Manifesto*, *End the Fed*, and *A Foreign Policy of Freedom* that's a collection of foreign policy speeches that Dr. Paul gave starting I believe in the late '70s, and then all the way up through the early 2000s. Which is such a great read, you gotta get your hands on it, *A Foreign Policy of Freedom*. And we'll be right back after this.

July 3, 2015

Horton: Our next guest today is the greatest legislator ever in all of world history, my hero and probably yours. His name is on most of my shirts, the great Dr. Ron Paul. Welcome back to the show, Ron. How are you?

Paul: Doing fine, Scott. Nice to be with you again.

Horton: Very happy to have you on the show, sir, and very happy to have gotten an advance copy of your brand-new book. I read the whole thing last night, *Swords into Plowshares: A Life in Wartime and a Future of Peace and Prosperity*. It's just great. So glad that you did this.

Paul: Thank you.

Horton: So appreciative of it. There are so many great points in here. I almost don't know where to begin. Much of it we've talked about before on the show in the past over the past decade, but I guess I'd like to ask you, first of all, about the national debt. It's over $18 trillion now. You talk a lot in the book about, "Well, it looks like the empire is just not going to come down until the dollar breaks, basically, until the economy and the people's will to live under an economy suffering under the weight of all of this, when it finally just breaks, then it'll all come home."

I wonder how far you think we really are from that. Because when you make the comparison to the USSR, hey, they were communists. They were going to implode anyway, right? Their economics made no sense. It seems like for all the Keynesianism, and all the intervention, and all the corporatism and, frankly, even fascism here in the United States, it's still a pretty resilient economy. There's enough market force to it that as you also say in the book, we can afford a lot of empire. I wonder if you think maybe this could last decades and decades still into the future or what?

Paul: Well, I'd bet against decades into the future because I think the debt is too great and we're not producing anymore. It used to be a lot of concern even back in the '50s. I remember when Barry Goldwater became famous in the '50s because he was complaining about the debt under Eisenhower. Well, he was probably a little bit too early. There's a big difference now especially since 2008, since that crisis and the one that we are still in: productivity is down. Structural unemployment is very, very strong and more and more people are unemployed. They give you positive signals, like the unemployment rate is 5.3 percent, but the jobs that are created are part-time and they don't — There are more full-time jobs lost, so the number of people actually employed goes down all the time when you take into consideration the increase in population.

So the numbers aren't there, but the question is: "Well, if it's so bad, why didn't the collapse happen two years ago or yesterday or why you don't you say it's going to happen tomorrow?" Well, there's one aspect of Austrian economics that more or less explains this. It's called the subjective theory of value. There's subjectivity involved in this. It's what people think is going to happen, so they can convey confidence to a degree — not forever. Right now, a lot of confidence has been conveyed to the American economy because like you said, if you look around, there's still a lot of wealth and there's still a lot of trust in the dollar.

But if you look at the true value of the dollar over the last 20 years or last 100 years, compare the value of the dollar today to 1913 — It used to be what you could buy for a penny when the feds started, you now have to pay 25 times that. That's steady. I see it like the foundation has been totally eroded; it's an economy built on sand and something's going to blow it down because it has a life that's sort of artificial.

We're on the verge of it. Sometimes we get special benefits. As long as we're the reserve currency of the world, this is going to last. Until somebody comes up with something else, or they reject all currencies and people just leave all paper currencies like people were leaving the euro — and the Greeks are suffering the consequences — that's going to have to happen around the world eventually, but there's going to be people then go to real money — gold and silver — or some currency that is maybe established. Maybe they will establish a currency someplace with Russia and China and have some gold backing to it.

We don't know what that will be, but there's no reason to be optimistic that in ten years from now, we will see economic growth and people satisfied and there wouldn't be because if we keep doing this — The discrepancy between the rich and the poor, that's the big political issue now. This is a consequence of this. This is why the middle class is suffering and the discrepancy is what is going to motivate all the politicians, but until they give a free market answer and emphasize personal liberty and emphasize no more wars, believe me, it's downhill for us.

Horton: Right. Now, speaking of "dollar hegemony," I know — and this is something we've talked about in the past as well — at the end of World War II, of course, America's economy outmatched the whole rest of the world basically. There's just no question why the dollar was considered as good as gold — and it was partially backed by gold at the time — so, having dollar hegemony as a legacy of that makes sense. But I wonder how far past the kind of legitimacy of that legacy do you think we are now? Because people say that it's the American empire itself that forces the world. Like our deal with the Saudis to denominate their oil sales in dollars, for example, and other kinds of contrivances like that.

Mirrors and wires and smoke and bubble gum and shoestring holding the thing together with American force is what makes the world continue to use the dollar in that way. I wonder is there anything else? Are they going to switch to the Chinese currencies or some kind of market basket of other currencies? Because they all have their own problems as you said. People, I guess, could just resort to bailing out of paper money altogether, but it seems like you're saying that there are no other currencies really to compete with the dollar that are much better.

Paul: Well, yes. But I think that is already starting. It's a consequence of our foreign policy for us all of a sudden deciding that we had to have the Cold War going and starting to attack everything that Russia says or does and pushing Russia away from us. Russia was integrating with Europe. The Europeans like trading with Russia, but we badgered the Europeans into accepting a negative Russian position, so we are forcing Russia to join with China and other far eastern countries. Now, some of the oil is being paid for in renminbi when they're using Chinese currency.

So, no, that's not the gold standard yet, but it all serves to weaken the dollar and also makes us more aggressive. I think our foreign policy is speeding this process up, not only because it contributes to the debt, but also because of our stupidity and just building more and more enemies. I see the day coming when finally, this breaks out that the hostility toward America is going to be unbelievable because it's been held in check. People haven't been quite strong enough to express themselves because if they do, they get sanctions put on them or we bomb them. But once we get a little bit weaker, there's going to be piling on. Right now, there's a strong talk about the Saudis going with Russia. Now, that is a big deal. We have been the protector of Saudi Arabia since World War II when Roosevelt made that commitment, but I think there's a lot of things going on that potentially could change things overnight. Not that I think it's going to be tomorrow or the next day, we are getting awfully close to this and — Yes, we put on sanctions and we put our troops around Russia and all these things, but there's going to be an accident and there'll be a false flag or there'll be some unintended consequence and this is going to break down. It's one of these things that you ought to be prepared, but not sit on the edge of your chair and say, "Well, tomorrow's the day it's going to happen." You can't do that, but just think of how many Greeks right now wish that they probably would have taken their money out of bank a little bit earlier. They had years to be suspicious of what was happening, but, "No, the government will take care of us. We live in a welfare state. They have always taken care of us before. They'll take care of us." But all of a sudden, the banks are closed. So debt is the big problem, and debt is what will bring us down. Not only do we have that $18 trillion national debt, we owe foreigners over $6 trillion. We're the biggest debtor in the world. Our debt is greater than our GDP. So economically speaking, we're in bad shape.

Horton: Alright. Now, this is something that you talked about a bit in your speech or actually kept going back to this in your speech at UT — the Future of Freedom Foundation thing a few months back — about how no matter what — I think you even said, "All of the worst natural disasters even happen at once, volcanoes and hurricanes and earthquakes — and a war and a currency problem. Don't worry. All we need is freedom and everything will be just fine." Now, for people who don't understand what you mean by that, what do you mean by that really?

Paul: Well, I say things like that and close to it, but I don't think I want to say everything is going to be perfect, but everything will be better. What I'm saying is that the only correction for excessive debt is liquidation of debt. This is why the Greek thing has been going on for five years. They won't accept the idea that the debt is unpayable. They only look around for victims — who's going to suffer the most, which banks are going to suffer the most, which group of people won't get their pensions and on and on — but the debt has to be liquidated.

The sooner you liquidate, the better. We prolonged the liquidation in our Great Depression in the '30s and early '40s. The Japanese tried to handle their debt by adding more debt. That's what we're currently doing, but if we allow the liquidation... Let's say that there were no bailouts back in '08 and '09, and no QEs and propping up and transferring wealth from middle class to the rich. If we had not done that, on the surface things would have looked much, much worse. You would say, "Hey, this is crazy," but if you do that and people have a right to work, a right to keep what they earn, they get their freedoms back, we stop the wars, we protect civil liberties and even if we lost everything, but if we have our liberties — I think it would have taken about a year to get back on our feet again. The best example of this is the depression in 1921. There was the liquidation of debt and the depression after World War I and the Wilson years and the war spending and all this kind of thing, and the GDP went down. I think it was down like 15 percent in one year, but the debt was wiped off the books.

That's what you need, but it's like painful treatment and nobody wants it. If you concentrate on liberty and concentrate on reality about when debts get to a certain level, they're never paid. It's just that they're looking around for victims. Adam Smith actually pointed this out pretty well that nations have this tendency to get this debt and they don't pay. So often, debt is liquidated by the debasement of currency. That's what we're working on — or at least Bernanke and Yellen are working on — so hard is to liquidate the debt.

They know what they're doing, but they don't come out and say, "We want to liquidate the debt and punish the purchasing power of all people." Even though that's exactly what they want to do, and they admit it. Along the way, they punish everybody who wants to save money and try to protect against this. I have strongly believed that if you take your medicine, things will look tough on us in the short run, but we would survive if we have our liberties. Today, the worse things get the more authoritarian our government gets. The more intrusion on our liberties, the more spying, the more wars we have. That's absolutely the wrong way to go. My vote is for liberty.

Horton: Yeah. See, I think that's such an important message because I was speaking a few weeks back with Professor Alfred McCoy who I'm sure you're probably familiar with and who is certainly an anti-imperialist. He was in no way trying to rationalize or justify the empire, but he was saying, "Boy, when the empire falls, when Russia and China and Europe finally integrate with…" — as you were talking about before — "when America succeeds in pushing all its former friends together in an alliance against us and our empire finally does break, it's going to hurt so bad." I was thinking, "Well, geez…" Because really, Dr. Paul, because I've been listening you for so many years now, it seems like that's really the best thing that can possibly happen. Never mind to the people of Iraq and Afghanistan, etc., but for the American people, even if we do have to suffer a pretty bad depression when the dollar breaks or whatever the problem is, as long as we have free market pricing systems and so forth, then it'd be okay.

Paul: We're working hard at it and I think there are some signs that the young people are changing their minds, but the real problem is going to be that they can't stop the momentum. Yes, they can temporize things, but the crisis will come and the financial system will break down and we will give up our empire, but if they haven't talked about the real saving grace of personal liberty, then there's no other choice but to have another totalitarian come on. Why should an avowed socialist get the biggest crowds right now? It's a government takeover and redistribute wealth. They're out there and there are others who lean toward fascism: "I'm a strong guy. I'm going to take over. I'm going to be the boss."

So, they're out there. Our voices are getting more numerous, but we're not louder. I'm not too worried about that. I'm worried about getting this 8 percent of the people who will be the thought leaders who will have an influence on the 51 percent, and that is where we're making progress. That's why programs like yours are so important to get more people to listen and say that there is a good chance that we can succeed because we have alternative ways of spreading our message. That's the only choice that we have, because most of us reject the notion — for practical reasons as well as philosophic reasons — that we can win this fight through violence. I just don't think that's the solution.

Horton: Right. Especially on Independence Day — which I guess that's probably the one American war that you and I would agree that we might be for — but it's that assertion of individual liberty that's at the very basis of American civic life, that we're all born free. Then, the entire Misesian vision and the libertarian story that you've been telling all these years is about how, "Hey, guess what? Conveniently, it's liberty that works." All this socialism and planning and whatever, all it does is create distortions and worse problems later. It's liberty that actually creates the ordered society that we need — it's the mother of it, not the daughter. And as you're saying, especially in times like this, that message is extremely important when so many demagogues are willing to say, "All you've got to do is surrender more your freedom and more of your power and we will take care of it for you."

Paul: Yeah. I think right now, we actually have an opportunity because our message wasn't listened to at all because there was a tremendous amount of prosperity and there was a lot of momentum — and there's still this prosperity on the surface, and all you need is a good lobbyist to get hold of it — but more and more people now understand that the system isn't working and that we can't depend on it. There will be more Greek failures. This, to me, is very, very important. Many times over the years I have said there's something wrong with us, us who promote liberty, because it's so wonderful, personal liberty — you can do what you want as long as you don't hurt people. You mean there is more prosperity and there's more peace, and we don't win the argument?

What's the matter with us? Because somebody thought they could get a free lunch forever, but right now, the free lunch is no longer to be free. That's why we have to make sure that they don't pursue it with more totalitarianism and say, "Oh, yeah. We screwed up. We didn't have the right regulations. We didn't print enough money. We didn't do this, and we bailed out the banks, and we should have given more money to somebody else." That is a challenge for us, but I think we haven't done a very good job, but we better do a better job to convince the people that something as wonderful as personal liberty and owning our own lives actually gives us more wealth. There are still too many that don't believe it, but we need more people teaching this and this is one reason why I've liked the Mises Institute because they work on trying to get more people into the universities and more people teaching this.

We have to use everything whether it's the internet or your radio programs and things like this to convince people to stop and think. You just can't keep doing the wrong things that have been so destructive financially and our personal liberties. Every day there's another nail into the coffin of the republic by some politician. This past week, there was a big nail into the coffin. We saw Jerry Brown out in California saying, "Nobody has any exemptions for saying that this government doesn't have the right to inject you with anything they want." We better wake up. That's all.

Horton: Alright. I'm talking with the great Dr. Ron Paul, the heroic Dr. Ron Paul, author of *Swords into Plowshares: A Life in Wartime and a Future of Peace and Prosperity*, his brand-new book coming out. It's not quite out yet. Am I right?

Paul: That's right. Within a few days, it'll be able to be pre-ordered. Hope everybody keeps their eyes and ears open for it.

Horton: Okay. Yeah. It'll be right there on Amazon. Of course, we'll link to it and all that at the website, etc. Again, *Swords into Plowshares*, a great book. You really do aim very high in this book too and talk about the abolition of war — shades of this book *The End of War* by John Horgan, where he says, "Hey, listen. We haven't succeeded in truly abolishing slavery from the planet, but it's virtually universally outlawed and the people who participate in it are being hunted." That's the way it's supposed to be — that's the best we can do I guess in a world of seven billion people — but slavery has always been with humanity since coming out of the grasslands.

This is a huge leap forward. You talked about the huge leaps forward that humans have made in the past few centuries in terms of material wealth and advancements in science and technology and medicine and different ways of taking care of each other and pricing systems and all of these things. You say, "Hey, it's real. It's possible. Imagine it, we could abolish war from the face of the earth."

Paul: Yeah. The world is so young, yeah. When you think about recorded history just in a few thousand years of history, and the Industrial Revolution is even much shorter. I would say there's every reason in the world to have some sort of optimism that the human race can change its attitude. It certainly became smart enough to have such tremendous improvement in material things. In the book I mentioned that we're all better off. We have such a higher standard of living because of the material benefits, but they use a lot of that for war, how to kill people. What we need is a little bit of intelligence and common sense on why the human race can advance in saying war doesn't make any sense at all.

Horton: Right. Especially as you're saying when the weapons that they can afford to make now include H-bombs and the kind of even conventional weapons that lead to such scales of slaughter that in previous centuries of humanity, people could not have ever imagined.

Paul: Right.

Horton: It's on the order of plagues. The amounts of death from the World Wars and the consequences in the 20th century. Now, there's something that's fun I like to talk about on the show. I don't guess I've ever talked about it with you, but I brought this up to people from time to time just to try to get them to imagine. What if Ron Paul had won in 1988, and the end of the Cold War had happened on his watch, and NATO had come apart just as quickly as the Warsaw Pact and we got our peace dividend, and instead of Greenspan inflating, inflating, inflating to disguise the cost of the creation of the world empire in the 1990s, we'd just gotten all the way back to — well, I don't even know back — went forward to some real libertarian economics in this country? Think how... There are our flying cars that we haven't had since the year 2000, right? There's all that great stuff that we all thought would exist by now. That's where it went, was the empire.

Paul: Right.

Horton: The counterfactual... The reason I like to bring it up is because, hey, you're real and it's a real possibility. It's something that really could have happened back in 1988. It would have been the perfect timing for the end of the Cold War. Then when all the neocons and all their warmongering and bluster about spreading our way of life to the rest of the people of the world, what could have been better than America under the Ron Paul administration for showing the world this is what it's like to truly have a Bill of Rights that means what it says, to truly have freedom and free markets.

Paul: Well, hopefully we could say it would have been helpful, but I'm cautious in saying that it would have been complete reversal of all those bad things happening because you still need a consensus and the consensus hasn't been there. Think about how Obama is still subservient to many of the neocons' ideas, but even when he makes a minor suggestion of just having a conversation with the Iranians and opening up an embassy, what is the consensus? "Don't let him do it. We're not going to have an ambassador and we're not going to allow any traveling." This consensus in the Congress by those good conservatives is to stop it all. That also is most important. Yes, an individual even from '88 or '96 or whatever that was determined… But quite frankly, if the sentiment is too strong, you don't stay in office. They have ways of silencing people if they're pushing things faster than they think they should be, but nevertheless anything anybody can do to promote the ideas is what really counts.

Horton: Alright. I'm sorry for keeping you over. Can I ask one more thing real quick?

Paul: Quickly.

Horton: Okay. You mentioned in here about the international institutions, the United Nations, the WTO and NATO and SEATO, the treaty organizations and all that. Are you that confident — especially on the UN — are you confident that the world would be peaceful, that America be more peaceful, without the UN Security Council, which, of course, the whole apparatus is created in the name of world peace?

Paul: Well, I think other things would happen, but I think the world would be much better off because I argue the case for smaller government: smaller units, secession, self-determination. When you have fast track legislation for international agreements that are done in secret, whether it's WTO or who knows what, it's going in the opposite direction. I don't think it solves the problem of the violence between states, but it would be greatly reduced. You look at the mess that's going on in Ukraine right now, the IMF is involved, our funds are involved, NATO's involved, and it would be more difficult. If you establish the principle of self-determination and us staying out of those affairs, then the neighbors over there would have to deal with it. Same thing in the Middle East.

I think the more organizations you have, the worse. When you think about the organizations that came out of World War I and the Versailles Treaty, and the artificial lines that were drawn, that was the real culprit, but we're still at it. Maybe the names of the organizations changed, but it's always these coalitions to tell other people to leave. Mainly, it has been so often a way of getting hold of natural resources. If people understood the free market, the best way would be to let people alone. What else can they do with their natural resources but sell them to us? I think that the international organizations are a danger to us.

Horton: Alright. Thank you very much for your time again on the show today, Dr. Paul.

Paul: Thank you. Very good. Thank you.

Horton: I sure appreciate it.

April 12, 2016

Horton: Welcome back to the show, Ron. How are you?

Paul: Doing well, Scott. Nice to be with you again.

Horton: Very happy to have you here. And everyone, you should know that Dr. Paul, while he was a congressman for a while, gave two of the greatest speaking tours on behalf of liberty ever, in 2008 and 2012, in the guise of presidential campaign runs, which were great. And he's the author of *Swords into Plowshares*, *The Revolution: A Manifesto*, and *Liberty Defined*. Of course, he runs, with Dan McAdams, the great Ron Paul Institute for Peace and Prosperity. Every day, they produce a great TV show called the *Liberty Report*, which you can find on YouTube.

Alright. So, in the file cabinet of "Ron Paul warned 'em," right there at the top, is Ukraine. You told them, "Don't mess around in Ukraine," and they went and did, Dr. Paul. And then, what happened?

Paul: Well, chaos. Sometimes, you wonder, are they stupid? Or do they want chaos? Or is it bad judgment? And probably a little bit of all that. But most of the time, wherever we go, whether it's Iraq or Afghanistan or Syria or Ukraine, it's always chaos that we end up with. I made an effort while in Congress, when I smelled it coming, I would make a statement and say, "Watch out, watch out. You can get into trouble." I can remember in 1998, I think, there was the Iraqi Freedom Act that they were passing. I said, "Well, you'd better watch out. This is going to give us a war there, if this is the policy that you're establishing." But no, the policies are really ridiculous, they're stupid, and the one in Ukraine, we're going to be putting up with that for a long time to come. People thought, at one time, that we were finished with Iraq. And now what are we doing? Sending more troops. I think the president just recently said that he's definitely committed to sending more if necessary. So things haven't changed very much yet.

Horton: Well, on the Ukraine one, it's funny. There's a clip that should be famous, anyway — I guess it is in some circles — of you being interviewed on Fox News two days before the coup d'état in Ukraine in February 2014. And they were saying, "Dr. Paul, how come you keep saying that it's a coup going on there?" And you said, "Well, because it is. Watch. And it's a bad idea, and no good will come of it, either." And then it was, I believe, two days later that the president fled, and the neo-Nazis took over all the government buildings in Kiev and accomplished the coup. That one should have gone viral. You know, here's Dr. Paul's prediction coming true within two days' time there. And I guess, in fact, it would seem that really the consequences of that coup in Kiev were even worse than you probably even expected.

Paul: Yeah, and that always seems to be the case. But it is a mess. I think a good thing to look at, to see exactly what's going on and a consequence of our policy, is the way their parliament operates, with fistfights going on. I thought, "Yeah, well, they're not killing each other," but it's not very dignified. It's not very civilized. But that's the way the whole country is. That country is poor, and they don't have a concept of liberty. It's a fight between, "Do we go with the Russians, or would you go with the NATO hoodlums? And do we go with the United States?" And it's inevitable that there will be chaos. It doesn't take a genius to figure this out, but for some reason their minds are just closed to using a little bit of common sense when it comes to our foreign policy.

Horton: Well now, at least the war is over for now. I guess there's some limited fighting in the east, but the Minsk II peace deal seems to be holding, even though it's not fully been implemented as far as all the different political agreements there. But the big news, as you wrote about in your recent column at the Ron Paul Institute, and at Antiwar.com,[8] was about the Dutch vote on Ukrainian membership in the European Union. And this was a referendum that came from the bottom up, is that right?

Paul: Right. They had to get many, many thousands, I don't know, 300,000 signatures or something, to have that referendum come up. Then it went down 62 percent. The turnout wasn't huge, but to those who came, I think 62 percent of them said that they don't want to have any part of joining with Ukraine.

Horton: And that was really what the fight was about in the first place, right?

---

[8] Ron Paul, "As Ukraine Collapses, Europeans Tire of US Interventions," Antiwar.com, April 11, 2016, https://original.antiwar.com/paul/2016/04/10/ukraine-collapses-europeans-tire-us-interventions/.

Paul: Yeah. It was the fight. Yeah, that was what was going on from the East and West. Of course, we've added fuel to the fire, because we have deliberately decided that we're going to put troops on the border of Ukraine to protect everybody against Russian aggression. Of course, I don't think they have strong evidence that the Russians are about to roll the tanks over Eastern Europe. But nevertheless, we have to put troops there. Just stirring up trouble. Stirring up trouble to justify more military expenditures, and the money keeps getting spent and wasted, and people — Even the Republican candidates now, even though those who should have a little bit more sense, what is the mantra? "We've got to rebuild the military." Well, who tore down the military? When did we become a military weakling? We have more weapons than everybody else put together, and all the candidates can say — of course, since Rand's gone from there — they can all say now, "Well, all we have to do is we have to rebuild the military." And you know who controls that kind of language. It happens to be the people who make money off the military.

Horton: Yeah. Well, and speaking of them, there's that great article "Lockheed Stock and Two Smoking Barrels," that explains that Bruce Jackson from Lockheed was behind the Committee to Expand NATO back in the 1990s, in the first place. Because it was all just about transferring those big-ticket jets, on American taxpayer dollars, of course, to arm up those Eastern European countries. So yeah, that certainly does have a lot to do with it. In fact, I'm going to ask you about Plan Colombia in a second, and the military-industrial complex there. But as far as NATO and the EU and all that, does the Dutch vote, do you think, does that provide a real break on integration of Ukraine into the EU? And the plans to eventually bring them into NATO there?

Paul: Well, I think they're going to have to reassess the whole European Union, because, of course, the June vote in Great Britain is a big vote, too, on whether or not they should just leave the EU. So I think that is all yet to be decided, but I think it's a very strong indication that the European Union might be on its last legs, which it should've never been established. What bothers me is that we do such a poor job... Superficially, if you take a position of not supporting the European Union, then you say, "Well, you're a bunch of isolationists." You know, that term.

But the whole thing is, integrating Europe is a grand idea. If you had a sound currency, if everybody was on the gold standard, and you liberalized traveling and trade, you could still have the French and the Germans — When they started talking about the European Union, I said, "I predict it's not going to work." Because for some reason, I think there is going to be difficulty for the Germans to get along with the British, and the British to get along with the French, and the French to get along with the Italians. The only way you can do it, you see, is if it's gradual and voluntary, rather than a government. It's the idea that you have another government dictating and ruling in who has to pay the bills, and then there are a bunch of socialists, and then you have bankruptcies like in Greece, and they have to be bailed out. Then the foreign policy complicates things when you think about the migration, and the people who are migrating now, a result of the wars that the Europeans and Americans have supported for years.

We'd do so much better if we were setting a standard for free market economics, where people say, "You know, that country is wealthy and free and safe, so maybe we ought to look at free market economics. That's what we want." But that's never the case. It's always force. Using force to tell people how to live, how to run the economy, and how we have to rule the world.

Horton: Well, speaking of that, if I can divert for a minute onto American trade policy. Bernie Sanders and Donald Trump, both, have harped on NAFTA, and the various trade deals with China, etc., and said, "And all this free trade is killing us. I'm for free trade, but, but, but," they say. In fact, Trump actually looks like he's already prepared — they are prepared, the Reagan Democrats, the union labor voters — are prepared to cross the aisle, possibly even, to support Donald Trump because of his opposition to China trade policy and that kind of thing. I know that over the years — I've followed your career since 1997 — and I know that you've always denounced NAFTA and denounced all these trade deals as well. But I know you have quite a bit different take, and think it'd probably be beneficial if people could hear why you're opposed to the same thing, but for just entirely different reasons there. So a lot of what you just said about the EU, too.

Paul: See, what they're doing is misleading the people, and saying that these trade agreements are for free trade and low tariffs, and then people get very nervous about it. But it isn't. It's for managed trade, to serve the interest of some special interest, and it has to do with more government. So there's a big difference. But this issue even splits the libertarians. There are libertarian groups, at least they claim they're libertarians, who are very strong for these trade groups, because they'll say, "Well, they're going to lower tariffs." And on occasion, they do lower some tariffs. But it's also management of lower tariffs.

Right now, Trump talks about China, and how much more tariffs he's going to put on, but the United States just got permission to levy huge tariffs on steel coming from China. But it's legal, because the WTO authorized it. So low tariffs are good, but I don't believe in these international government organizations that happen. Matter of fact, the Constitution said that foreign trade should be dealt with by the Congress, not by deferring to the president or an international body. I think that's where the big mistake is. Then, they turn around and say that we are the isolationists, and we don't want to trade because we don't want to support these treaties. But these people who accuse many of us as being isolationists, are the ones who are always putting on sanctions on countries, and stopping trade, and invading countries. Then they claim that we who believe in true free trade are the isolationists. So it's an educational problem that we have to keep plugging away to make sure that people understand our position, rather than being criticized falsely.

Horton: So, when it comes to especially China and Mexico, for example, our biggest trading partners: If it was Sanders or Donald Trump in there, do you think their policies would lead to a trade war? Or could they get us a "better deal"?

Paul: Well, I don't think things will get better. I think that even if they did bully their way through there, and interfered with trade, and raised tariffs and all, it would be much, much worse. Because it would hurt everybody's economy, and there would be a trade war. I think it would be a trade war to go on, because they're not going to move in the libertarian direction, they're going to move in a more authoritarian direction, and just saying, "Well, it's that we're not getting our way on these international deals, and we're going to have our way." Well, I don't think that's going to work very well. Even if they did, what are the Chinese going to do? They might decide to sell some of our treasury bills to penalize us. So who knows what would happen?

Paul: But under the circumstances, the problems are so big, economically, that tinkering around the edges, which is what this would be, won't work. They're not talking about what needs to be done, when you need to look at monetary policy, and central banking, and deficit financing, and all these other things that need to be changed. Tinkering like this about a trade agreement, I don't think that's going to be the solution. On occasion, I guess, they might accidentally improve things. Sometimes they do lower a tariff. But overall, it's a big problem, and Europe is witnessing that problem, because they still have the socialist welfarist mentality, and we have it as well, too. So changing a treaty or an agreement with China is not going to solve all these problems.

Horton: I actually thought of you this morning when I was reading this thing out of Hillary Clinton's interview with the *New York Daily News*, where she cites the wonderful progress of Plan Colombia, saying it must be what caused the current peace talks between FARC and the government there. So what we need is another one of those, but for Honduras, and Guatemala, and El Salvador. I remembered something that you had said years ago, about whenever Joe Biden, when he was still a senator, and his counterparts in the House, would hold their hearings and pass their bills in favor of Plan Colombia, that there was only ever one interest group that showed up, and they had nothing to do with Colombia at all. It was just Bell Helicopter at the House of Representatives, saying, "Dr. Paul, we'd really like you to vote for this." Is that right?

Paul: It was. And as I recall — I haven't refreshed my memory on this, but I remember this coming up — they wanted to send helicopters, and there was a big faction, and there were two helicopter companies and they couldn't agree, so the solution for Plan Colombia was one company got half of the helicopters, and the other company got the other half. So we gave them away, and the taxpayers got stuck. And they were dealing with a situation that had to do with Americans' appetite for drugs, and the willingness to break the law in this ridiculous War on Drugs, and it was all a consequence of that. It was sort of like dealing with the Mexican-U.S. Border without taking into consideration the chaos there about the drug lords. And that's what was going on in Colombia, as well.

But yes, it was the special interests, the military-industrial complex, no matter how little, how big it is, somebody's out there to look after their money. So even though what they do so often leads to war, my guess is because I want to think a little bit better of them than it appears, is they probably don't say, "Oh, let's go have a war." They keep talking to themselves, "Well, let's do this, and this will prevent the war." And they don't understand unintended consequences, and they don't understand all that can happen by doing this, and how it gets out of hand.

But they continue the prospect, and I think the only solution is looking toward the principles of a noninterventionist foreign policy in a clear sense. We've had those leanings in our early history, but right now, I think we have to be more dogmatic in believing that, yes, we can live in an integrated world. We can have trade, and travel, and friendship, but we don't need to be throwing our weight around and enforcing our will on other people and picking leaders through a military empire and belief in pre-emptive war. That's where the real danger is.

Horton: Thank you, again, for your time, Dr. Paul. I sure appreciate it.

Paul: Okay, Scott. Good to be with you.

Horton: Great to talk to you again.

Paul: Mm-hm.

Horton: Alright, y'all. That is the heroic Dr. Ron Paul. Check out the Ron Paul Institute. They put out great antiwar propaganda all day long, seven days a week. The great Dan McAdams, Dr. Paul, Adam Dick, and others there at the Ron Paul Institute.

June 8, 2016

Horton: Welcome back to the show, Dr. Paul. How are you, sir?

Paul: Thank you, Scott. Nice to be with you. Doing fine.

Horton: Very happy to have you here, sir. I've got to tell you, I've really been missing you this year during the presidential campaign. We've got right authoritarianism and left authoritarianism pretty well represented. But I just don't hear that cry of freedom out there. And I was thinking back to what I like to call the greatest speaking tours on behalf of individual liberty ever — your previous presidential runs, especially the last two. Obviously '88 counts too, but '08 and '12, that was the real greatness. That's where you really changed the world.

I don't know if people even remember anymore. But you used to go around telling people all the time, especially during those campaigns, "Hey, all we need is freedom and everything will be fine. Everything will work itself out. We don't need power to fix it." I think, Dr. Paul, people just don't believe that. Maybe they believed you then, but nobody's telling them that now. They just don't know why that should be true when they look around them and everything seems so messed up.

So I was wondering if you could remind them, make that case. Especially in economic terms, everybody is so worried about the economy, and how things are, and we see, especially on the right side this year, Donald Trump saying, "I'm going to take control of this economy and I'm going to make it right."

Paul: Well, I think what we're facing and why it's difficult is that we're fighting a culture of dependency. The entitlement system is alive and well and we were challenging it and we were getting people to listen. But now, you see that even the word socialism doesn't scare people off — they sort of gravitate to that. I think the fear has been built up, but the people don't quite understand that what they're afraid of and they come to the conclusion that they think this dependency on government can be fixed by having more dependency and the fear can be removed by continuing to do the same things that have made people so fearful. So, if they've messed up the economy, and it's the Federal Reserve, well we just need more credit and take interest rates down to zero and all this. Of course, if it's entitlement, you know, everything is free, and it's not just Sanders that says this, Hillary says it too. But then there's others from the right who say, "I can fix everything. Just hand it over to me."

I think the test that libertarians ought to look at when they're wondering about this… Because I get people that will come in and if I say something reasonable about Bernie Sanders being against corporate welfare, they think, "Oh, this is a good deal, we've got to work together." And what I think people should think about, along these lines, is that if they decide that there's a problem with government, they should challenge that this so-called bipartisanship that Republicans and Democrats are really enemies of each other. They're really working for the same thing and that is Big Government.

The real key question they ought to ask, if you come to this conclusion that philosophically the parties aren't that far apart and that it's more freedom that you want and you understand this, which individual that we've heard from so far — nobody since Rand left — will any of these people now that are left, will they shrink the executive branch of the government? It's the branch of government I think is the biggest threat, and the Supreme Court next. I think the Congress is sort of lackadaisical and they don't do anything.

But I cannot see, with either one of the two leaders actually even setting a goal, "I'm going to shrink the power of the executive branch of government because they are out of control," because right now people are scared, and they are dependent and therefore they don't want to hear that. They want to be taken care of.

Horton: Yeah, I'm sure you've noticed, Donald Trump doesn't talk about freedom or liberty, those are not part of his sales pitch, whatsoever. And when he talks about cutting government, he says, "I'll cut waste, fraud and abuse," which is the Al Gore line.

Paul: That's always a big fake, you know about that. It's the philosophy of government. What should the role of government be? Should the role of government try to make us better people individually, morally speaking, and teach us habits and how we get along with our fellow man? Then they get out of control because they shouldn't even be doing this, and people should be left alone if they're not committing violence.

But this whole idea that we've been taught for many, many decades now, probably a hundred years, is that you just can't let an economy run roughshod over the people. This sort of came out of the Depression, the idea that it was laissez-faire capitalism and the gold standard that ruined us and gave us the Depression. So they really, really believe that government has to manage the economy.

And, of course, they have this attitude that because we are such a great nation, we're exceptional and nobody else is strong, and we have the military, that we have a moral obligation. They don't even see this in terms of preemptive foreign aggression. They see this as a higher ideal of moral obligation to bring about peace. But they never look at the total failures of the foreign policy. How many countries have we messed up in the last 15 years? And it continues and they're not backing off, they're looking around for more fights. It's just like the NATO-U.S. buildup in Europe, being antagonistic toward Russia right now, and our idea that have we have to go 8,000 miles in the other direction to see what we can do to provoke something with China.

Paul: People have to wake up that the government can't be the solution if it's been the problem. Of course, libertarians see the government as the problem. We have a lot more confidence and faith in liberty. But people have to have an incentive. People have gotten benefits from the government because we've been very wealthy, and we've had a fair amount of freedom. We have been prosperous, so they're very dependent on it. That's one of the downsides of liberty. You can get fat and happy then think, "Oh, all I have to do is go to the government to get my share." And, of course, what happens then is the incentives are taken away, the productivity is demolished, and people get away with borrowing money — people and governments — for a lot longer until eventually the bubble bursts. I think we're in the midst of that occurring. I think what we have to look forward to, unless we wake up and provide the opportunities for the people, that there's going to be a major, major, economic calamity and I think that it's at our doorstep.

Horton: Well, and this is one of the areas we're you've really made such progress too, is in spreading the understanding of Austrian School economics. If I have to boil it down to the one overriding most important aspect of that, that would be the way that the government central bank, backing the expansion of bank credit, causes the artificial booms and the real busts.

I think, as you mentioned before with the Great Depression, they always say, "Well, laissez-faire caused the Depression, so government had to solve it." Once people learn the truth that the Federal Reserve predated the Depression by a generation there — or well not quite — and really helped to cause it in the first place, that really turns some light bulbs on, you know?

Paul: Right. If you had to narrow it down, we talk about the Fed and central banking, why it's not legal under the Constitution, it's not moral when you think about it. But if you had to narrow it down with the current system, what particular program do they mess around with that allows this to happen? And that is the manipulation of interest rates below market rates. Of course, we've been doing that for a long time, especially since Bernanke's time and that is why this bubble is so big because we've destroyed the pricing structure of capital.

So this disturbs savings, this disturbs productivity and, of course, under these circumstances, Mises predicted that you can expect the middle class to be wiped out under these monetary conditions. That's where we are right now. I don't see this as a political struggle, I see this as a philosophic struggle. We should use, of course, the political system to bring these ideas to as many people as possible.

But ultimately, the people have to believe that liberty is successful. That we will thrive, we'll have a middle class and it will be more honest and it will not serve the interests of the one percent. When they come around to that — and I think that we'll have the opportunity once it's noticed that even this token effort of manipulation of the redistribution of wealth it will fail — that's when the real challenge will be. Are we going to look for a very, very much stronger executive branch that's going to take charge or are we going to argue our case and win the argument that what we need is a greater incentive system with an honest monetary system and an honest tax system.

Horton: Well, and it's hard for the average person, usually, to understand anything about central banking and boom and bust cycles. We can't see the Fed from wherever we are. It's far away. But what we can see is Mexicans. Why, they're everywhere! I'm pretty sure that Lou Dobbs said that they're the reason the economy sucks. Maybe we should just round up 11 million Mexicans and get rid of them, Dr. Paul. What do you think of that?

Paul: It's a tough argument to make because the people are so resentful. The one thing that I have noticed, especially living in Texas and knowing who does the work in Texas, one of the qualities of an American citizen has always been hard work and savings and self-reliance and take care of oneself. But, as I look around, when the hard work has to be done, there's usually not average American citizens who are not employed, because they're not lining up to do the work that others will volunteer to do if they can just get into this country.

So, in many ways, I think the problem… I don't believe in illegal immigration, but I think there should be a much different system because those who come are very appreciative of an opportunity to come and be able to work here. They have a great work ethic and that used to be an American value. But the welfare state and the entitlement system and the dependency has taught a lot of Americans to not really take any job they can get. I don't believe the clichés of those who want to change. I don't fault the people who have some gripes, but what they say is, "Well, if you allow one person to come here illegally, he's going to take a good job away from somebody else." I just don't think that is true.

A matter of fact, if we really had a free market, we would have a shortage of labor and that would expand our markets. Then you could still do that legally because there would be a need. But right now, it's so out of balance, sort of like monetary policy being out of balance, and savings. But the labor market's way out of balance too. It's very easy for the demagogue, and we find a few of those in politics, to blame somebody else. They don't ever look to our own policies. Our politicians say… Where we're at fault is that we've been following a philosophy on economics that's completely wrong. It's completely failed.

The 20th century sort of solidified the idea that Nazism and fascism and communism didn't work. But here we are now being very tolerant to the whole idea of socialism. One thing that's helping us on the argument of socialism is people are pointing out, "Well, okay why don't you look at Venezuela?" And that's really the answer rather than getting too academic.

Horton: Right. Yeah, a libertarian can explain why Venezuela ain't working but anybody can see that it's not working. That's definitely for sure right now.

Alright now, so what about trade? Because, of course, you're Ron Paul. I know that, and I think everybody knows, they should know, that you're not for NAFTA, you're not for GATT, you're not for the WTO, you're not for all these large international agreements and yet you are for free trade in every single way. Yet, Donald Trump says, "Look, the Chinese, the Japanese, the Koreans, they're eating our lunch. They have tariffs on our goods, but we don't have tariffs on their goods and it's not fair and we need better deals." And so where do you really come down on this?

Paul: Well, I don't want any tariffs, especially punitive tariffs or competitive tariffs — they're wrong. But if you just look at recent history, if you look at tariffs on steel, we're the one that initiated that trade war going on with China right now. Most people think, "Well, if you don't have an agreement, which is 100 percent even-steven, then you're being cheated."

But people should relax a bit. If you have this competitive economy and somebody's stupid enough to subsidize their exports, Milton Friedman, in this area was very good, he says, "Take advantage of it. Let them subsidize it." Yes, in the short run people get very annoyed by that; but ultimately, it doesn't take away jobs. It might make us adjust a little bit.

I remember when there was so much complaint about "those dirty old Japanese cars" coming into this country. But American cars were lousy. Because they couldn't ban all imports and the imports were better, all of a sudden, the American cars seemed to get better and catch up a little bit. No, I believe in competition. I believe strongly the more you trade with people the less likely you are to fight with people. I've been always in favor of trade with Cuba and I think we should be trading with Cuba. That's something people have to be confident about that trade is a benefit. But they can see only the very short-term and then once again they're told, "Well, if you have trade, they're going to steal our jobs from us." Well, how do we know that? Maybe it'll give us an incentive to make something else.

If we have the environment, I think we can compete with anybody. The environment to me would be very, very low taxes. No income tax. Regulations should not be done by thousands and thousands of pages in the Federal Register. It would be a lot easier, and we wouldn't drain the resources by artificially pumping it into the military-industrial complex. We're subsidizing one industry against the other. This is the reason we aren't doing as well, and that compounds. But people who are trade protectionists never want to say that maybe there are some things that we haven't done right either.

The one reason... You mentioned that I was against those trade groups, like the WTO and all. I've always argued that they're not for low tariffs. As a matter of fact, they're just the manipulators. That's where you go when you want to raise tariffs. "Well, he did such and such;" "Oh, okay, you can do this." It's more government. One thing that I read recently that I found fascinating is that we don't have a precise trade agreement with Great Britain. And yet for years and years and years we've always traded. So we don't need trade agreements, that just invites people — the politicians and the special interests — to control these things. So I think big business controls these trade groups, whether it's NAFTA or whether it's WTO or IMF. They get the influence and the smaller companies, competitive companies, they don't have the same representation in these groups like the large corporations would.

Horton: You brought up Russia there, so let me ask you about what Hillary Clinton said in her big speech the other day about — "Russia is messing around," I think she said, "on NATO's very doorstep."

Paul: (Laughs)

Horton: I wondered… You obviously clearly objected to that, that framing of the issue earlier in the interview here, a little bit unprompted. But I wonder if you could explain to the people who really don't know. Because after all, Putin makes a pretty good bogeyman, why not?

Paul: Well, it made me chuckle a little bit because today on the *Ron Paul Liberty Report*, Daniel McAdams and I discussed this very thing, the NATO buildup on the Russian borders and these war games that they're playing and all. Putin is no angel. But he's at least dealing with his borders. And I keep trying to make the point, what if Russia were like the Soviets and were building bases and missiles in Cuba, we'd probably object.

What if Putin tomorrow said, "Well, we want to spread our defenses a little bit better and Venezuela needs us, so we're going bail them out and they're going to give us a couple bases." That's all we ever do around the world — 130 countries we're always manipulating. But if Russia did that, the American people would be hysterical about it.

But to go over there with NATO and have these war games, it's nothing more than a manipulation to spend more money for the military-industrial complex. Actually, it's a war on our national security and our safety by getting ourselves involved. I don't think they're over there, that they're planning in six months we're going to attack Russia. But who knows what could happen in between? Accidents are going to happen, there are false flags and people get blamed for things that they didn't do.

We're doing it all the time. Since 2014, they've had 16 war games in NATO dealing with Russian threats. I think people should try to be more objective about it. But the bottom line is, it's very expensive what they're doing on our part. Also, it doesn't help our national security. It endangers our national security by doing this.

So there's really no purpose in this and it makes the Europeans, of course, to be more dependent on us. So we're over there in Poland right now. And Poland is pretty inept, and they sort of like us to back them up.

But the other thing that I strongly objected to in the program today, and which I have in the past, and that is, when we have obligations, we've signed NATO and NATO says we have to do this. Well, NATO has no moral right or constitutional right for us to sign a NATO treaty 10, 15, 30, 40 years ago. We have all these treaties to obligate this generation and our kids to automatically fight if there is a war, which would be costly economically and it would also involve our troops. I just think these treaties are absolutely immoral and illegal and we should work to get — not just modify them and get a better deal — I want to just get out of them.

Horton: Alright. Thank you again for your time, Dr. Paul. I sure appreciate it.

Paul: Okay Scott, good to be with you today.

Horton: Great to talk to you.

March 15, 2017

Horton: Welcome back to the show, Ron how are you sir?

Paul: Thank you, Scott, good to be with you.

Horton: Very good to talk to you again. Listen, so there's so much going on, and you guys do such a great job covering foreign policy on the *Liberty Report*. So I really feel privileged to talk with you again to cover a little bit of this stuff. First of all, North Korea. It looks to be worse and worse of a crisis there, and I know you're something of an expert on the issue. What do you think Trump should do in the face of Kim Jong-Un firing off these missiles towards Japan and these other provocative moves?

Paul: I think it was yesterday we mentioned it on the show, and I believe I concluded at the time: Just come home. We don't need to be over there. He's a problem, there's no doubt about it, the neighbors shouldn't be too happy with him. But I think for us to go over there and have these big military buildups — The operation that they're practicing right now, 300,000 troops are involved, 10,000 of our troops and then South Koreans. And to go over there and do that and put some missile defenses that even China does not like, it doesn't make any sense.

And I remember so clearly when the Korean War started — because it's still the same war — it was back when I was in high school, and the war was going great until all of a sudden the Chinese entered into it and the whole picture was changed. And we're still there, and even in the presidential campaigns, I kept saying, just bring the troops home, and that's still my position.

If he is a threat to their neighbors, they have to deal with it. But I think that for us to go over there... And then with Trump actually threatening, "Well, we may just go in there and kill them, or use a drone missile," or what-not — that's just stirring up a lot more trouble than we need, because many times it gets out of hand because the navy is involved, with what we're doing in that area, that there could be another incident. The more we're involved, the more likely it is that either somebody could create a false flag, or it'll be done deliberately. The Vietnam War was expanded by us deliberately lying about something that was happening. But there are others that can do it, and there are accidents that can happen —

unintended consequences — so it's sort of a mess.

Horton: You know, I kind of don't understand, why have all the troops there? If we wanted to float our whole navy offshore, and say don't you ever mess with the South, that would be one thing. But why have tens of thousands of American infantry on the ground when the South Koreans have a big enough army to do all of that part of the dying in the war themselves?

Paul: Well, interventionism generally doesn't make much sense if you look at it in a sensible way. So, no, it doesn't make any sense whatsoever. Then you have to think well, why is that? We have to fortify these guys and equipment, so the military-industrial complex is involved. We have the neocons who are always looking for another war to fight.

So I think it's part of that, and they just believe in intervention, they believe in this moral responsibility that we have. But I think your question is more of a tactical question, that you could almost still say we're going to be there, we're going to take care of things, but why do we have to be right on your property? And it's probably some finances, but generally speaking most of the people finally get tired of our occupation, whether it's in the Philippines or in Japan, they get tired of us from being there and want us to leave.

But there are a lot of financial benefits to the government. Sometimes the militarism benefits the government in charge because the governments use that to make sure there's no overthrow of their own government — that certainly has been the case in the Middle East. We generally don't give weapons, just because they're going to fight on our side against our enemies, it's sometimes just to maintain the power that they have established in their own government.

Horton: Yeah, I mean it's interesting that Clinton had a deal with the North Koreans and George Bush at the end of his term in 2008 could have had one before… He started to get another deal before he sabotaged it himself again.

But then Obama never really tried to deal with the North Koreans at all, it doesn't seem like. He just seemed like, "Well, we'll just leave everything running at idle for eight years and pass this problem off to someone else." But I guess I don't understand what's so difficult, about — As you say, there are obviously these vested interests in the status quo, but we've seen politicians be able to overrule things like that before, like Nixon going to China or something like that. George H.W. Bush pulled all the nukes out of Korea and reduced the number of overall nukes by a couple of ten thousand I think.

So these kinds of changes can be made. I just don't see what's so hard about shaking hands and at least not being best friends, but a drop in all the tension.

Paul: Well, it makes a lot of sense, but that doesn't mean the governments are going to follow any common sense. I use as an example of when it gets really serious about it, and that it's best to talk to somebody that we should follow the lead of Kennedy when the Cuban Crisis was on. He and Khrushchev talked because it was a very dangerous situation. So I think people don't want to, out of just sort of a strategy… The Korean leader wants to look tough for his people, we have to look tough for our people, and we're not going to get pushed around and we have this moral responsibility.

A lot of it is money and power. But a lot of people get sold on this idea that now that we're the superpower, we have this moral responsibility to maintain peace and spread the American goodness and the American message which some people believe, but other people believe that's just an excuse. But the combination of all — The American people on the whole aren't all that annoyed by us going over there. But then if you looked at it, maybe conservatives would be more responsive with the spending. So far, they haven't been. How many dollars, how many billions of dollars have we spent keeping troops on the land over there, whether it's in Korea or in Germany, or all these other places — and then the Middle East, I mean just so much — But conservatives aren't concerned when it comes to militarism. They never vote against anything hardly, about the military. And I think that's a big problem, too.

Many of them are just military Keynesians. They might say now we don't really want to fight them, but we've got to be strong, and that's how you have peace — peace through strength. But when you talk about building major weapons systems, like the F-35, you get all the congressmen involved. Every state gets to make a piece of the pie. So then the members of Congress think, "Well, you may be right, this is a dumb weapon, we don't need it, but I don't want to go home and explain that to the people." My job is at stake, and it's good for our economy, it's good for our state. They don't understand the principle of what would happen if we didn't spend that money on these weapons that don't work or getting involved overseas.

It's sort of a theoretical position where you can't quite visualize it, what might've happened if you didn't waste it in this militarism. Of course, they also are able to use being patriotic and being pro-military. If you don't support it, you don't support the military, if you don't support it, you're not patriotic, you're not a good American, and I've heard that for a good many years.

Horton: Yeah. So 15 years into the terror war in the Middle East, we've got al Qaeda and ISIS-type groups in quite a few different places, obviously Iraq and Syria, and then there's Yemen and North Africa and there's always still Afghanistan. And it seems like all indications are — I saw you and Dan talking about this on your show too — that basically Trump's telling the military and the CIA both, "Gloves off. This whole al Qaeda thing, you guys go ahead and take care of it. Knock the hell out of 'em," as he said in the campaign.

And yet you wrote this article about Syria saying this isn't going to work — but you know, I don't know. On the face of it Dr. Paul, it might seem to people that wimpy old Obama with all his rules and regulations wasn't letting the military get the work done, but now if James Mattis and his Marine Corps want to finally go ahead and take care of this problem for us once and for all, surely they could, right?

Paul: Yeah, not only does it not work, these interventions — I would say us getting involved in the Korean War was a bad thing, it's still going on. We did it under authority from the United Nations, it was a bad thing. It didn't work well when we got involved in Vietnam; things are much better in Vietnam since we left. So it doesn't work.

But many times, it's not only that it doesn't work, it causes a lot of harm, because I think you know, the blowing up of the Middle East and the creation of a lot of homeless people… I make the assumption that most people that are marching out of the Middle East and looking for a place know who's behind the encouragement of it, but there's a lot of people, the migrants are just trying to get out of the way. So that's a consequence of what we've been doing.

So not only do these efforts not work, they create new problems. Right now, Trump was over there talking yesterday talking with the defense minister of Saudi Arabia, and they both agree that we have to have these safe zones and keep the people over there so that they don't have the incentive to migrate to Europe. But then you have the cultural Marxists who — That is exactly what they want them to do. So it is significant — it's still as far as I'm concerned, to try to sort all this out — it's still much better to accept the notion of what it would be like if you had a noninterventionist foreign policy, willingness to talk to people like you indicate we should be, trade with people and recognize that everybody has shortcomings, and I'm convinced the Founders are right, the more you trade with people and the more voluntary travel there is, the less likely you are to have wars. And, of course, that's what has been one of my goals ever since I've been in politics.

Horton: Yeah. And I really encourage people to read your book, *A Foreign Policy of Freedom*, a collection of foreign policy speeches going back I believe to the late '70s, at least the very early '80s. There's just so much great history in there, in that great book. And then, of course, there's *Swords into Plowshares*. And you know, truly Dr. Paul, I say this every time but it's only because I'm so grateful that I have the opportunity to: I really do believe — I don't think it's really in question — that you have done more to spread the philosophy of natural rights theory, of sound economic theory, and of peace, and of the normalcy of peace and the insistence that war must only be the gravest exception in defense of our rights — and you've done more to push this stuff, and to change the world, to orient the world that way, really than anyone I think in world history and certainly for the rest of all of our lifetimes, and so I feel very privileged to have a chance to talk with you again, thank you.

Paul: Very good, nice to be with you today.

Horton: Alright y'all, that is the heroic Ron Paul.

May 15, 2017

Horton: Alright, well I'm nervous and excited and everything like I always am when this happens. I've got Dr. Ron Paul on the line. Welcome back to the show, sir. How are you?

Paul: Thank you, Scott. Good to be with you.

Horton: I'm very happy to have you here on the show. Everyone, you know Dr. Paul, greatest congressman ever, greatest presidential candidate ever, if you ask me, did two great speaking tours on behalf of peace and liberty, back in 2008 and '12, running for president. He wrote a bunch of books including, *End the Fed*, *A Foreign Policy of Freedom* and *Swords into Plowshares*, is the most recent one, which is just great. Of course, today is the tenth anniversary of the big showdown with Rudy Giuliani. Now, I'm not going to make you sit through all of this sir, but I want to play a little bit of this clip.

[Begin clip from Fox News broadcast of Republican presidential candidates on May 15, 2007]

Paul: Intervention was a major contributing factor. Have you ever read about the reasons they attacked us? They attack us because we've been over there. We've been bombing Iraq for 10 years. We've been in the Middle East. I think Reagan was right, we don't understand the irrationality of Middle Eastern politics. So right now, we're building an embassy in Iraq that's bigger than the Vatican. We're building 14 permanent bases. What would we say here if China was doing this in our country or in the Gulf of Mexico? We would be objecting. We need to look at what we do from the perspective of what would happen if somebody did it to us.

Wendell Goler (moderator): Are you suggesting we invited the 9/11 attack, sir?

Paul: I'm suggesting that we listen to the people who attacked us and the reason they did it and they are delighted that we're over there, because Osama bin Laden has said, "I am glad you are over on our sand, because we can target you so much easier." They have — already now, since that time — have killed 3,400 of our men and I don't think it was necessary.

Rudy Giuliani: Wendell, may I make a comment on that? That's really an extraordinary statement. That is an extraordinary statement of someone who lived through the attack of September 11th, that we invited the attack, because we were attacking Iraq. I don't think I've ever heard that. [*End of clip*]

Horton: Now, I have to stop it there, to let you know sir that at my apartment that night, at this point my friend Mike stood up, his face was as red as blood, or fire maybe, and I thought there were terrible curses being hurled and I could have sworn he was going to grab my TV and throw it right out the window. It's a miracle that he didn't, but he let Giuliani continue here. Oh, he said — What he said that wasn't a cuss was "That's not what he said!"

[*Clip continues*] **Giuliani:** ...before and I've heard some pretty absurd explanations for September 11th. And, I would ask the congressman to withdraw that comment and tell us that he didn't really mean that. Congressman? [*End of clip*]

Horton: Now, at this part, of course, in my apartment, we're just on the edge of our seats — absolute pins and needles. "Oh my God, what's he going to say, what's he going to say?" And, of course, any other politician in all of world history, would have backed down before Rudy Giuliani and would have said, "Oh no, I'm sorry, please, I didn't mean that." But you responded:

[*Clip continues*] **Paul:** I believe very sincerely that the CIA is correct when they teach and talk about blowback. When we went into Iran ... [*End of clip*]

Horton: Alright, and then the rest is history, of course. That was the moment. You won the polls all that night. Boy you must have felt lonely up there. But you won all the polls that night and then that was it. There's an entire documentary called, *For Liberty: How the Ron Paul Revolution Watered the Withered Tree of Liberty*, and it's such a great documentary. I'm sure you've seen it, and it shows that this was the moment, this was what made the difference. Finally, someone — one man in all of Washington, D.C. — was honest and told the truth about who started the war and what happened there. And millions and millions of people were won over to your message of peace and freedom, virtually in that instant. So, I guess first of all thank you and then can you tell us a little bit about what that moment was like for you up there, sir?

Paul: Well, for me personally, it wasn't as dramatic. Maybe it was important, and it was challenging, but it wasn't as dramatic as it was to the people who were watching it. Because over the many years of what I was doing and saying and promoting in Washington was always challenging the status quo. I just figured, "Well, this is routine operating procedure, why shouldn't I expect them to react exactly this way?" But, so I was, in a way, neither angry nor upset. I thought obviously the crowd was much more for Giuliani, and so I assumed that this would be the routine reaction.

But — and you recall Kent, our campaign manager, Kent Snyder at the time — after we were walked off the stage we were walking together and he came up to me and he said, he says, "Guess what, you're winning all the polls." And that was the first time that I realized there was a significance there, because the polls and the stations — You know how Fox would rig the polls against me.

So, it was a time, after I stopped to think about it, it gave me a little bit of hope that the world isn't quite as bad as we might think. And that's one of the reasons why I have remained to be optimistic, that there are people out there that will join us in this cause of peace and prosperity and liberty, but they have to hear the message.

And, that's our biggest challenge, because there's so much propaganda and so much control and even back then, especially in 2007, I was not very much involved with the internet and didn't understand it. And yet, today I have my own program on a daily basis on the internet. So we reach a lot of people, but back then, it didn't dawn on me that we don't have to depend on Fox and CNN and MSNBC, because they're all the same. You know, they're all pro-war and none of them came to my defense, though that is what I expected. Just as in Washington the Republicans and Democrats represent one party. But to me, it was enlightening and encouraging. It's always nice to find out you have some friends out there that happen to agree with what you're trying to do. So I was very pleased.

Horton: Right. Yeah and I'm sorry I left that out of your bio there. It's RonPaulLibertyReport.com for your great show with Dan McAdams, the great daily show and, of course, as is my preference, always putting foreign policy first. Very important stuff there daily. Now, so, at the time I went immediately, and I rushed to write up this article at Antiwar.com, it's called, "For Those Interested in Facts, They Hate Our Foreign Policy,"[9] and it's my big defense of you.

And I was in a panic: "Oh my God, we've got to defend Ron!" But then it turned out that I didn't need to defend you, that everybody that heard you — I mean, other than the people who are most firmly invested in the deception — they knew that you were right. They knew that it was true. What did you say, other than, "Come on guys, you remember the 1990s, the first Gulf War, the Clinton years." We were bombing them, as you said, at that point we'd been bombing them for more than ten years.

Everybody just knew that that was right and the way I've always put this, because there's such a huge and important lesson here — I don't know if I really follow as well as I should, but I think what really happened there in essence, sir, was that you gave people a permission slip that they could be antiwar without changing any other part of their identity, right? "If antiwar means Susan Sarandon and Jane Fonda and Michael Moore, then I'm not that, I guess," sighs the entire right half of American society, right? But then, here comes little old Ron Paul, Republican congressman from Texas, white and Protestant and — I mean this in the nicest way, sincerely — the most square sort of personality, married to your high school sweetheart, scandal-free in all that sense, all the grandkids and everything, perfect postcard. And you said, "Oh, I'm way more antiwar than Michael Moore, forget about it. You guys could be for abolishing the Pentagon and still be just as red, white, and blue as me."

As you told the *Washington Post* back then, "Nah, we can defend this country with a couple of good submarines." And it just blew everybody's mind, that they said, "Oh, okay, so I don't have to leave my church, I don't have to leave my job, I don't have to quit my softball team, I don't have to stop being friends with my friends, I don't have to stop thinking about myself the way that I thought about myself. The rest of my identity's intact, but I don't feel this pressure any longer to be part of the pro-war consensus just because I'm some kind of right-winger."

And so, overnight millions of people — tens of millions of people — just snapped right out of it, because of you. You gave them a permission slip, you gave them the hall pass, that it's okay to leave GOP consensus on this issue.

Paul: Well, it was certainly an interesting event. If you would have asked me on whether or not I anticipated something like that, obviously not, and

---

[9] Scott Horton, "For Those Interested in Facts, They Hate Our Foreign Policy," Antiwar.com, May 19, 2007, https://original.antiwar.com/scott/2007/05/19/for-those-interested-in-facts-they-hate-our-foreign-policy/.

sometimes, when it's a spontaneous answer you don't always know exactly what will come out. But the one thing that listening to it as you replayed it — It refreshed my memory because I didn't realize that I had brought up Ronald Reagan, which was an appropriate thing to do because I had previously mentioned him, I think, in another question that Ronald Reagan explained in his memoirs that he made a mistake about the marines in Lebanon and that 243 marines were killed and he admitted he made a mistake and he came up with a statement that he didn't realize how irrational the politics of that region was and if he would have known that those marines would still be alive today.

That to me, is the astounding question that Reagan did come around on that, not that he joined us in the antiwar position, but he did have the honesty to at least admit that, that that was a serious mistake that he did. And figuring out the politics of that region, we're no further along on that than ever before. That alone should have made us all cautious and it should have made all the conservatives cautious, because they admired Ronald Reagan.

Horton: Well, you know, you're famous now for having given all these speeches back in 1997 and 1998, during the impeachment of Bill Clinton, notably. You warned that this policy... What we ought to be impeaching him for is bombing Iraq and that this kind of policy is going to create more terrorist attacks against us. In 1997, I found a speech where you said, "Mr. Speaker, the Saudis are warning us that we're driving their local population crazy with these bases there and we've got to get out. We need to take these warnings seriously."

There's just so many of those from back then and yet, everybody else somewhat pretended and maybe a lot of them really were caught by surprise and it was sort of... It really was the planes looked like they came out of the clear blue sky in the pictures on TV. So even in the Congress they pretended that history began the day before yesterday and now what are we going to do?

But, you had a good answer, a ready-made answer, just like the neocons had a ready-made answer: we've got to attack Iraq. You had a ready-made answer; you said let's do a letter of marque, instead of an authorization to use military force and an open declaration of war. Let's do a letter of marque against al Qaeda. Can you explain what that is, sir?

Paul: In the Constitution, the term is marque and reprisal. It says that the Congress gives authority to individuals that said that you can, under a legal document, if you carry this letter that you can defend yourself rather than being the aggressor, you're legally acting defensively. It was mainly used on the high seas and there weren't very many federal crimes in the Constitution, there were only three, but piracy was one, so it was a big issue for the people at that time. It probably should go without even the letter, that you can defend yourself.

But it actually said that they could defend themselves or go after somebody who has been molesting them. So, it narrowed... It means you don't ignore what they've done to us, but you narrow it down and give people authority, but you don't declare war, you don't draft people, you don't run up the bills, you just allow the people technically legal endorsement by the government that you can go and pursue the bad guys.

Horton: Yeah and now, there seems to be a question, I guess I'm not exactly certain of whether by definition it has to be privateers and mercenaries who are hired to carry out the order, or whether really the point is that the target is specific. That in this case, for example, you could send the special operations forces, or the army rangers, or marines.

Paul: Yes.

Horton: It's just that the target would be this group of bandits, this group of outlaws, rather than the government of Afghanistan, for example.

Paul: You know, that is true, they don't designate that. Let's see if I can remember the details. When we had the crisis in Iran, when they had captured our people at the embassy, and they were being held hostage. Near that time, some oil company employees were held, and I can't remember who the oil person was, he did it himself and probably just did it unknown, but he had his own private little army.

Horton: That was Perot, right?

Paul: Ross Perot, that's right. Ross Perot went over there, and he got them back. And I got to thinking, well, maybe we need — I probably even mentioned it back then — what we need is to talk to Ross Perot and to go and deal with these people, because it wasn't the country of Afghanistan, obviously, that orchestrated this. Obviously, the country of Iraq and that's where we went first — So that made no sense, it was just an excuse. That was the neocons taking advantage of an incident to go and do what they wanted to do anyway. They actually admitted it. "This gives us an opportunity to remake the Middle East. We've been wanting an excuse for this. We were waiting for a Pearl Harbor event." They put that in writing. It was so blatant. But yeah, I think Ross Perot had a standard on what could have been used under this marque and reprisal.

Horton: Well, as you know, I've got this book coming out about Afghanistan. I found these quotes from General Zinni, the former head of CENTCOM and Gary Berntsen, who helped lead the CIA effort in Afghanistan at the very outset there. And both of them basically admit — Now years later in 2016, they said, "Yeah," — in other words, in brackets, "[Ron Paul was right,] this whole war could have been over in six months. None of this had to happen. The entire terror war, none of it had to happen at all." They just had a few hundred guys, they could have rounded them up, wrapped them up and that would have been it. Happy New Year everybody. And then here we are in 2017, still talking about this mess.

Paul: When we were debating in Congress, sort of giving the authority to go into Afghanistan, I can't remember which State Department person was there — I remember he was a neocon. I said, "Okay, I don't want you to go in there, but what will it take to change your mind? How many Americans — and I wanted a specific number — how many Americans have to die in how many years before you'll say, 'Well, it was a mistake.'" I said, "How many people — If so-and-so number died in five years, would you reassess things?"

And you know, I was thinking, the way they're going we could be there five, six, seven years — and here we are sixteen years and thousands of people killed, not only the people killed on our side, but the people we killed on the other side, who never attacked us, had nothing to do with threatening our liberties at home. Our liberties at home were — Was our own government more than anybody else.

Horton: Yeah, it is absolutely incredible to think and here we are, as you say in your most recent article at the Ron Paul Institute for Peace and Prosperity here, McMaster and Mattis are pushing for a whole new escalation to begin under President Trump, so we're just…

Paul: Another "surge."

Horton: About to start a Chapter 3 maybe here.

Paul: Yeah, what a shame.

Horton: Yup. Alright now, I have to tell you also, sir — well and this is more of a personal thing — but it's also the 20th anniversary of your return to Congress, which is a hugely important thing to me and to my life. And

I can tell you, I'll never forget in the middle of the night watching reruns on C-SPAN in 1997 and there's this little old congressman from Texas saying, "I have some papers here in my hand, Mr. Speaker, from the British newspapers today, about how President George H.W. Bush was selling chemical weapon precursors to Saddam Hussein and some even during Operation Desert Shield in the run up to the war, Mr. Speaker."

And I went, "Oh my God, I can't believe it," and I looked, and it said: "Ron Paul (R-Texas)" at the bottom. And I just — you know me, I'm from Austin. I just… My mind just exploded. I couldn't believe it, that a Republican congressman, would dare to — you didn't use the word — but you were basically accusing Bush Sr. of treason, in essence. And in fact, when you first started running for president, I went back and found that speech in your archives, that exact speech, in the records. I think I still have it saved somewhere.

But that absolutely changed my life and I was already a Harry Browne libertarian and everything, but that just meant so much to me and I spent years — I know this isn't really asking a question, I'm just flattering you and everything, but I'll beg your forbearance. I spent years telling people in my taxicab, "Did you know there's one good congressman? Oh, yeah. No, he's great, check it out." And I would give copies of your speeches to people in my cab. I was a pretty obnoxious cab driver, I'll concede.

But then, my favorites were — One speech was, "A Republic, If You Can Keep It," and then the next one was, "Sorry Mr. Franklin, We're All Democrats Now." And I just loved these things and I would just give them to people in my cab all the time and it was… You know, I was the Ron Paul evangelical. And it was such a miracle really when you ran for president, because we all knew. I remember talking with Eric Garris at Antiwar.com as soon as we found out you had the exploratory committee. Because we knew that you had one hardcore, dedicated fan in every single neighborhood in America. Just one, but in every neighborhood. So how's this going to play out? What's going to happen?

We had all this potential, just lying there and then, once you set that match with the Giuliani speech, that's what, of course, turned the world upside down and helped do so much to get the word out there. But, I just want to tell you, as long as we're doing anniversaries and everything today, that that was my introduction to you and your character and, of course, then I read pretty much all your speeches and articles and newsletters and everything you ever wrote after that. And I've been very honored to have you come on my show all these times to talk with us and all this stuff as well. So a big Thank you, sir.

Paul: Well, great and it's great being on your program and you've done a lot of hard work. Just keep working at it, you're doing great.

Horton: Alright, well thank you very much sir.

Paul: Alright, good to talk to you Scott.

October 2, 2017

Horton: Welcome back to the show, Dr. Paul. How are you doing, sir?

Paul: Good, Scott. Nice to be with you and congratulations on your book, *Fool's Errand*. It's great! And one thing on your subtitle: It's an understatement — *Time to End the War in Afghanistan*. I mean it's so necessary, but it's such an understatement. It's been a long time that it's time to end this war. It never should have started, but congratulations.

Horton: Well, thank you very much, Dr. Paul. I really appreciate that a lot — and your great blurb. Of course, you're in it. If you want, we can talk about it. You did vote for the AUMF, but at the same time, you recommended against it. Do you want to go back to 2001 with us a little bit there?

Paul: Yeah, and it does raise questions because I did vote for it because of the obvious problem that we were facing. I wasn't very happy with it, but I didn't think that you could do nothing.

I think the way it was written wasn't too bad. It was to address the subject of those people who participated in 9/11. The disaster is — and should have been the reason that you can't condone it or think it's a solution — is that they abuse it. They're still using that authority to use military force even today. In any place they go, it's being used, and they argue about that.

Some of the more libertarian members are trying to force them into another vote and remove those things, but it's the abuse of the rules, the abuse of the Constitution, it's abuse of the legislation and Congress doesn't do anything about it.

Obviously, those were very difficult times, but if they would have used that authority to deal with the people who participated in the attack, it would have been a lot different.

Horton: Well, and in fact, the Democrats did take out a lot of the worst language that Cheney wanted to include. It's just that, in the end, it didn't matter anyway.

Paul: Right.

Horton: The quote in the book on this subject — There is a nice block quote from you as you were introducing your Marque and Reprisal Act where you emphasize that what we have to do here is get the guys who did this, sure, but do it in such a way as to prove them wrong about us and to prove that we don't have a quarrel with Muslim people or Arab people in general and that there's no reason for this war to escalate into some kind of stupid clash of civilizations that we don't need to have here, and that's, of course, exactly what they did instead.

Paul: Yeah, and we got a little attention on that, a little discussion, but that would have been the last thing the neocons wanted. They wanted escalation. They wanted to remake the Middle East. As soon as it happened, they immediately invaded Afghanistan and, of course, ignored bin Laden and different things.

Marque and reprisal was written into the Constitution early on by the Founders to try to limit the need or the use of military force rather than declaring war. It was an in-between, but it permitted people to take it upon themselves. It was certainly used in the war on piracy. It was a legal document. They actually carried something on the vessels and other countries recognized it. It wasn't just somebody trying to start a battle with somebody, but they were acting under the authority of the government. It was a letter designed to do very limited things.

At the time, I was desperate to look for something other than what we ended up with because I knew it wouldn't be good, what the consequences would be, and this was just an excuse. That was my immediate reaction on 9/11. We as libertarians and noninterventionists have now been given a much more difficult job presenting our case.

Horton: So I brought you on to talk about the problems with North Korea. I saw your most recent episode of the *Liberty Report*. I'm sorry I left that out the introduction. The *Liberty Report*, it's the greatest show. It's the wonderful and heroic Dan McAdams and Dr. Paul every day on YouTube — or four or five days a week — on YouTube and at RonPaulLibertyReport.com. It's really, really great.

I saw a bit of the latest one here where you guys were talking about the North Korea thing. As you say, "Well, geez, it would be such a bad war that's probably not going to happen." They would need a real excuse, something new to happen rather than just to go ahead and start the war as they are now.

In fact, James Mattis had said before that if we had a real war in Korea, this would be the most bitter fighting of our lifetimes. He obviously meant to include Vietnam in that and maybe even the first Korean War in that depending on whose lifetime we're talking about, right?

Paul: Right.

Horton: But then we see the Twitter wars, and my confidence that "Don't be an alarmist, Scott. It's probably going to work out," is starting to recede here and I'm beginning to worry that this idiot president could really get us into a war with North Korea here. What do you think?

Paul: Well, I think that is the great danger. Interestingly enough, I just did today's program for the *Liberty Report* and it was on the subject. It had to do with Trump versus Tillerson.

Tillerson actually was pursuing this, with talking to the North Koreans, and it leaked out. I don't know, maybe the neocons leaked it out that he was just because they wanted to undermine it. Here he is practicing some diplomacy and Trump goes nuts and publicly he goes after Tillerson: "It's a waste of time. Save your energy. We'll do whatever has to be done. Nothing is off the table." They always say that, which really bugs me because there is something that is off the table: common sense and diplomacy. They will not consider it.

They won't even allow the secretary of state to talk to somebody. And yet, of course, a nuclear first strike is not off the table. They always imply that it is. It's a foolish policy and this confrontation in open public — it's hard to believe.

How much can Tillerson put up with, this insulting in public? Tillerson is a long way from where we are, but at least he is sensitive about maybe not starting this war. Now I don't know what is going to happen. Trump is unpredictable. Is he going to get rid of Tillerson now? It gets to be a real mess and it comes from the top down. That's too bad.

Right now, this little episode with Tillerson, I sort of like the idea that he at least talked to them. Why shouldn't he talk to them?

Horton: Well, I wonder, do you think it's a possibility — not that this is a good excuse for it or anything — do you think it's a possibility that it's quite deliberate, and that they are playing "good cop, bad cop," like Richard Nixon saying, "Henry, tell them I'm drunk and crazy and I might nuke them," to try to coerce the North Vietnamese and that kind of deal?

Paul: Yeah, that's always possible, but Tillerson sure is exposing himself to too much ridicule if he puts up with all of this. It's hard to say. I imagine we'll find out if this sort of fades away and Tillerson wins the argument and Trump backs off, that's one thing. But what if Tillerson gets kicked out? Which is always possible once he starts talking this way. He does that for a while and then he either backs off and lets it go or then he gets rid of the person, but that wouldn't be good for the little bit of hope that we have that we will come around to some common sense.

Horton: Well, and you know, it was also really a problem, I thought, Trump's tweet where he says, "We've been trying to deal with 'Rocket Man' for 25 years, and it didn't work for Clinton, or for Bush, or for Obama," and this and that. Maybe it's just a Twitter character limit problem, and we all know that he knows that that was Kim Jong-il and that he's dead and that this is the son. So, if we're trying to be charitable… Let's be charitable and say that Trump knows that it's really not the same guy for the last 25 years, but that that's more or less what he meant because it was a Twitter miscommunication thing there.

Even then, assuming he understands, it seems like such a poor way to frame it because, of course, the son is not the father. The father is dead. He came in saying, "Oh, the new guy, the son here, Jong-un, he's a smart cookie. Maybe we can deal with him," and this and that. He got roundly criticized for being naïve and saying we can deal and paying a compliment to this guy.

Paul: Yeah.

Horton: It just seems like such a poor way to frame it; that there is no point in making a deal with this guy or talking with this guy because the deal with Bill Clinton fell apart, when we all know that was George W. Bush's fault, not even Kim Jong-il's fault in the first place.

Paul: Yes, but nobody wants to look at our own policy as being part of the problem. But even in '94 under Clinton, Clinton did have some agreements, which he's being ridiculed for now and Trump says he caused all the trouble because he gave them nuclear weapons and all these things, but the agreement was broken by the United States. There were a couple things we promised to do, and they would back off and the door was open, and we would recognize certain things and the neocons went nuts. They started immediately undermining that.

Paul: Then when Bush got in, they really totally destroyed it and they wouldn't have anything to do with the agreement that the North Koreans had agreed to. They said, "They wouldn't have listened to them." Well, that's what they're saying, but is that true? Is it always just the other side's fault or is it our fault that we back off on some of these agreements?

Just like they're attempting to do or at least talk about backing off of the agreement with Iran. This is not all just Un's problem, it's all of our problems because of the aggressiveness of our government. Besides, no matter how bad this guy has to be… I compare it to what it was like in the real Cold War when I was in the military in the '60s and missiles were in Cuba. We didn't have to confront or badger or claim or fight or drop bombs. The whole thing just dissipated.

Now I say we spend more time worrying about bombs that don't exist, whether they're in Iran or North Korea, than we worried about 30,000 of them when they were held by a ruthless nation like the Soviet system. It's just people who are agitating for more warmongering and war profiteering.

People who do believe in a global system, as long as it is run by the United States and they're in charge, this is all about the empire, I think.

Horton: Well, you know, people keep asking me if it's about Afghanistan or the Islamic State or Russia relations or Korea or whatever: "What should we do?" Somebody asked me — I gave a talk in L.A. about the book the other day and they asked me, "What can we do?" I said, "Go back to 2008 and elect Ron Paul, otherwise, I really don't know."

But then, I can sort of see the criticism that maybe I'm kind of utopian, that I think well, if Ron Paul was here, he would have ordered every admiral in the world "sail home — that's it, it's over!" But that sounds too utopian and too perfect, so maybe Dr. Paul you wouldn't have been able to do that or maybe you would.

What would things look like with Korea now if you really had been the president of the United States to handle this?

Paul: Well, it would have been difficult because if you're too blatant and too blunt and start moving, you know what happens to people that would do that.

Horton: Well, I know you'd have brought your own private security with you.

Paul: Yeah. (Laughs.) But if you could do it, I would do it much quieter and not just antagonize all your political enemies, which are most of the Democrats and most of the Republicans. You'd have to find a nucleus in each party to work with and then quietly just back off. Just start coming home.

You're the commander in chief. You don't have to do that. But the power of the military-industrial complex, the Deep State is pretty powerful. I think we have a ways to go changing people's ideas and that's what you work on every single day, trying to change people's minds about this and the time will come. Because I think the majority are still with us on this. They get their minds changed with the propaganda.

Before we went into Iraq when I was giving a lot of speeches on that, the people — You did polling and the people would say, "No, we don't need this war. We don't need this war." But then after a while… Right now, I think there's been so much anti-North Korea scaremongering going on, I think the majority of the American people think we've got to attack them. They can be influenced, but they also can be influenced with ideas.

That's why I think us speaking out and talking to young people, maybe a few of them will find their way up to be an influence on policy. I think we have to remember, as much as we fear their guns even coming after us, we also have to remember that ideas are more powerful than the guns and ideas have consequences.

Our ideas are alive and well right now. I'm making the argument that some people are writing quite frequently about the libertarian movement and the early stages of the Tea Party Movement from 2008: "It's all over. It's done with. They don't exist." But the fact that they're attacking some of us I think is showing that we are alive and well.

That's the only thing I know to do is keep pursuing it. That's why I'm delighted to see you on the air and talking and writing books because we need you, but we need thousands more people out there. That's how the large majority of minds finally get changed.

Just think, I lived through those days of the Vietnam War. What a tragedy that was. It took a decade of demonstrations in the streets to finally to say to the government, "Enough is enough. You've done all this killing. Quit, quit, quit."

It's never fast enough, but when we have victory, it will be that we'll prevent them from getting involved. They won't be using and abusing the authority to use military force and never going deliberately to the Congress and finding the proper way of doing that which would be to declare war, which they have no interest in doing.

Horton: Alright now, I'm sorry, do you have to go, or do you have time for one more?

Paul: One more. One more and then I've got to go.

Horton: On Korea here, the great Peter Lee, the "Chinahand," on Twitter, pointed out this article in the *Los Angeles Times*. It was quite cynical. It said, "Listen, we could make peace with North Korea. We could have an end to the Korean War, a real deal and have a sound agreement and back down on this brinksmanship, but if we didn't have North Korea to hold over the head of South Korea and Japan and threaten them with and protect them from, then they could spin off away from our orbit, imperial orbit, quite frankly. And then, God forbid, they could not just declare independence, but maybe even fall under the dominion of the Chinese."

And so — I mean I know it just sounds to me crazy in the first place. I know you disapprove. I can hear you scoffing now, but wait, all morality and ideology and everything aside, maybe in terms of *realpolitik*, America really has something to lose if we don't have something to threaten Korea and Japan with to keep them in our orbit, whatever all exactly that means. What do you think, sir?

Paul: I think South Korea is in a box. I think basically they would like to do a lot more with North Korea, just that simple token effort of sending a couple dollars up to North Korea, a couple million dollars, to help the people suffering from our sanctions for example.

At the same time, they have to say what the American government wants as far as the exercises go. We have to show strength and it's sort of a conflict.

And even the new president I think is more sympathetic to negotiation. I think the best thing that could happen would be for us to just get out of the way and let them deal with it, let the South Koreans deal with it and I think the Japanese would be better off. I think our goal of maintaining our sphere of influence and our empire is a driving force and unfortunately, they have the bully pulpit more than we do.

Horton: Well, do they have a point at all though, that we would what, lose out on some trade deal or some kind of thing would hurt our economy or hurt anything but the power and influence of those in D.C.?

Paul: If we had more of a better relationship with North Korea?

Horton: Yeah, and if Japan and South Korean then felt more independent from the Americans without that threat over the long term. That's the so-called concern in this article, that this will hurt us somehow.

Paul: Some people might say that and who knows exactly? But no, I think things would be better. How much trade do we do with China now? They're just not going to change that. I think the results would be a lot more. That would be sort of like the saying, "We have to make South Vietnam pro-West because if not, they're going to be part of the domino theory and they're going to be locked in with communist China and communist Russia."

But lo and behold, we finally lose, we walk home with our tail between our legs and what are we doing? Trading more with them now than ever before. So I don't think that they can make these predictions that if we get out of the way... And I always make the statement, "We win a lot more in peace than we do in war." This idea that we use our military to protect our interests and our trading, I just don't think that's true. What we have to do is emphasize the benefit that free trade is a benefit to both sides.

Horton: Alright, well thank you so much again for your time Dr. Paul. I appreciate it so much.

Paul: Good to be with you, Scott.

Horton: Alright you guys, that is the greatest American hero ever, Dr. Ron Paul. I mean that seriously. Who has ever done more in the history of mankind to spread the ideas of individual liberty and for that matter, peace, sound economics, and on and on and on? Dr. Ron Paul, the author of a bunch of great books and our good friend.

Okay, there you go... and blurber of my book *Fool's Errand*. How do you like that? Okay, thanks again. You guys can find all my stuff at ScottHorton.org, LibertarianInstitute.org, FoolsErrand.us and follow me on Twitter @scotthortonshow. Thanks again you-all.

December 1, 2017

Horton: On the line, I have got the greatest American hero ever, Dr. Ron Paul. He's got a brand-new book out, it's called *The Revolution at Ten Years*.

Horton: Welcome back to the show, sir. How are you doing?

Paul: Thank you, Scott. Nice to be with you, doing well.

Horton: Good, good, very happy to have you on the show and I love your book.

Paul: Good.

Horton: You're, you know, probably two-thirds of the reason I'm good on everything. I've had you to look to for a solid 20 years now, since 1997 is when I first found you on C-SPAN, as I told you before. And you're why I was good on the dot-com bubble and you're why I was good on the housing bubble and, you're a big part on why I've been so good on war all this time and I owe you a lot. I have to tell you, too, and I know I always talk at you instead of asking you questions when I have you on the show — and I know you already know this — but I just want to tell you from my angle, I have met so many people, I mean I couldn't count the number of people who are libertarians because of that time you whupped Rudy Giuliani in that debate.

Paul: (Laughs.)

Horton: They call it "the Giuliani moment," but I think people kind of forget that — You had such success, but what it was, the argument was the most bitter pill that you were trying to get the American people to swallow, that George Bush and Bill Clinton got us into this mess, that history didn't begin on September 11th, that America started it in the terror war, and you said that at a Republican debate, and people, not necessarily Republicans, but millions — tens of millions — of Americans were receptive to that, because they could tell you were bravely telling the truth. This was not a great political point to make if you're trying to be popular. This was the truth, the hard truth, and you respected them enough to tell them the truth, and the light bulb just went off. I know you already know this, but it's millions, and millions, and millions of people are libertarians because of your courage, sir.

Paul: But Scott what you're touching on is really what the book is about. Because the question is: Did Giuliani win and is his movement winning, or is our movement winning the revolution that came to light back during those campaigns? Of course, I don't call it the "Ron Paul Revolution" as much as it is a movement for liberty, a libertarian revolution. And yet on the surface, many people would say — and I acknowledge this — they say, "Washington hasn't changed, they're still warmongers, we're still in debt, we still have the Fed, and what did you guys do?" How can you have this as a revolution? But then when you come along and you have access to and you participate in the public arena, that you meet people that are actually very knowledgeable about this, and they're laying the groundwork for the necessary changes that will come after this whole thing falls apart. Of course, I believe that the libertarian revolution is alive and well, and that it's a philosophic revolution and numbers are less important than determination, and when a system fails it has to be replaced.

Just remember, not very many people in 1988 were predicting that the Soviet Union would disappear. Nobody was doing that and yet it self-destructed. I think what we have is self-destructive and it will have to change. Nobody's certain when and how it will be replaced, but I think we have a real shot at it because of what's going on in a quiet way, academically speaking. You're on the radio and doing the work but there's a lot of people doing it. We have the Mises Institute which is really influential in teaching young people the philosophy and going to college campuses. I get encouraged, but most people would think, "What are you guys talking about? Bernie Sanders has control of the college campuses." Well I disagree with that and I try to make that point in the book.

Horton: Right, yeah. Well, certainly there are a lot of young people who probably would be Bernie Sanders types except for your intervention in their intellectual development there, with the Ron Paul Revolution. So, here's my concern though, what if America the country can afford America the government and America the world empire? Maybe Osama bin Laden's trap worked on the Soviet Union because they were communists and their economy was a joke anyway. Then the oil price crashed — that was it, they were out. Yet here in America, we haven't had a war here in what, 165 years? Where you look at all the freeways, and all the factories, and all the trucks, and all the people, all the universities, all the capital that the American people bring to bear. What if we can afford an empire for another few lifetimes?

Paul: Well, I don't think you believe that. It's a challenging question. I don't believe that because this is all based on debt — it's debt and spending. They're working really hard on taxes, but taxes are secondary to the spending because taxes try to pay for all the spending, and it's the spending that counts. Because of our system, based on the dollar, which allows us to run the world because it's the reserve currency of the world, it allows us to run up this debt, and the government prints the money. And the Federal Reserve builds that system that you're talking about. It finances welfare and warfare.

But it's every bit as factitious as the Soviet system. It's a little harder to identify because on the surface what you describe... I think of that too, I would go around the cities where there's a lot of homeless people where you don't really see them. And think about the lower 50 percent of the population that are getting poorer. I think, well it doesn't look that way. But it really is, it's based on debt, and you and I could do very well if we decided to go into business, and the business wasn't a good business, but the banks are loaning us a million dollars a week. We could look pretty good until the debt comes due. And the debt is coming due, it comes due for a government and a country a little bit differently than it would be for you and me. If we were involved in that, the bankers would stop us.

But the only thing that's going to stop this system is the value of the dollar and it's overburdened now. I think that that time will come, but exactly when that will arrive, I don't think anybody can be certain.

Horton: You do talk about sound money in the book, and you talk about... And we've talked before about just how amazing it is that before the crash, this was all in the year before the crash. Boy, can you imagine if only the crash had happened in '07, how different that campaign would have been? Man... But anyway, before the crash happened, you got the kids chanting "End the Fed." You got people interested in monetary policy, which we all learn in first grade when we learn how to count quarters, we learned that George Washington is on there because the government makes sure the money is fair, and that's all you need to know. And that's all anybody needs to know, they go their whole life thinking that, believing that. And yet you made this a huge issue for — obviously it is a huge issue — but you drew people's attention to this issue in a way that I know you could have never anticipated. But so, if I give you a real short crack at it now, what would you tell people? Why is it so important that we have sound money, Dr. Paul?

Paul: Well, you're right, I was pretty surprised during the campaign that it did catch on. But stating the facts sometimes can be very appealing and I think there's more unhappiness than people realize. I think the reason that, although they booed when I was explaining to Giuliani about the foreign policy, it made a lot of sense to a lot of people who had already come to that conclusion, but they were afraid to say that. I think the Federal Reserve is the perpetuator of all of this. I called them once "the biggest taxer" because they're the ones who tax us through the inflationary tax, and they're the facilitator, they allow this to exist.

I started off with a serious concern about economic policy in the 1960s when I came across Henry Hazlitt, Mises, and Hayek, and I started reading. "Well, these guys are onto something and they're predicting this Bretton Woods is going to fail. Boy, that would be a big deal." Of course, August 15, 1971 was a big deal and we're still suffering the consequences and...

Horton: You're talking about when Nixon finally closed the gold window.

Paul: Yeah, when there was a bankruptcy, we no longer could promise to pay for our currency. Of course, already by then, the American people were denied the right to own gold, but foreigners could still put down their $35. But the gold was being drained from this country. Finally, Nixon said, "No more, we're going to stop doing this," so they declared bankruptcy. The '70s was a very, very bad economic decade. But we've been up and down ever since, we've gone through Nasdaq bubbles and housing bubbles, and now we're back in another bubble and that crisis will come. But I think it's going to be different. It's going to be a lot worse, there's no margin they have. Before, they could pretend we're going to stimulate the economy by spending more, printing more, and lower interest rates. How do you lower interest rates once they're down to 1 percent, or negative interest rates? They don't have any leeway.

So the bust always comes, and the reason you can predict this is the fact that all bubbles are artificial, and they have to be corrected. They come from the fact that the Fed creates artificially low interest rates and extra credit and causes the malinvestment that causes the bubbles to form. So they're there and they will have to be corrected. But I think the monetary policy... Actually, it fascinates me about how it works, and when you mention that some of these young people in college campuses were catching on, I don't think it's that complicated. This happens more than once, where they'll come up to me and they'll say, "Boy, I understand what you're saying, I get it." Then they'll say, "It's just common sense. Don't you think that's about what it is?" Yeah, this is common sense. Why should a secret group of individuals be able to just decide what interest rates should be and what the money supply should be, and then become regulators too? It's so far removed... I was on a show yesterday and I said that what's going on has nothing to do with free market economics, this whole thing is distorted, and it's destined to fail, and I think the cracks are already there.

Horton: Yeah. Well, and that's the whole thing about it, too, that whenever I interview Bob Murphy or Mark Thornton about the business cycle, I always try to set it up by saying, "Hey, you don't have to agree with us libertarians about any other thing at all, but the Austrians have figured out this boom and bust." And look, any of us who've lived a few decades, our lives are a history of booms and busts in our states, in our towns, where we live. We can't ignore the fact. They teach us the Fed is here to prevent that kind of thing, and yet it's always either… And I think everybody knows it, right now we're at the height of a bubble, whether we can personally feel it or not, we can see the stock market bubble and see where we're at. I don't know how long until this one busts, seems like they're already deflating now, so…

Paul: Our greatest challenge is sorting all this out, because we understand why when the bailouts come, they go to the rich, and the poor don't get help, they lose jobs and they suffer the consequences of price inflation and they get poorer. That causes wealth maldistribution and a lot of anger, it sets the stage for the socialists to come in, so it's not illogical for the Bernie Sanderses to all of a sudden arrive: "Well, there's a gross distortion, see what freedom does, see what capitalism is all about, look at what it does." The libertarian free market explanation is crucial and it's vital for us to talk about it, because no matter what you like, we should have a much better alliance with progressives because true progressives are very much antiwar, yet they have to realize how does it get financed and who benefits. Welfare, in many ways, is similar to warfare because the industrialists, the weapons manufacturers, are the ones that benefit from all the war. We should have more coalitions, but I obviously think that understanding monetary policy is vital because we will have a bust, it's going to be terrible. And who gets blamed?

Paul: In the depression, in the '30s, it was those terrible capitalists and the gold standard that got blamed. Yet it had nothing to do with free markets and sound money. As a matter of fact, it was the violation of sound money in the '20s that caused the problem.

Horton: Well in fact, even in '08 they pretended that you'd been the president for eight years and said, "Oh yeah, see, it's the laissez-faire free market policies of George W. Bush that got us into this mess," as though all the history between 1933 and 2008 never happened.

Paul: Right. (Laughs.)

Horton: This is the thing with the progressives, right, is that they don't understand or believe — They think we're corporate shills, we all work for the Kochs, or whatever it is. They don't understand that we want the economy to be so free that these very powerful banks, and insurance companies, and arms manufacturers are free to fail and go out of business, so that we can move on in a society without them, and that we think that the best way to get rid of Citigroup is to have a free economy rather than the State regulating them which is never going to happen, right? The State just regulates them right into the position they're in right now.

Paul: And they need to understand why inflating a currency also leads to the point where average people's real wages don't go up, matter of fact they go down. When we talked about 1971, getting off the gold standard completely — Real wages have essentially stood still. The wages don't go up but the cost of living always goes up, which prompts people to spend more money to pass out more welfare, which means they're going to print more money and create more inflation, which caused the problem in the first place.

Horton: Right.

Paul: For a while, that seems to work because the currency can be strong and the country very wealthy, but eventually you consume the wealth and then the production goes down. Trump, you know, harped on, "No more production, we've got to force people to do this and that because we're not producing enough." But just having a soaring stock market isn't the answer to the problems that we have.

Horton: Yeah. Alright, well listen, I'm sorry, I know you have to go, but I really appreciate your time on the show again, Dr. Paul.

Paul: Great, Scott. Nice to be with you.

Horton: Always great to talk to you.
   Alright you guys, that's the American hero Dr. Ron Paul. The brand-new book is *The Revolution at Ten Years*, and there's so much other great stuff in there about the police state, about populism, and, of course, war, the drug wars and all these things. It's the *Ron Paul Revolution at Ten Years*.

April 18, 2018

In an interesting turn of events, in the spring of 2018, Dr. Paul interviewed Scott on his show, The Liberty Report, co-hosted by Daniel McAdams, about his book Fool's Errand: Time to End the War in Afghanistan.[10]

Paul: Hello, everybody. Thank you for tuning into the *Liberty Report*. With me today is Daniel McAdams, our co-host. Daniel, good to see you.

McAdams: How are you this morning, Dr. Paul?

Paul: I'm doing very well and we have a special guest today and we're excited about that, and I'm going to hold up a book that he's written, and we'll do a little discussion about his book, but he's also been involved in the libertarian movement for a long time, has a radio talk show and I've been on it at least three or four times. He might even tell you how many times I've actually been on it.

But he's been in this business promoting libertarianism for a long time, but especially in the last 15 years. But the book is something that is dear to our hearts. It's on foreign policy — and guess what? He's a noninterventionist, and he writes about Afghanistan and it's called *Fool's Errand: Time to End the War in Afghanistan*.

Scott, welcome to our program and let's end that war as quickly as we can.

Horton: Thank you very much for having me, Dr. Paul.

Paul: Okay, very good.

Horton: As you know I consider you to be the greatest American hero ever.

Paul: Oh, calm down.

Horton: So I'm very happy to be here with you.

---

[10] Ron Paul and Daniel McAdams, "Fool's Errand – 17 Years In Afghanistan," The Ron Paul Liberty Report, April 18, 2018, https://youtube.com/watch?v=yelwRfZBGy4.

April 18, 2018

Paul: So what got you first involved in the libertarian movement? You've been involved even before you had your radio program and you — How many interviews have you done now? I was making fun of "a few interviews," but you've had quite a few, haven't you?

Horton: Yes, it's 4,600 and something interviews now, going back 15 years to April 2003.

Paul: Right.

Horton: At the beginning of the war in Iraq.

Paul: And your site is ScottHorton.org?

Horton: Right.

Paul: And you post them there?

Horton: And that's 30 interviews of you so far.

Paul: Oh, boy. Thirty! That ought to be enough.

Horton: Not quite yet. I've got some questions still.

Paul: Well and also, I see it a lot of times on Antiwar.com. It pops up there, too, so you've worked with Antiwar. But what got you motivated on this other than the fact that the war in Afghanistan is insane? I was kidding you before, I said, you better start making notes about writing the next book. When are we going to stop the war in Syria?

Horton: Yeah, I know.

Paul: And it goes on and on. But, of course, our goal should be to stop all these ridiculous wars of aggression, you know.

Horton: Right.

Paul: That's where our real problem is. But I'm sure that you keep up to date on these various invasions that we have made, and we've just finished this weekend… I guess you are very much aware of what was happening and probably not too encouraged by our reaction in Syria.

Horton: Yeah, it could've been worse. It doesn't appear that the policy has changed back to regime change against Assad. But, of course, any time that they're bombing the Shi'ite partisan forces there, they're risking killing Iranians and possibly even Russians on the ground there and that kind of thing really could escalate.

Paul: We talk a lot about Syria recently because they've been more in the news, but Afghanistan's been in the news for a long, long time. And the way it started we could spend a couple hours going into the details of that — and you have detailed a lot of this. But do you see similarities between how we slip into wars and get involved in Afghanistan and yet we never seem to learn?

Horton: Yeah, it is. It's the same in Afghanistan as it is in Yemen, Somalia, Iraq, Syria, and Libya. Once they get in there, well, it's just another government program. They never can solve the problem that they claim that they're there to fix and so they just make matters worse and that gives them more to do and so here we are, working on almost 17 years later and still occupying Afghanistan.

Paul: Daniel, do you have a question for Scott?

McAdams: Yeah. Scott, I've known you for a number of years. I've been on your show. Actually, just this last week I was on your show and I love your show. You've really built something. But one thing is your reputation as a meticulous researcher. You always dot the i's and cross the t's when it comes to these things, and I really think that's important at a time when people throw out opinions left and right. But I would like to talk about your book with that in mind. I remember, because we talked as you were writing it, and you agonized blood, sweat, and tears pouring out of your body as you were writing it, getting everything right. Walk us through writing the book and tell us what it's about if you can.

Horton: Sure, thanks. Yeah. I'm a big fan of yours, too, so thanks. Okay, so the book actually started out, it was going to be refuting the War on Terrorism in general. Then I basically got stuck in the Afghan quagmire and Chapter 2 ended up becoming a whole book. So Chapter 1 is "Getting into This Mess," for anybody familiar with Dr. Paul and the blowback argument. Chapter 1 is all about how Jimmy Carter through Bill Clinton's policies is what provoked the al Qaeda war against the United States. Then, with the rest of the book, basically, I make the case that first of all, we didn't really have to invade. We could've negotiated with the Taliban to give over Osama bin Laden. But if you don't buy that and you say, "No, we really needed to just bomb al Qaeda, not arrest them," then okay, but we still didn't have to fight the Taliban. And even if you say, "No, but the Taliban hosted Osama bin Laden for five years so they had to go because I'm just so angry about 9/11," then okay, even if you had to carpet bomb the Taliban, you didn't have to create a new government in Kabul. And then you definitely didn't have to stay and build up this new government and take on all of its enemies as our own enemies.

So now that our government has done that, we have picked a fight, to oversimplify it slightly, with the plurality Pashtun population of the country that we absolutely cannot defeat, our side cannot defeat. So they got into a war they didn't need to have and then they built it up so big that now they're stuck in a quagmire and can't get out of it.

McAdams: And our friend Eric Margolis, whose opinion we both value very much, his point all along has been, basically, we're taking the side of the communists in Afghanistan. We always have since we started.

Horton: Right. Yeah, we switched sides. Really, it's the guys that we were backing…

McAdams: From the terrorists to the communists…

Horton: That's right, the guys that we were backing in the 1980s against the Soviet sock puppets, the sock puppets are the ones we're backing now — the Tajiks and the Uzbeks and the Hazaras in their war against those mujahideen.

Paul: You know there are so many ideas and different things happening, whether it's the drug war or foreign policy, monetary policy and all these things. But I want to ask a question or get your opinion about libertarianism. Where is it going? There are articles now coming out and saying the libertarian moment is over and done with and if we went up to Washington and I shook hands with some of the people I know, you might see why they have that opinion. If you turn on the evening news, you might get that opinion. But I make an effort to try to refute that and also to come down on the side of optimism. So tell me where you stand on that, on the unfairness of saying libertarianism is… It's almost like it's orchestrated to show that we don't exist anymore. At the same time, it's always painted so negatively.

Horton: Right. Well, part of our problem is we eschew power. So instead of doing everything we can to insinuate ourselves in Washington, D.C. and take over policy creation, we kind of stay out here in the hinterlands complaining because we don't really want to do that much participating. And frankly, without you on the national level being interviewed on the cable TV news shows regularly, as it used to be when you had your seat in Congress, we don't quite have the leadership that we used to have in terms of publicity — although Rand has been doing some really good stuff, especially lately. But so, I can see, again, agreeing with you, I can see why the TV people and the Washington, D.C. establishment types as far as they can tell, we're sort of absent. Yet out in the country, it's not like that at all, I think, primarily, because of your two presidential runs. That did so much to boost the discussion about real economics — Austrian school economics — peace, and limited government and all of these things. And to show people, especially by example, that you don't have to be a liberal or a leftist or some Michael Moore millionaire communist hypocrite to be antiwar. You could be a Texas conservative Republican and be more antiwar than those people, even.

I think that that is the real appeal of libertarianism. That's obviously my focus, as well as yours. My primary focus is foreign policy. It's the worst thing our government does and it's also the comparative advantage that we libertarians have, is that we stay antiwar when liberals are in power.

Paul: Right.

Horton: And when Donald Trump, somebody like Donald Trump, a populist right-winger who makes some antiwar promises, when he breaks them, we're the ones who stay consistent. So whenever the parties in power shift back and forth, we get the flotsam and the jetsam. Everybody disappointed in Obama for not following through on ending the wars and everybody disappointed in Trump, they come back to us.

Paul: I think what sometimes happens is people don't realize the difference between political power, and you sort of alluded to that… At the same time, ideas are pretty important, and they sort of are in the background.

Horton: Right.

Paul: But it makes a difference. That's why I was surprised so often in campaigning. I thought, well, nobody knows about this. And all of a sudden, I mention something — the drug war, foreign entanglements, and noninterventionist foreign policy — and there's support out there, so the ideas have been out there. So I think if we're looking to see that libertarian ideas can only be present by a political knowledge and a political presence, I think you can be discouraged. But I think the ideology is so important because I think with the drug war, we've made progress there until we got the current attorney general. But I don't think he's going to get anywhere. I think nullification has been heard, I think the Federal Reserve has been out there and in spite of the disaster of the foreign policy, I think the American people actually are with us on foreign policy. Why are we going into these wars? That's why the work that you do, and all of us try to do, is getting the truth out. Because I think truth is more powerful than all the power of these politicians — truth wins out in the end.

Horton: Absolutely. Well, and especially when their policies are completely crazy and wrong and immoral. You know, backing al Qaeda, the only enemies of the American people, against Assad because he's allies with Iran, who they may be the enemies of the American empire in the Middle East, but they never did anything to us. Yet our government prefers al Qaeda to Iran and Iran's friends. So that's a pretty easy argument to win, because we're right and they're not.

Paul: Daniel?

McAdams: We talked a little bit about politics, now I'd like to get your take on this, Scott. A two-part question: Do you believe that Trumpism has hurt noninterventionism? And if you do, is it temporary or has he done permanent damage? Not just noninterventionism but libertarianism in general.

Horton: No. I mean, I really think that Donald Trump is a side issue, really, to noninterventionism. I mean, he ran on promising war crimes. "We're going to kill not just ISIS; we're going to kill their family members. We're going to bring back torture, it doesn't matter if it's good for getting intelligence, they deserve it anyway, we're just going to punish them with it." Right? So his instincts are very right-wing nationalist. And so, as part of that, that meant that he was against overthrowing secular dictators — at least he finally learned a lesson after Libya, which he supported the war in Libya. But he learned a lesson finally after that, that enough of overthrowing these secular dictators in favor of these jihadists. So, I mean, I think overall, he's actually still better than Hillary would've been on Syria, even last Friday included in that. I think if it was her, Zawahiri would probably already be on the throne in Damascus.

But I think he was elected in part because half of what he said sounded kind of antiwar. And I think that overall, the populist right rank and file in

America, sort of the Tea Party-right Republican voters, they're sick and tired of this. They don't even necessarily have really good arguments; they just look at how long it's been. How can it take 16 years to kill 400 men? What is going on? Right? You have these families, they've lost one son in the wars, they don't want to lose their other son in the wars, it's still going on and they can't stand it. So now when Trump bombs Syria, the polls show that Republicans support that, but I don't think with George W. Bush numbers, and I think that their overall sentiment of being over this foreign policy and wanting to see an end to it is still there.

McAdams: That's a good point.

Horton: So I guess it remains to see how much more damage he does as president. But I'm told, and I won't say who but — and I won't say I believe this either necessarily — but I know somebody who knows somebody in the White House and they say that Trump absolutely wants out of Syria and wants out of Afghanistan, John Bolton notwithstanding. He does not want a war with Iran, he wants out of the Middle East and to spend this money at home like he always says. There's this brand-new article in the *Washington Post* this morning, or last night's *Washington Post,* where they say — it's about Russia specifically — but they say there's Congress's foreign policy, there's the president's foreign policy, and then there's the executive branch's foreign policy. They just refuse, they're just completely insubordinate, they refuse to do what he said. So they tricked him when he kicked all those diplomats out, they told him "Well, what we're going to do is we're going to kick out the same number of diplomats as our European friends." Well, they meant all the European countries together. He thought that, and when he found out the next day that the French and the British had only kicked out four each, and that the Americans had kicked out 56 or something, that he went absolutely ballistic.

McAdams: Wow.

Horton: They're basically framing him up and doing everything they can to try to prevent him from doing the right thing as far as the Russians go. Honestly, I think that it's going to end up blowing up in their face. I think the American people agree with Trump that we do want to get along with Russia. I was thrilled — Weren't you guys thrilled when you heard that he invited Putin to D.C.?

Paul: Yeah.

Horton: And that's what he should've done on the very first day in office, he should've invited Putin to D.C. and just shoved this whole Russiagate argument right back down the throats of Democrats and the CIA.

Paul: Scott, how do you think this will end? You've written about this in great detail, it's been going on for a long time, it can't go on forever, but it can go on for a long time yet — these wars can last. But do you think it's going to end? Some of these things, whether it's economics or foreign policy, I claim it's an overwhelming task to convert the people in Washington, not the American people — I can't see next month or next year after the next election, that all of a sudden the majority will be agreeing with us. So what do you think the odds are that eventually that's the way it will end, or do you think that something like going broke might play a part in this? Because it doesn't look like we're going to all of a sudden have the right kind of people there. Not that we shouldn't keep trying, and even if you have somebody moving us in a direction, it's beneficial. It just seems like they're dead set. And the power and the clout of the neocons and the media and all is so strong that I keep thinking that the American people have to support getting out of there. But the big question is, is how do you think it's going to be resolved?

Horton: The American people in the polls have been against the Afghan war since at least 2013. They even said it was not worth fighting in the first place, even including September 11th — no fake weapons of mass destruction in Afghanistan. They still are saying we should've never even gone at all. In this book *Fire and Fury* about the first nine months of the Trump administration, there's a quote from Dina Powell who was the deputy national security advisor, saying, "Look, at the end of the day, the bottom line is if Trump pulls the troops out of Afghanistan, then he loses a war. And Trump can't lose a war." So they're just talking about politics there and I just think that that's wrong. I think especially that Donald Trump, being Donald Trump — never a senator, never a governor — he didn't vote for this, he has nothing to do with it, he could've easily just come in and said, "This is all Bush and Obama's fault, it's not my fault. The Pashtuns of Afghanistan are not our enemies, and now they're not again and we're just going to leave. We're not calling it a loss or a victory, we're just coming home and if the government in Kabul can't stay, then blame that on George W. Bush and Barack Obama, the dummy and the coward," or whatever his bad names.

And then he could do it. And I think the American people would just applaud. I think it's only in Washington, D.C. they say that, "Oh, that would be bad." But part of this though too is, they say well ISIS is there now. Well these are still just local Pashtun fighters. Local militia men, not real ISIS international terrorists at all. But the story that they claim is that Obama didn't create ISIS by backing al Qaeda in Libya and in Syria and then that blew up in his face. No, he created ISIS just by pulling the troops out of Iraq. So the lesson is you can never pull any troops out of anywhere, because then anything bad that happens in that country will be your fault.

Paul: And not enough troops.

Horton: Right, exactly.

Paul: Send in more troops.

Horton: So now anything bad that happens while our troops are still there, well that's just despite their best efforts. Right? But I just think that's wrong, and I think the American people are over it. I think if Donald Trump ended the Afghan war tomorrow, and told the American people, "Look, you're going to hear a lot of criticism about this, pick which side you're on." I think the American people will side with him, hands down.

Paul: I think you're right. Scott, I want to thank you for being with us today. It's a great book here, I want to put it up again for our viewers to see because Scott writes well and he also is on the side on nonintervention, he knows about Afghanistan and he knows how to apply that to our total foreign policy. Scott, thank you very much for being with us today.

Horton: Thank you, sir, really appreciate you having me.

Paul: And I want to thank our viewers for tuning in today and please come back to the *Liberty Report* soon.

November 15, 2018

Scott Horton Speech, "New Media and the Terror Wars," presented at the 2018 Mises Institute Symposium with Ron Paul: "We Need Alternative Media," in Lake Jackson, Texas.

Jeff Deist: I'm sure most of you know our next speaker. Scott Horton is someone who really has single-handedly changed that narrative that we've spoken of, especially when it comes to the war in Afghanistan. I mentioned his book is called *Fool's Errand*. If you haven't read this book, be ready for some footnotes because Scott annotates everything. He has done — I just read this last night in his lifetime of doing various radio shows — he's done 5,000 interviews and almost all of them fighting against this crazed warfare state that we find ourselves in. Please welcome Scott Horton.

Horton: Alright. So Jeff Deist asked me to speak today on alternative media, but this is my first opportunity — and maybe my only opportunity — in my life to share a stage with Ron Paul. So first I'm going to tell you about Ron Paul.

Lew Rockwell and Jeff Deist, Ron Paul's former chiefs of staff; Dan McAdams, of course, Ron's closest advisor for twenty-something years and co-host with Dr. Paul of the most important show on YouTube, the *Liberty Report*; Carol Paul, his loving wife since sometime in the 1960s, I guess: You all just don't understand the greatness of this man. You all don't love him like I do. Ron Paul is simply the greatest hero in American history. He's certainly my greatest hero, and being a skater and a libertarian, I have a lot of heroes. Seriously, I have a bust of Ron Paul in my office. His name is on the super-majority of my shirts.

Dr. Paul is the best kind of libertarian. He always knows his facts and opposes the very worst things about our government the most and first — and he always tells the truth. As Anthony Gregory says, "Ron Paul makes Thomas Jefferson look like James Madison." And what is Ron Paul's libertarianism, but true American liberalism — that Jeffersonian liberalism untainted by socialism and progressivism and only a little bit of conservatism. And that's okay, because Ron Paul's conservative personality, his purist capitalist economics, and Republican Party political affiliation helped him, during his presidential runs in 2008 and 2012, to open the minds of millions of Americans to adopting an antiwar position they had previously been persuaded could only be held by hippies and Hollywood know-nothing, know-it-all liberals.

Have you all ever seen the great documentary *For Liberty: How Ron Paul Watered the Withered Tree of Liberty* by Rye and Kealiher? It's more than a documentary about Ron Paul's 2008 campaign. It's about the birth of a whole new libertarian movement in America. It's more — and it's better — than you would think. It's really a wonderful film. I hope you'll all look at it. The key to it, of course, was Ron's clash with Rudy Giuliani over the causes of the War on Terrorism in the May 2007 GOP debate. "The U.S.A. started it," Dr. Paul insisted, prescribing Americans the most bitter pill. But millions of people rallied to his message. They knew it was true. They hated the war, but they didn't want to identify with utopian and helpless hippies or Michael Moore, the gluttonous Hollywood millionaire communist hypocrite. Ron Paul told them they didn't have to: If you like your identity, you can keep it.

So let me ask you — and I've been giving a lot of speeches since the book came out, and to a lot of Libertarian Party groups — I like to ask, how many people here are libertarians because of Ron Paul? Oh, man. Well, it is a Ron Paul event. Okay. And now how many of you are libertarians because of the Giuliani moment — the fight between Ron Paul and Rudy Giuliani in 2007. Okay. We have a few. At every speech I give where I ask that question, hands go up, and you'll see in that documentary *For Liberty* just how important that was.

Now my Giuliani moment story is actually from ten years previous, in 1997. I was up late in the middle of the night. This is when Ron Paul had just come back to Congress from his semi-retirement and return to medicine. And I looked and it was C-SPAN reruns — three in the morning or something — and there's this little old congressman saying, "Mr. Speaker, I have here in my hand, proof published in the British papers today that President George Bush," this was Senior, "was selling chemical weapons to Saddam Hussein, even during Operation Desert Shield in the buildup to the war in the fall of 1990, and I'd like to enter this into the federal record there, sir." And I thought, "Oh, my God, I can't believe this. A congressman just accused George H.W. Bush, essentially, of treason on the House floor." And then I looked at the bottom and it said: Ron Paul (R-Texas). And I thought, "No way. You have got to be kidding me."

And in fact, in 2007 when he started running for president, David Beito and I started writing articles together to run at LewRockwell.com supporting his candidacy. One of the things I did was I went digging through the speeches and I found that speech from 1997 and I really had remembered it right. That there he was, that courageous to accuse a

Republican president of not just violating the law, but violating the very concept of what most people would think it would mean to be the president of the United States. I've been a big fan ever since. In fact, I used to drive my cab around, and I would give copies of his speeches to the people in my cab. You can imagine, right? "Hey, did you know there's one good congressman? No, really, one — and he's really good." And there were these two speeches, they went together: The first one was, "A Republic, If You Can Keep It," and the second was called, "Sorry, Mr. Franklin. We're All Democrats Now." And these were some good times there, passing this stuff around.

One more story. In 2005, just before… in fact, the day that Katrina hit New Orleans, which was really the beginning of the end of the credibility of the Bush administration. But that day it was Ron Paul's birthday party, and they held a barbecue as they do usually — most every year — for Ron Paul's birthday party. And he got up there and he gave an antiwar talk to a room much smaller than this. This is before the presidential campaigns. The room was entirely full of almost all just local Republican voters and constituents. And he got up there and he gave an antiwar talk and he said, "Listen, I know the president is from Texas, he's in my same party. I feel a lot of pressure to support what he's doing. I know a lot of you people support what's going on in the war, but I'm here to tell you it just isn't right." And then he went through and he explained how America started the terror war, how the September 11th attack and the rest of them were blowback from American imperial policy in the Middle East.

I sat there and I watched a room full of Republicans nodding. They knew that even if they didn't agree with him 100 percent, they knew he was telling the truth and they knew that they trusted him. They knew that he was doing what he thought was right, and that was good enough for them — and good enough to really move that needle. And you know what? I have to think that after a week of George Bush and his government doing nothing to help the drowning people in New Orleans, that those same constituents must've been thinking back on Ron Paul's speech just as so many other Americans were looking back at the Bush government and wondering whether these guys really know what they're doing like they said they did in the first place. And it was really something to see, anyway.

And also, I want to say about Ron Paul that I've interviewed him on my radio show 30 times now, since 2004. He always knows what he's talking about on any issue no matter what. It's not just that he knows about economics and knows about libertarian political theory. But if I ask him about Korea, he knows everything about Korea. If I ask him about Afghanistan, he knows everything about Afghanistan. If I ask him about Iran's nuclear program, he knows everything about Iran's nuclear program. He really is an expert and, of course, always tells the truth. Now, you might remember from the clash with Rudy Giuliani, the argument was two parts. The first part was, "They hate us because we've been bombing them for ten years before 9/11 ever happened." That rang true and people got that immediately, but then he said something that confused people, even supporters. He said, "But now bin Laden is glad that we're there. Now we're doing exactly what he wanted by invading."

And people thought, "Well, I don't get it. You're saying they attacked us because they want us to leave. Now you're saying that they're glad that we're there." Well, he was right about that. I want to share with you this one small part from my book. It's *Fool's Errand*. It's on sale now — audio book available, if you think you could stand nine hours of this. In 2010 — this is when bin Laden was still alive — his son Omar, who's one of his non-terrorist sons, Hamza is the bad one — Omar bin Laden gave an interview to *Rolling Stone* magazine. He said:

> "My father's dream was to bring the Americans to Afghanistan. He would do the same thing he did to the Russians. I was surprised the Americans took the bait. I so much respected the mentality of President Clinton. He was the one who was smart. When my father attacked his places, he sent a few cruise missiles to my father's training camp. He didn't get my father, but after all the war in Afghanistan, they still don't have my father. They have spent hundreds of billions. Better for America to keep the money for its economy. In Clinton's time, America was very smart, not like a bull that runs after the red scarf. I was in Afghanistan when Bush was elected. My father was so happy. This is the kind of president he needs, one who will attack and spend money and break the country. I'm sure my father wanted Senator John McCain more than Obama in 2008. McCain has the same mentality as Bush."

When the reporter asked Omar bin Laden if he thought Osama bin Laden will launch any more attacks against the United States, he replied, "I don't think so. He doesn't need to. As soon as America went to Afghanistan, his plan worked. He's already won."

And so this really goes to show the important point. As Dr. Paul said in that debate, "If we think we can just go around the world doing what we want and not have to suffer the consequences, not to study the truth of what's really going on, then we do that at our own peril." And that's the situation that we find ourselves in today where after 18 years, our government is still following Osama bin Laden's script and reacting exactly in the way that he wanted them to.

Of course, it was not all about the wars, though that was the key. Ron Paul, before, during, and since his presidential campaigns — and if you saw his speech, his little talk last night was really great — Ron Paul stands for what is after all the essence of the American creed: unalienable natural rights for all people. During his two campaigns, he gave what amounted to the greatest-ever speaking tour on behalf of peace, liberty, a free economy, sound money, and the rest.

Those campaigns certainly did more to advance the ideas of liberty than anything else in our lifetimes — perhaps in history. He changed the world.

His warnings about the then-coming 2008 crash also has helped to prevent the worst anti-capitalist narrative from becoming dominant. They did try to blame George Bush's laissez-faire free market policies, but it didn't really stick — because of the work that Ron Paul had done in attacking the economy from the free market point of view before the crash ever happened. And part of this was because Dr. Paul put on this massive propaganda campaign for freedom right when Americans really needed it the most. Okay, it might've been a couple of years early, but still — what Dr. Paul did was remind American society that liberty brings us together, that it allows us to tolerate each other's differences of opinions and actions.

Freedom is what we all have in common. It's at the end of the day what we all care about the most and agree about: freedom of religion, freedom of speech, a free press, guns, fair trials for the accused, protections from torture, the right to keep what we earned to take care of our families and our businesses. But in America today, the failures of the Bush-Clinton neo-liberal, centrist consensus in the post-Cold War era had become too dire to propagandize away. In reaction, the worst of the left and the right are becoming more socialistic and more nationalistic — then, of course, they react against each other even more, and it really is a shame. The neoliberal, so-called moderate centrists have just about ruined everything. They take our libertarian concepts of self-government and property rights and pervert them into an international crusade to install a global regime of what Bill Clinton called "free markets and democracy," meaning, really, policies that favor American business interests and installing and backing compliant governments around the world — with bloody force if necessary.

We libertarians have Murray Rothbard. The neo-liberals have Thomas Friedman. He says global trade and capitalism can only exist with the mailed fist of the U.S. government to enforce it. It turns out the government is looking for work and so they agree with him.

And what they've done is they've killed millions of people. They've spread chaos across Southwestern Asia, wasted uncountable trillions of dollars, disgraced all of our names, doing it all in the name of the American way, dragging the good name of individual rights, market economics, and regular elections through the mud just as so much of the rest of the world are also undergoing major reactions against this peculiar American freedom of the neo-liberals. Corrupted by money, power, and the ideology of American exceptionalism, which claims that murder is just fine when U.S. government employees do it in the name of freedom and progress — they've dealt these concepts significant blows.

But Charles Krauthammer and the "unipolar moment" are both gone. The world wonders what is next. The horrors of the totalitarian states of the last century show us what could happen if humanity embraces new consolidations of power by strongmen of the left or right against the crumbling American order.

But there is hope for America. After all, at the root of modern liberalism is the belief in equality and freedom for all and at the root of American conservatism is the attempt to conserve that same old liberalism of the American Declaration. Under these traditional viewpoints, the U.S.A. isn't supposed to be a world empire anyway. It's surely the path to our self-destruction. So the American people and our country are actually giving up nothing that we should want to have when we give up our world empire.

In peacetime, as Dr. Paul said last night, so many of the rest of our problems will be much easier to resolve. I look at the division in the country now between left and right, and obviously there were lots of problems in the 1990s, too. But I chalk the current level of division and vitriol between left and right in America up to George Bush's decision to invade Iraq in 2003. Half the population damned and cursed the other half for refusing to support America's war to defend this country from Saddam Hussein who attacked us on September 11th. And the other half of the American population said, "No, you dummies. Saddam didn't do it, or the war would have started a year and a half ago." And the level of contempt and hatred between the two sides in fighting over that… And then, of course, once the torture scandal broke and Bush and the Republicans insisted that the entire American right line up to support their torture policy, it just helped to double that feeling of division that the left and the right, the blue and the red, are no longer members of the same country.

And this is why Ron Paul's message is so important, as the centrist so-called moderates — really the worst extremists of our era — are discredited and fade away. Dr. Paul shows the country why our radical opposition to the disastrous policies of the liberals and conservatives is the true moderate middle of American politics — in a "moderate is Walter Block's middle name" kind of way. The reason we all fight so terribly is because the government has made it so there's so much at stake. By insisting on the de-politicization of American life, we will see so many of these conflicts fade away.

Now is the time for our movement to supplant the consensus of the liberal Republicans and conservative Democrats who are running this country into the ground with libertarians trying to call their most destructive policies to a halt. We have already seen some advances on this front, due in no small measure to the catastrophes our opponents have created. The politicians are the enemy, but the masses of Americans really aren't so bad. When the gap between the truth and the conventional narrative is so vast — and when the gap between the truth and the way things should be are likewise so vast — this is the best opportunity for libertarians to not only recruit new people to our movement, but to help lead the best of the left and the right, to help them to get their priorities straight to help us end the very worst things our government does first — just as Dr. Paul does.

Now Jeff wanted me to talk about my own experience in alternative media, so I'm going to do that. Otherwise, I would just continue talking about how much I love Ron Paul for the rest of the day, or maybe to talk to you about Iraq War III again. But this realignment between the best of the left and the right, this has been my mission since I started on pirate radio in Austin in 1998, to try to bridge that gap between the populist left and the right, to fight the elite and protect freedom. I admit it hasn't worked that well, but I'm trying.

I've never really tried to join up with mass media. My first show was *Say It Ain't So* on the community pirate radio station Free Radio Austin 97.1 FM in Austin, which was mostly hippies and Earth First! environmentalists... and some right-wing militia guys. We're all fighting the power and exemplifying that same spirit, that same agenda here.

After the FCC cracked down on Free Radio Austin, some friends of mine started another pirate radio station, KAOS Radio 95.9 FM, which lasted through almost all of the George W. Bush years. This is where I started the interview show under the name of Philip Dru back in 2003. I also used to call Congressman Paul's weekly update recorded message — (888) 322-1414 — and play that live over the air every week. And Jeff — where's Jeff? I'm sorry. I did lie to you a couple of times. Jeff wouldn't let me interview Dr. Paul on pirate radio, so I told him it wasn't.

Hey, it was wartime. (Laughter.)

It still is.

Then, of course, there's Antiwar.com, where the show has been featured since 2007. This is where we get the most bang for our antiwar buck, probably anywhere — and all credit to Eric Garris, Jason Ditz, Justin Raimondo, Angela Keaton, Margaret Griffiths and the rest of the crew there at Antiwar.com.

And possibly interesting to you guys — curiously even to me I guess — is that I've been on KPFK 90.7 FM in Los Angeles for seven years now. Now, every single other host on there is a leftist. I'm the only libertarian on there. My show is called *Antiwar Radio*; I'm on every Sunday morning, and even though I don't quite fit in with the rest of the crew there, they don't mind my point of view on other matters. They figured, I guess, that even though I'm bad on everything else, at least I'm really good on war. It goes to show that that's their priority. It is Pacifica, after all. It was founded for antiwar purposes generations ago and so they still had their priority straight and allow me to do my show there. At first it was hard for them to understand that I'm not from somewhere to the right of Dick Cheney, but they figured it out. It took them a while.

Now something that's been very important to all of us, of course, has been the advent of Facebook and Twitter and the huge effect that they've had on the internet for good — and for ill. The promise of these sites, of course, is the potential for a great expansion of all of our audiences. Though from the beginning, they've also been a double-edged sword killing great comment section communities and blogs from all places on the political spectrum. I got fed up and quit Facebook back in 2014 when they first started really changing the algorithms to punish alternative media. I would post an interview of Ron Paul and get just a few likes and shares. Whatever exactly they thought of me, I was sure that more than just a couple of my 6,000 friends and followers would want to listen to and like such posts. The people who hung around on my Facebook page, the community of people of friends there, vanished. Facebook started demanding money to show my posts to anyone. I called their bluff and walked away.

Now Twitter is doing the same thing to their timelines and are banning people with unpopular opinions. The centralization of the internet onto these sites is already showing its major weaknesses: that one can be made to disappear from discussion at the whim of a few Silicon Valley executives in bed with the government and corrupt think tanks like the Atlantic Council, which is funded by arms dealers and foreign governments primarily to promote the permanence of the NATO alliance. If you don't like their policy, then you're a Russian agent and have to go.

Honestly, I was really happy to quit Twitter. I was wasting far too much of my time for far too little reward on that site and cold turkey was the only way to go. My temporary ban, along with Dan McAdams, during the Peter van Buren troubles a couple of months ago just gave me a good opportunity to finally do so.

A worse stage of internet oppression now looms. First, they came for the extreme right and the truthers, de-platforming them, as they call it, from virtually every Web 2.0 service and even including kicking them off of major corporate servers like GoDaddy.com. At this rate, banning their servers from access to American ISPs — banning them from the internet entirely — is not far off. Nor is the targeting of libertarians and leftist alternative media sites, many of which have already been de-ranked by Google and ghosted and banned by Facebook and Twitter. Facebook purged at least dozens — maybe hundreds — of libertarian-minded political pages like those of Copwatch and The Anti-Media just a couple of weeks ago. In reaction to this, we have seen the advent of a few alternatives such as Mastodon and Minds. Perhaps one of these will take off. Perhaps someone will invent a stand-alone app that negates the need for us all to join any one site in order to network with friends, family, and ideological fellow travelers and opponents.

Now here is why all of this matters so much. This week the *New York Times* finally ran two major stories on the suffering of the Yemeni people at the hands of the American-Saudi war there. The administration now finally says it's time to start wrapping things up. After three and a half years of slaughter. At the end of 2018, public pressure, including perhaps especially through social media, has really helped regular people from the right, left, and libertarians to force at least some congressmen and senators to introduce resolutions to try to stop this war, and finally for the *New York Times* to admit how bad things there have gotten. The fact that the Saudi crown prince tortured and murdered a regular writer for the *Washington Post* the same way that they and the United Arab Emirates had been torturing and murdering Yemenis for the past few years also seems to have helped to raise awareness of the tragedy of the U.S.'s war there as well, of course.

But right now, we're still dependent. Our pressure from below can push, but it takes the *New York Times* and the *Washington Post* and the pressure on them by us for their change in narrative to really change the narrative where it counts in D.C. I'm sorry to report that's true, but I think this week's *New York Times* story has helped to prove it.

Right now, I'm actually trying to get away with reforming the transcript of a talk I gave on the internet to turn that into my next book about the War on Terrorism. And I'm thinking about getting another old-fashioned daily radio show. So I'm not really sure if I'm using these technologies right. I seem to have gotten a better reaction from the book than 5,000 interviews over all these years. So I guess people really do still crave the deep dive and the old technology to get the real truth through.

But as the great comedian Bill Hicks once said, "You do what you can." So let's all do what we can to spread the message of peace and liberty while we still can.

You are all ideological capitalists and I supply books. Say's law says that you have to demand them. I'm pretty sure that's how that works. Thank you all so much.

January 18, 2019

Horton: Introducing the great Ron Paul, one of my very favorite guests, if not my very favorite. Dr. Paul, welcome to the show. How are you doing?

Paul: Nice to be with you, Scott.

Horton: I'm very happy to have you on the show. I have a very broad question for you, if I can formulate it right. I just kind of want to know what you think about American politics right now, particularly in regard to Donald Trump's foreign policy. I am amused, actually, watching the *Liberty Report* and seeing just how bemused you are by all of this. It's fun to imagine what you must really think about what all is going on with this chaos here. And so, I'd just like to hear it.

Paul: Well, evaluating Trump is difficult for everybody, because it vacillates a bit. But, if I looked at it in very, very general terms — One way you can look at is how much suffering goes on with our military personnel and how many people are out there shooting and killing somebody that we don't need to be shooting at, and if you look his two years compared to Obama or Bush or any of them, it's been relatively better. But the policies are still there, very much interventionist where it's in too many places. There's lots of threats. And then, yesterday was how tough we're going to be to build all these huge weapons in space, and because there's a lot of danger out there.

At the same time, a couple of weeks ago he says, we're coming home from Syria. It made the neocons go nuts. I think there's a problem that goes on in our foreign policy. I think his instincts are better than his ability to carry them out, because he's up against great odds when you come to the media and the organized Democrats and Republicans, and this whole shift just due to philosophy of economics and foreign policy. But just the fact that they hate Trump. So all the Democrats now are pro-war and they put pressure on him.

It should be, if you had the right coalition under these conditions, he could even do better and get the troops out of Syria and get the troops out of Afghanistan. But then, when you look at it and analyze it, he's up against the people who support the Israeli position, the Saudi position. And it's very difficult to do it. It's just too bad that the American people don't shout a little bit louder because when I campaigned, I did get a favorable reaction to stating as clear as I could: Enough is enough. We don't need this. It drains us. It makes us poorer. People die. They received it well. But, right now, I think the noise is all coming from under control of the neocons, and, of course, they control the media quite strongly.

Horton: Well, it really is interesting though to see, isn't it? How Donald Trump is effectively leading the right on this issue. They're willing to… and maybe they already really did agree with him. He did win the primaries against all of his interventionist opponents. While promising to crack down on terrorist groups, he promised to stop with the regime changes, and end the permanent occupations, and pacification campaigns, and these kinds of things. And they responded very well to that.

And the recent polls showed — and this got most of the attention, how bad the Democrats are now on this — but it showed that the American right is really moving much further to a noninterventionist position in support of him.

Paul: Yeah, I think that is the case, but you might not hear that on the evening news, because a certain group of conservatives are noisy enough to… Especially when it comes to passing some resolutions in Congress, they go along with the Democrats and they get some of these things done. But no, I think there's a big opportunity.

I think the Democrats are actually going to split on this because there's a lot of traditional progressive Democrats that aren't all that happy about this war mongering. And I think you're right that there are people speaking out on the Republican side. But we still have a long way to go because when you look at the top leaders in the Republican Party and in the Senate, a good many of them, if you look at a Mitt Romney type, they're closer to the establishment Democrats. So the establishment Republicans and the Democrats are pro-war. And that's where our big problem is.

Horton: Well, so your son, Senator Rand Paul, said the other day — I guess he had met with Trump or had spoken with Trump — and said that he had promised he's really serious about, at least on Syria and Afghanistan, he reiterated that we really are getting out of there. Although, he only ever said he was ordering half a withdrawal from Afghanistan so far. But that sounds like maybe he's implying a further and maybe a complete withdrawal sooner rather than later. But what do you think?

Paul: Yeah, well I'm hopeful. I keep my fingers crossed, and I think he's sincere. But measuring the opposition is the tough thing. How much noise can he put up with and how much beating up by the media can he stand without caving in?

The other thing, Scott, that really bothers me, is some of the times when things don't go as well as they should for Trump, it's his own people that he appointed. That's a real tough thing to figure out. He has some neocons in places where they shouldn't be. When you can look at Bolton and Pompeo, he's in a hard position there. They're going to be difficult to handle. They might give some token support to the president, but behind the scenes, I don't think we can trust them.

Horton: Well, that's one thing that I guess we all wonder if he's even aware of. We all know that we don't have that deep of a bench of noninterventionists who have the credentials to really serve in the White House or something like that. But we do have one good bench worth, right? They talk about Jim Webb, and there's Col. Macgregor, and, of course, Doug Bandow and Ted Carpenter from Cato, and a few others there. I mean, these are enough to really — and, I think obviously, Senator Paul could fit as secretary of state — and they could make a great Republican noninterventionist team right there.

Paul: Oh, it's there. It's whether or not they can pull it off, because of the resistance by these smaller groups of special interests. They're in positions of power when they control the evening news incessantly. It makes it very difficult. I think the groundwork is there, and there's some good people there, and it would be much better, but I'd feel better if they would have been quietly appointed two years ago.

Horton: Well, so now what do you make about the actual withdrawal from Syria? Does this seem like they've really succeeded in putting that off? Or do you think that…

Paul: Well, they definitely succeeded in slowing it down. The attitude has changed. There may be — If you want to give them a little bit of room for it, you might argue, well it might take a little bit of time, because Trump made it sound so immediate. If we had an immediate need to send in thousands of troops some place which was justified, we could move troops pretty darn fast. But, all of a sudden, moving them out is more difficult. So I think that they've been slowed up. I think that, when he has an interview in talks with Senator Graham and the other neocons, he listens to them. And, yeah. I think it's been slowed up. I don't think it's totally dead, because he's going to try to live up to it, but I don't know. A good question would be, has there been any literal evacuation yet?

Horton: Right.

Paul: And I think I read, and you may know the number, but I read, and I was even shocked because I didn't know the number, how many military bases or units that we have in Syria. It's not like five or ten. They're all over the place. And they have to close them down. I would say forget it, just get out and change your policy. But that's opposed by a lot of people that are going to really object. I know Israel wouldn't like that, and Saudi Arabia wouldn't like that. I don't know what's going on, but I don't think they are going to get them out of there real fast. But we have to give them support, and that's what you do. You try to get as many people thinking along the lines of giving the support to the president.

And, since you watch my program, you know that every chance we get we give support. But then we get worried about him or he's changing his position, we try to boost his confidence.

Horton: Yeah, of course. Just like under Barack Obama, he signs the nuclear deal with Iran, he's Obama the Great, for a day anyway, because it's the policy that counts and certainly if he is going to do the right thing. You may have seen — I don't know if anybody really covered this very much, and I'm sorry because I don't catch every show — but there was an NBC report that the White House was talking about getting out of Somalia too. And that was a story from about a year and a half ago as well that he was questioning, well, why are we even in Somalia? Where is Somalia? Right? Like you can imagine Trump being frustrated about that.

Our guys getting shot in Somalia, at same time, he ordered an escalation there. And then, in one report, the military was really digging in their heels and said, "Well we haven't heard anything about that. We're not leaving Somalia." But it's just another one.

Paul: Yeah.

Horton: I guess I'm grateful that he even knows we're there and is mad about it.

Paul: Yeah. You know, on all these interventions, the simplest and clearest message that we can send is, show us where we got involved and things got better. Syria is a typical example. Obama says, Assad has to go, and then a few years later, then we started putting troops in there and helping in all sorts of ways. The whole mess of it, the reason we can't leave is because of what we've helped create. The warmongers, and the neocons, are saying, if you leave, al Qaeda is going to come in and it's going to be disruptive, and we have to stay there because it's a mess. Yeah, but the mess came from us being there. But they aren't willing to listen to us there, because they have ulterior motives. But the American people will listen to that message. You make a good point. They did listen to Trump because he was not endorsing everything we talked about, but he was leaning in that direction. What are we doing over in these places? And he still won the election.

Horton: Yeah. Well, and you're right again, of course. If you look at what's going on right now where the obvious solution to, for example, protect the Kurds from a Turkish invasion, if there is a solution at all, it's to allow the Kurds to negotiate with Assad and make a deal to bring the Syrian army back in there. But the Americans still don't want to concede that. It's this guy James Jeffrey who is telling the Kurds that they're not allowed to, I guess they're trying to negotiate that anyway. But, as long as America is there, that prevents the Kurds for making the peace with Assad that they need to protect them from Turkey, so.

Paul: See, they don't want...

Horton: The problem solves itself if we just quit it.

Paul: Yeah. They don't want to admit that Assad actually won, you know? He's representing a country. Yes, it's far from perfection, but what we've given them for the past ten years is a heck of a lot worse than it was like when he was maintaining an authoritarian approach to the problems that he had in Syria. But it's awfully strange that so many people can't see this. But I think the ulterior motives are the toughest thing, whether it's an oil pipeline here, and the energy, and the Kurds are involved, and it's on and on.

And that's why I think our philosophy is so attractive. You know, it's sort of like people wanting to manage the internal affairs of our next-door neighbors and say, "Oh well, you should be doing this." And that would be insane to go into their house and say, "Well, what we want you to do — These are the habits you have to follow." You'd be shot or thrown out within a few minutes. But for us to go into these countries and, even with good intentions, and try to micromanage their countries, that's going to create just more chaos. And that's what's happening.

But I don't know how many places that they can use as a good example of us restoring good government. We can hardly tell them to look to Iraq.

Look how much good we did in Iraq, and how much good did we do in Afghanistan after 17 years. The evidence is so strong, I think that we have to keep plugging along and keep working on improving our arguments, because I think we have truth on our side.

Horton: Yeah. Well, you have a career of being right. I mentioned at the beginning of the show your book, *A Foreign Policy of Freedom*, which is a collection of foreign policy speeches going back to, I guess, the turn of the Carter to the Reagan years there, in the late '70s/early '80s and through those terms in Congress, and then, I think some in your inter-Congress years, a couple, but then when you went back to Congress in 1997. It's literally decades of you warning caution that, if we back the mujahideen in Afghanistan against Russia that we might have some bad consequences from that. Or if we get in this war with Saddam Hussein in 1991 that there could be some blowback coming down the line, and this kind of warning. Not just to say that you told them so, which you did, but that all you had to do was to have the proper principle and an honest analysis of it, and you proved the case that anyone or many people could have and did get this right all along. That it really didn't have to be this way at all.

Paul: Yes. Yeah. And, to me, is such an easy message. We take a principled position of noninterventionism and it gives us good results. The others are very difficult when they're interventionists and they're so-called pragmatic and realist, they have to go in there and dissect out, "Well, on the one hand we should help this group. On the other hand, we should help this group." And they still believe that, if we do the right thing, we're going to be bringing about peace and order. That's when they get into trouble. That's how we ended up in Korea, and Vietnam, and all over the Middle East, the whole works. So the message of noninterventionism and defending that is a lot easier than picking and choosing between the Turks and the Kurds.

Horton: Yeah, absolutely. Well listen, I'll let you go, but thank you so much for your time again on this show, Ron. It's great to talk to you.

Paul: Scott, nice to talk with you again.

Horton: Okay guys, that's Ron Paul. He is at RonPaulInstitute.org, for the Ron Paul Institute for Peace and Prosperity. And, of course, just check out the channel on YouTube for the *Ron Paul Liberty Report* as well.

June 14, 2019

Horton: Alright you guys, introducing the great Dr. Ron Paul, a former congressman from District 14 in south Texas, and presidential candidate and author of a great number of wonderful books including, *The Revolution: A Manifesto*, *End the Fed*, *Liberty Defined*, *The School Revolution*, *Swords into Plowshares*, *The Case for Gold*, *The Revolution at Ten Years*, and my favorite, *A Foreign Policy of Freedom*, a collection of speeches from the early '80s through the early 2000s. Really great stuff there. He also is the founder of the Ron Paul Institute for Peace and Prosperity, which he runs with the great Dan McAdams. They also host a show, four days a week on YouTube, called *The Liberty Report*. You can find all those archives at RonPaulLibertyReport.com. It's the best show, anywhere.

Welcome back, how are you doing Ron?

Paul: I'm doing well, Thank you, Scott.

Horton: I really appreciate you joining us on the show today. I wanted to start off with giving you an opportunity to talk about this event that you're doing in D.C. on August 24th.

Paul: Yes, and I think this is either our third or our fourth year that we've done it, and it will be on foreign policy. Daniel is excellent in putting all this together, and he has all our speakers lined up. I don't have the names in front of me right now, but it's held at the hotel that's at Dulles International airport, so it's real close there. People do fly in, and we usually get people from around the world there, so we're looking forward to having it again.

Horton: Great, and then people can find out all about that at RonPaulInstitute.org.

Paul: Right, on the web.

Horton: Great, okay, then also I have an announcement: Today, later this afternoon, I'll get to my 5,000th interview, and that includes, with this one, 38 of you. And I'm putting out a book, which is almost done. I've had to go through it a few times, editing it, but I'm putting together a book. It will be called, *The Great Ron Paul: The Scott Horton Show Interviews, 2004–*

2019. So I'm happy to announce that and with you on the show here, and I thank you very much for your permission to go ahead and do that this way.

And it's really great. I've had to read it three or four times through now, and I'm just so proud of it, and my association with you: The fact that you were available to say all these things on my show, all these years. And it's such an education. I think everyone will really like it.

The only bad part is, it's a little annoying how much I like you, but people are just going to have to suffer through that, because I really do consider you the greatest hero.

Paul: Well, I have a special interest in this because I like people who are energetic, have their own method of getting a message out. People ask me, "What should I do?" I say, "Whatever you want to do." And you did your thing, and you've done it, and you've done it for a long time, so you've talked to a lot of people. You ought to list the number of people you've talked to over the years. It must be in the many, many thousands.

Horton: Yeah, I'm not sure exactly the total number. You know, 317 of them have been with Gareth Porter.

Paul: Wow.

Horton: So I do have my favorites that I do interview regularly, including you and Dan, of course. I just got off the line with Bob Murphy again, so it is that kind of a show.

Paul: Yeah, but I'm talking about the people you have reached.

Horton: Oh, I'm sorry.

Paul: You know, your listeners. That's why I encourage people like you to do your thing. You came up with it, somebody probably didn't come to you and offer you some money to put on this program, and you've been working at it, and you deserve a lot of credit.

Horton: Well, thank you very much, I appreciate that, and yeah, I have no idea the numbers. And I guess I settled overall a long time ago, for knowing that I can't really change history or anything like that, but I can help to change people's lives, and help to inform people who are looking for the truth, which is something that I've taken as a great inspiration from you, all this time, too.

Back before you ran for president, and were world-famous, you were sort of this little old congressman, all alone in the House of Representatives, just consistently telling the truth, and setting the example that's what you've got to do, just stay at it. And it's come to so much since then. I mean, really, especially now in 2019, just looking back at the last decade, it's so easy to see the tremendous influence that you have had in American society and for libertarianism around the world and everything. Your name is on people's tongue all the time.

Paul: Thank you.

Horton: Yeah, it's really great. So, let's talk about the news. Oh wait, before we talk about the news, let's talk about the funny thing you said about the news on the show yesterday. I love this quote. You said, "The only time they tell the truth is when they admit they lie."

Paul: You know, sometimes, I'm sure you've had this happen, sometimes when you're the most spontaneous, you can blurt out a good one.

Horton: Yeah, that was a great one, definitely.

Paul: I looked at Daniel and sort of chuckled over the whole thing, and I said, "Yeah, I'll take that one." But that is the sad story, and then just compounded today, because here we are at Pompeo telling more lies, which you can't say they are lying, but boy, it's sure a gross distortion of what was going on there. Now it looks like what he was saying yesterday, was not true, that they had evidence, you know, a smoking gun, and that they know exactly how the Iranians shot up those vessels. What is so disgusting is, why don't the people realize that that's how they put us into war, they lie us into war. And these guys actually admit they tell lies. So we should be awake from all their shenanigans.

Horton: And then I think you are referring there to the story in NBC news where the owner of the Japanese tanker says that it wasn't a mine, it was a flying object that hit his ship.

Paul: That's right. That's exactly opposite of what Pompeo is saying.

Horton: It's kind of funny in a way, how bad they are at this, that their lie can't even hold up for one day.

Paul: Yeah, and that's to our benefit. All we have to do is expose them because you wonder how anybody could trust them.

Horton: And now, you know, something that you and Dan talked about on the show, too, was that, it wasn't even just the Iranian president, it was actually the Ayatollah himself, who was sitting down with the Japanese prime minister, essentially, right at the time that this was happening. It's almost inconceivable that they would do such a thing.

Paul: Yeah, it is amazing. The longer I've been in this business, I still am amazed. I'm not totally shocked that this is happening, but it still is amazing that they don't even think about it. We think maybe they are over the top, but they keep at it. I guess there's a lot of gullible people out there that just buy into these distortions that they give us.

Horton: So, I'm sure you saw this. Your son, Senator Rand Paul did great yesterday on the Senate floor. He gave a great speech about arming the Saudis, I think UAE and Bahrain. Or was it Qatar? I forget. Three of the four of those. He sounded just like you, saying that so often we end up in conflict with countries who are armed with weapons that we have sold them.

Paul: You know years ago, I would make a statement because, even though I didn't have all the details, but it would happen occasionally, but it probably happens more than we realize, is that on all these weapons sales, and all these alliances that we have, that we end up fighting those people that use those same weapons against us.

And the other silly thing is, is we go, and we bomb so often these countries, and put on sanctions, and we destroy a lot of property, then you know, which is an expense to the people to pay for all the bombs. But then we frequently go back and repair the very damage that we did to these countries. So it makes no sense, whatsoever.

Horton: Yeah, well unless you have a contract for Kellogg, Brown and Root to rebuild the broken thing, I guess. It's in their interest at the expense of the rest of us.

Paul: Yeah, that's probably the way it works. The military-industrial complex is very broad.

Horton: By the way, what did you think of Donald Trump and his statement? You know, he's so blunt, whatever it is he's talking about, where he just said, "Hey, get real. We have a military-industrial complex."

June 14, 2019

He said, "There are people in this town who love war."

Paul: Yeah, I think it's great when we hear that, and we have to praise him when he does it, and encourage him to do it more, and to be cautious when he contradicts himself. But no, and Rand confides a little bit with me, that he thinks Trump really has beliefs that are very tolerable, and very much in our direction, but I don't think any one person completely understands what makes his decisions from, you know, which sometimes appears like a flip-flop. One day, he takes the troops out, and the next day, he puts them back in.

But I've always wanted to believe that Trump has good instincts, because he has said some good things, and sometimes he's consistent, and sometimes he's consistent in what he believes in, but sometimes he's consistent in and sticks to some things that I disagree with. But the one thing for sure, he has shaken up Washington, and for the most part, they deserved it all.

Horton: Yeah, sort of regardless of even his policies, just the fact that he got elected was certainly a repudiation. He beat a Clinton and a Bush in one year, to get into that spot. That's meaningful, that the people would support even Donald Trump, if it's at the expense of those two dynasties, or that one dynasty, in a sense.

And so that brings me kind of to what I really want to talk to you about. It's that at this point, at the end of the 2010s now, and through the first Trump term, what's more and more a consensus about the death of neo-liberalism as the path of the American center, that the American people have rejected it because, even though it does have, in a sense, sort of this pseudo-libertarianism; an embrace of capitalism, and of freer trade, although it is the managed, globalist kind of trade that you have opposed in the past — we could talk about that — but it's come with all this war, and all this debt, and the terrible boom-bust cycle, that all of us libertarians have warned about. So it's just been rejected. Now we have people moving further to the left and further to the right and then reacting against each other even more.

It just seems to me like now, more than ever, it's important that people hear, especially the Ron Paulian libertarian take about what the real American consensus is supposed to be about. It wasn't really the American way that failed, it was the Bush-Clinton post-Cold War neo-liberal consensus that failed. But that wasn't what we were all supposed to be doing here.

Paul: What you're talking about is very important because we see things happening. This was certainly the case in the '30s. There was a major depression and there had to be some analysis, but the analysis turned out that the people believed that there were too much free markets and a true gold standard was in existence, that sort of thing, in the '20s.

So they blamed that, and they moved, of course, toward the New Deal, which changed things a whole lot. Right now, we're at a similar situation, although the statistics say that everything is rosy, we know that they aren't, and the spending continues, and the deficit is out of control. And there's a lot of people now who claim they understand it perfectly, and they're getting elected to office.

When you see some of these very, very far left individuals getting elected, that means somebody is paying attention, but the big question is, is this very narrow in certain districts where they have already known as progressives, and if this is a good time to use it as an excuse to move in that direction, or is it national? I tend to think that it isn't a national movement. I think people are waking up and in that way, you could argue the case that the establishment has been deeply challenged by Trump, and it should be used as a shift away from government, and hopefully we can make the shift away, and then refine the best way we can, you know, the market economy.

Of course, I've talked about the Federal Reserve, as well, because for a sound economy, you have to have an understanding about the monetary policy, and that is a big one, too. That is as powerful and monolithic as is the military-industrial complex.

Horton: Well, you've always said too, sort of secondary to the war, but really intertwined entirely with the issue of American so-called global hegemony — or empire, dominance, or whatever euphemism — is inflationary money.

It's all part of it, and then comes… It's not just the consequences for the Yemenis and the Iraqis, and the Americans who fight and are killed and wounded in the wars, and all of that. But it's at the expense of our entire society — and now with the global economy, even the whole world gets disrupted by this massive American boom-bust cycle, that's driven by that paper money. That was a huge part of your appeal in your presidential campaigns. I remember you talking about how surprised you were about how resonant that was with people, that the government causes the boom and the bust.

We have to end the Fed and that's something that people knew was right, and they knew it was important, and especially it was reinforced how important it was because no one else would say that, even though that's the obvious truth of the thing.

Paul: Well, the one thing I tried, and I continue to try doing is, that is work with people who are honest progressives. And I have been able to get them to look more seriously at the Federal Reserve, and making the point, which I believe is accurate, that the Federal Reserve probably is much more beneficial to the very wealthy, and the banking system, and the war mongers and all, even though it's necessary for the welfare state too. So they throw a bone to the welfare recipients, and the liberals go along with it. But there are many progressives, you know Dennis Kucinich, frequently he and I worked together when he looked at this honestly with the war issue and the Federal Reserve.

So this is an issue that I think we can bring people together with, rather than making the disagreements even broader, so I think as long as we stick to those principles, we can get more people to join us, but right now, on the surface, and what is reported by most of the media, you know, is that this is the age of socialism about to be on our doorstep. I don't believe that's true, because it doesn't work, and I think it's a distortion of what's really happening.

I'm still encouraged when I go to the college campuses. I do meet a lot of young people that do not spout the trashy stuff that we see reported so often.

Horton: Okay, so, that's really interesting. In a sense, it's a left-wing argument for the gold standard, saying that the inequality, which is the huge issue in liberal politics, which it is something, right?

CEO pay in ratio to the average employee pay at X corporation; those kinds of numbers are completely through the roof. We have what they call the "financialization" of the economy where these guys, in the midst of that giant boom before the bust, you have people making absolute fortunes, trading these ridiculously fraudulently pieces of paper around, and all of these things. These are all problems that, by the left, are typically identified simply as symptoms and problems of capitalism, itself.

But your argument is that it's actually taking us off the gold standard, that has helped to precipitate that. Can you explain that a bit more, please?

Paul: Well, I think that Mises has helped me understand that because he claimed that if you destroy the monetary system, and get away from sound money, you will destroy the middle class. When you have sound money, you have a bigger middle class. America was generally known, in a very positive way for having a very strong middle class. Today it is dwindling. So the people who make the complaints, that come up with the idea that what we need is socialism, they're very annoying, but I think they're spotting the problem, and you touched on it with your statement, is because there is a discrepancy.

The money that was used, the trillions of dollars that were pumped into the system, you know since the last recession started in '08, '09, has gone into the coffers of the big banks, and big corporations, and buy backs, and mergers and the big salaries. But actually, the average person is still in big trouble, and no matter how they give you these statistics, there's a gross distortion of how they report unemployment and inflation, you know, they keep arguing, "there's no inflation, no inflation." Yet, the Austrian School of Economics teaches that you can't control where the inflation, that is the creation of money goes, and quite frankly, I think it's right now, going into debt. And that's a bond, and that's buying bonds, the bonds bubbles.

I mean you can't help the person who wants to save and take care of themselves, by not being able to make any interest whatsoever, and not they're talking about banks charging you if you want to put your money into the bank. It's a total mess, and it's because of the dishonesty in the monetary system.

Horton: And then also, of course, especially with the military, as you've written and talked about so much, that you have all these corporations that make massive fortunes straight off of treasury dollars, where they don't participate necessarily in the free market at all, or even the rigged market at all. They simply deal with the Pentagon as their customer and make "cost plus" on weapons that don't work, or who knows what.

Paul: Yeah, that is, you know, good evidence for us to be used against these wild-eyed liberals. If you can find one that's more honest about things, and have them look at it independently, because those corporations do benefit. And this whole idea that nobody can ever question the military spending, conservatives or liberals. I mean, right now, there's no effort whatsoever, to work together and cut back spending because they are locked into it.

It's politically so difficult, and also, they hide behind the intellectuals from our universities, who probably 85 percent of them say, "Well, don't worry about the deficit you guys, you conservatives and libertarians. You worry too much about the deficit, but you shouldn't do that."

So that's probably the number one reason this continues because it's the difficulty of coming back. Politically it's very, very hard to vote against the interest which seems to be short-term. If you have benefits going to your district in the next year, and you vote against it at the next election, they give you trouble. Sometimes I wonder how I ever got away with it, but I believe if you couldn't vote against all the spending and then you have no credibility.

Horton: Yeah, well, I think probably it was because you delivered two-thirds of the population of your district in your obstetrician's office, right?

[Both laugh]

Paul: Yeah, you know it's funny, I had contacts with George Bush socially … It was a little bit easier, but I was so annoyed with the foreign policy. But there was one time we were in a crowd and we were meeting over a hurricane incident, but he said, "Okay, we'll hear from Ron Paul. He delivered more than half the babies in this county, and that's the reason …"

So, he was sort of giving me a hard time about one of the reasons why I was successful. But I wouldn't deny. I think it was helpful, but also, I hope there were people who understood what I was doing.

Horton: Of course. I was just teasin' ya.

Paul: If I would have been way, way out… I always got a big charge out of… You've known me for a long time. I was always against this ridiculous drug war, and we're living in the Bible Belt. How can I do this? I always voted, and preached that, and was a libertarian, but the district never held it against me, which I thought was pretty amazing.

Horton: I remember, that was actually one of my original introductions to you back then, was the Democrats attacking you for that, and showing a clip of you saying, "We need to repeal all the drug laws," at a Libertarian thing, and then having your head float around the screen, and this and that. But it never stopped you. And just the same, I sat there and watched you preach antiwar stuff to a room full of Republican constituents again, before you ran for president and became world famous. There were some national libertarians who had come, but essentially, it was a room full of all your own constituents at your birthday party down there in, I guess, 2004 or '05, and you got up there and said antiwar stuff.

I could tell that they didn't agree necessarily with everything that you said, but I could also tell that they respected you for your opinion and your honesty, and that it certainly was no deal-killer to them in the way that you were going about it. I'm sure it's the same thing with the drugs, because you always say exactly the right thing, which is, "Hey look, I'm a doctor and I'm an economist, and I know about this stuff." And what you say, of course, makes sense.

So, in speaking of the economist thing in the last couple of minutes here, I wanted to ask you about the trade because, of course, this was a big part of what got Trump elected too, was he ran against the centrist Republican-Democrat, Clinton-Bush consensus for NAFTA and GATT, and the World Trade Organization, and all this stuff. We've talked about this before, that you're really for real libertarian free trade and open trade, and none of these international organizations. But essentially these groups have regulated toward freer trade, and it seems like, maybe this part is wrong, but it seems like that has been such a shock to the American people that they can't stand it, and that's what they hate about the Bushes and the Clintons the most. Because after all, before NAFTA, and before the World Trade Organization, America had all these protectionist walls and so American industry was built up under all this protectionism. But then, Newt Gingrich and Bill Clinton came and took it all away, all at once.

So maybe that's an overstatement, but that's how it feels to the American people, and they want their old, high-paying blue-collar factory jobs back, and they're gone, and they blame the center for that. So now Trump is ratcheting up, especially with China, but also with Europe, and some threats with Mexico, tariffs, and trying to bring back that old system. So I just wondered, I know you don't take either side in that fight between those two but how would you explain to the American people that it really should be?

Paul: Well, I do it two ways. I have never been in favor of more government, bigger government, international organization, even though a lot of libertarians like the WTO and these things, because they said, "We'll move it toward less tariffs and freer trade." Well, I didn't trust them, but I didn't think it was the right thing to do. A country doesn't need to belong to the WTO in order to work one way or the other. Besides, I thought the organizations became political and some companies got better benefits than other companies, so I didn't like that idea.

The other thing is, I think the executive branch of government has too much to say about it, although Trump is getting some credit for some of the things that he has moved along by the use of tariffs, and the threats of tariffs in forcing people to do something, but quite frankly, I think we're better off if we followed what they put in the Constitution, and that is, the Congress is supposed to be involved in this. You know, foreign trade is supposed to be a congressional function. I think we've given way too much power to the executive branch, and even if they can pull one off and did something, and it was better than what was happening, the next guy, if he has this much authority, they use it to do it.

This is what's happened say, on foreign policy, on going to war. Both parties like that. They don't want to give up on that. The War Powers Resolution, which tried to curtail that, is opposed by all presidents,

June 14, 2019

Republican and Democrat.

So I don't like bigger government, and I'd like to see us follow a closer position following the Constitution on congressional authority. But Scott, one thing right now is pretty bad is, congressional responsibility sometimes isn't much to brag about.

Horton: Right. Okay, but so, what about the idea though, that if we do have really just Ron Paulian policies; no tariffs, open trade, that because of labor costs in poor countries, the American people will simply just lose all their jobs, or enough of the jobs that they wanted to keep, to Mexico or Indonesia or China or elsewhere, that it causes this much of a disruption, that they're willing to put in a guy like Trump to try to solve it for them in this manner?

Paul: But, see I don't believe in taxing the people, and tariffs mean you tax the people. I can remember going through all of this in the '60s and even in the '70s when our automobiles weren't in very good shape, and all they wanted was protectionism. They got a little bit, but they didn't get a whole lot, and the Japanese were whipping us to no end. I think if you can't compete… and your point is the toughest one to defend, and that is, wages are lower. But wages being lower benefits the consumer.

This is always the thing. Mises has always said that the whole market system is designed for the consumer, not for the working man, and not for the businessman. It is geared to provide services and goods at the best price and let the consumer make all the decisions. So if we as a country can't provide the cars in competition because there are subsidies, well, if they're better cars at cheaper rates, why take that away? I mean, if you can get a car for $1,000 instead of $2,000, you've got a good car and you have $1,000 left over, and then maybe we would clean up our act. Maybe we have too many regulations, maybe we have too much wages propped up too high. You have to deal with that.

I don't think the answer is just retaliate with put-on tariffs and tax the American people. This whole idea now that we just put in $50 billion dollars because we collected a lot of import taxes, I mean, that came from the American consumer. I think we haven't seen the end to that yet. I think that's all in motion right now, what the consequence will be, because so far there's been a lot of talk about the tariffs and on the surface, it looks like it may have achieved something, but ultimately I'm still going to argue for free trade.

Horton: All right, since this is going to be the last chapter of the book coming out here, I guess I ought to ask you to say one last thing here about empire and individual liberty.

Paul: Well, the bigger the empire, the less liberty there is. When the government spends the money that means the people have less money. Even if you can borrow, even if you can print it, ultimately, empire needs a lot of money, and that requires a greater handicap for the people.

So, I do not believe the republic can be defended in empire. I think the Romans taught us that once they went to empire, they lost their republic. That's what's happening to us now. If you look at the last hundred years, the republic has disintegrated to a great deal, and that is why the empire is so detrimental.

The biggest problem we have here is teaching people that what we're talking about is not isolationism, I don't like isolationism. I think the isolationist are the ones who want to put on tariffs, and impose our will, and tell people what to do. I want to trade with people and visit with people. I just don't want these international organizations, which are very opposite.

An empire always undermines the personal liberties and they do it through an attack on the finances.

Horton: All right, well thank you so much for your time again on this show, Ron. Great to talk to you, sir.

Paul: Good, Scott. Thank you.

Horton: All right, you guys. That's the great Ron Paul. And one of the books that he wrote that I left off the list there is a really great little primer, *Mises and Austrian Economics: A Personal View*. It's really a good read. I think you might like it. Add it to the pile there, and again, check out the Ron Paul Institute for Peace and Prosperity, covering everything, and they're good on everything over there, day in and day out. And, of course, the *Liberty Report* with the great Dan McAdams at RonPaulLibertyReport.com.

All the audio files are available in the archives at ScottHorton.org, YouTube.com/ScottHortonShow and at the following web addresses:

https://dissentradio.com/radio/04_05_30_paul.mp3
https://dissentradio.com/radio/04_10_16_paul.mp3
https://dissentradio.com/radio/05_12_17_paul.mp3
https://dissentradio.com/radio/06_12_13_paul.mp3
https://dissentradio.com/radio/07_04_03_paul.mp3
https://dissentradio.com/radio/07_08_17_paul.mp3
https://dissentradio.com/radio/08_03_06_paul.mp3
https://dissentradio.com/radio/08_09_26_paul.mp3
https://dissentradio.com/radio/08_11_21_paul.mp3
https://dissentradio.com/radio/09_02_18_paul.mp3
https://dissentradio.com/radio/09_04_22_paul.mp3
https://dissentradio.com/radio/09_05_29_paul.mp3
https://dissentradio.com/radio/09_09_23_paul.mp3
https://dissentradio.com/radio/10_01_21_paul.mp3
https://dissentradio.com/radio/10_03_04_paul.mp3
https://dissentradio.com/radio/10_05_12_paul.mp3
https://dissentradio.com/radio/10_06_18_paul.mp3
https://dissentradio.com/radio/10_08_27_paul.mp3
https://dissentradio.com/radio/10_11_23_paul.mp3
https://dissentradio.com/radio/11_02_24_paul.mp3
https://dissentradio.com/radio/11_04_01_paul.mp3
https://dissentradio.com/radio/11_04_22_paul.mp3
https://dissentradio.com/radio/11_06_03_paul.mp3
https://dissentradio.com/radio/11_11_23_paul.mp3
https://dissentradio.com/radio/13_04_26_paul.mp3
https://dissentradio.com/radio/13_06_10_paul.mp3
https://dissentradio.com/radio/13_08_22_paul.mp3
https://dissentradio.com/radio/15_02_12_paul.mp3
https://dissentradio.com/radio/15_07_03_paul.mp3
https://dissentradio.com/radio/16_04_12_paul.mp3
https://dissentradio.com/radio/16_06_08_paul.mp3
https://dissentradio.com/radio/17_03_15_paul.mp3
https://dissentradio.com/radio/17_05_15_paul.mp3
https://dissentradio.com/radio/17_10_02_paul.mp3
https://dissentradio.com/radio/17_12_01_paul.mp3
https://dissentradio.com/radio/18_04_18_paul.mp3
https://dissentradio.com/radio/19_01_18_paul.mp3
https://dissentradio.com/radio/19_06_14_paul.mp3

About the Host/Editor

Scott Horton is director of the Libertarian Institute, editorial director of Antiwar.com, host of *Antiwar Radio* on Pacifica, 90.7 FM KPFK in Los Angeles, California and podcasts the *Scott Horton Show* from ScottHorton.org. He's the author of the 2017 book, *Fool's Errand: Time to End the War in Afghanistan*. He's conducted more than 5,000 interviews since 2003.

Scott's articles have appeared at Antiwar.com, *The American Conservative* magazine, the History News Network, *The Future of Freedom*, *The National Interest* and the *Christian Science Monitor*. He also contributed a chapter to the 2019 book, *The Impact of War*.

Scott lives in Austin, Texas with his wife, investigative reporter Larisa Alexandrovna Horton.

https://antiwar.com
https://foolserrand.us
https://scotthorton.org
https://libertarianinstitute.org

https://twitter.com/scotthortonshow
https://youtube.com/scotthortonshow
https://facebook.com/scotthortonshow

https://twitter.com/libertarianinst
https://facebook.com/libertarianinst

About the Guest

Dr. Ron Paul, a former twelve-term congressman from Texas, is the leading advocate of freedom in America today. He has devoted his political career to the defense of individual liberty, sound money and a non-interventionist foreign policy. After serving as a flight surgeon in the U.S. Air Force in the 1960s, Dr. Paul moved to Texas to begin a civilian medical practice, delivering over four thousand babies in his career as an obstetrician. He served in Congress from 1976 to 1984, and again from 1996 to 2012. Paul ran for president as the Libertarian Party candidate in 1988, and for the Republican Party presidential nomination in 2008 and 2012, sparking the "Ron Paul Revolution," and helping to spread the ideas of peace and liberty to millions.

He is the founder of the Ron Paul Institute for Peace and Prosperity and co-host of *The Liberty Report* with Daniel McAdams and Chris Rossini.

Paul is the author of the books, *A Foreign Policy of Freedom*; *The Revolution: A Manifesto*; *Liberty Defined: 50 Essential Issues That Affect Our Freedom*; *The School Revolution*; *Swords Into Plowshares: A Life in Wartime and a Future of Peace and Prosperity*; *The Revolution at Ten Years*; *The Case for Gold*, with Lewis Lehrman; *Pillars of Prosperity: Free Markets, Honest Money, Private Property*; *Gold, Peace and Prosperity: The Birth of a New Currency*; *Freedom Under Siege: The U.S. Constitution After 200-Plus Years* and *Mises and Austrian Economics: A Personal View*.

He and Carol Paul, his wife of sixty-two years, have five children, nineteen grandchildren and ten great-grandchildren.

https://ronpaulinstitute.org
https://ronpaullibertyreport.com

Special thanks to Steven Woskow, Aaron Keith Harris, Mike Dworski and Grant F. Smith.

Selected praise for Scott Horton's previous book, *Fool's Errand: Time to End the War in Afghanistan*

"In *Fool's Errand*, Scott Horton masterfully explains the tragedy of America's longest war and makes the case for immediate withdrawal. I highly recommend this excellent book on America's futile and self-defeating occupation of Afghanistan." — Daniel Ellsberg, *Pentagon Papers* whistleblower and author of *The Doomsday Machine: Confessions of a Nuclear War Planner*

"The real story of the disastrous U.S. war in Afghanistan must be written so that future generations may understand the folly of Washington's warmongers. Scott Horton's Afghan war history is an important contribution to this vital effort." — Ron Paul, M.D., former U.S. congressman and author of *Swords into Plowshares: A Life in Wartime and a Future of Peace and Prosperity*

"Scott Horton's *Fool's Errand* is a deeply insightful and well-informed book on America's longest war, explaining why it remains as unwinnable as it ever was. It appears at an important moment as the Trump administration is once again reinforcing failure." — Patrick Cockburn, Middle East correspondent for the *Independent*, author of *The Age of Jihad: Islamic State and the Great War for the Middle East*

"An incisive, informative analysis of the Afghan fiasco and how we got there, scrubbed clean of propaganda and disinformation. Horton captures the situation very well indeed. I much enjoyed reading it." — Eric S. Margolis, author of *War at the Top of the World: The Struggle for Afghanistan, Kashmir and Tibet* and *American Raj: Liberation or Domination? Resolving the Conflict Between the West and the Muslim World*

"*Fool's Errand: Time to End the War in Afghanistan* is a spectacularly researched and sourced book, and it provides a refreshingly rational analysis of America's Afghan quagmire. I would recommend this book to anyone who wants to know the truth of this nation's longest war." — Lt. Col. Daniel L. Davis, U.S. Army (ret.), senior fellow at Defense Priorities

"Scott Horton has a far better record on Afghanistan than the Pentagon or the White House. He has been pointing out the follies of U.S. intervention there since it started half a generation ago. *Fool's Errand* vividly exposes the pratfalls, atrocities, lies and incorrigibility of our never-ending Afghan crusade." — James Bovard, columnist at *USA Today* and author of *Attention Deficit Democracy*

"Scott Horton's *Fool's Errand: Time to End the War in Afghanistan* is a definitive, authoritative and exceptionally well-resourced accounting of America's disastrous war in Afghanistan since 2001. Scott's book deserves not just to be read, but to be kept on your shelf, because as with David Halberstam's *The Best and Brightest* or Neil Sheehan's *A Bright Shining Lie*, I expect Horton's book to not just explain and interpret a current American war, but to explain and interpret the all too predictable future American wars, and the unavoidable waste and suffering that will accompany them."
— Capt. Matthew Hoh, USMC (ret.), former senior State Department official, Zabul Province, Afghanistan, senior fellow at the Center for International Policy

"*Fool's Errand* is a hidden history of America's forgotten war, laid bare in damning detail. Scott Horton masterfully retells the story of America's failed intervention, exposes how Obama's troop surge did not bring Afghanistan any closer to peace, and warns that the conflict could go on in perpetuity — unless America ends the war. As Trump threatens to send more troops to Afghanistan, Horton shows why the answer to a brutal civil war is not more war, which makes *Fool's Errand* a scintillating and sorely needed chronicle of the longest war in American history." — Anand Gopal, journalist and author of *No Good Men Among the Living: America, the Taliban, and the War through Afghan Eyes*

"Scott Horton's *Fool's Errand: Time to End the War in Afghanistan* is a brilliant achievement and a great read. I recommended it to the faculty at the Army Command and General Staff College to be part of the course work. It's that important." — Col. Douglas Macgregor, U.S. Army (ret.), author of *Warrior's Rage: The Great Tank Battle of 73 Easting*

"In *Fool's Errand*, Scott Horton informs us of just how non-masterful has been the U.S. approach to Afghanistan — policy-wise, strategically, and even tactically. Having watched this debacle from very close-by for four years and for twelve more in academia, I totally agree with Mr. Horton, but he has done a much better job than I could of telling every single American citizen precisely why." — Col. Lawrence Wilkerson, U.S. Army (ret.), professor of government and public policy at the College of William and Mary and former chief of staff to Secretary of State Colin Powell

"A lot of people think of the war in Iraq as the bad war, but Afghanistan as the good and justifiable war. That convenient view does not survive Scott Horton's careful and incisive demolition." — Thomas E. Woods Jr., author of *Nullification: How to Resist Federal Tyranny in the 21st Century*

"Scott Horton is the first to pull together all the strands of the story of America's longest war in one book. He tells it straight, with an unblinking eye for all the lies that have accompanied each twist and turn of the war. Read it if you dare to know the full truth about this sordid exercise in American imperial power." — Gareth Porter, historian and journalist, author of *Manufactured Crisis: The Truth Behind the Iran Nuclear Scare*"

America's longest war — in Afghanistan — has until now been among America's least documented. Horton brings together far more than 16 years of conflict, drawing in sources from well before most Americans even heard of Osama bin Laden to show how the Afghan quagmire's roots are deep. The title tells it all, however: this war cannot be won, and 'victory' will be in the form of escape. Meticulously researched and footnoted, *Fool's Errand* is required reading." — Peter Van Buren, retired foreign service officer and author of *We Meant Well: How I Helped Lose the War for the Hearts and Minds of the Iraqi People* and *Hooper's War: A Novel of WWII Japan*

"Why is the United States still fighting in Afghanistan? In this timely new book, Scott Horton explains why America's longest war is strategically misguided and why getting out would make the United States safer and advance America's broader national interests. Even readers who do not share Horton's libertarian worldview are likely to find themselves nodding in agreement: the war in Afghanistan has indeed become a 'fool's errand.'" — Stephen M. Walt, professor of international affairs, Harvard University, co-author of *The Israel Lobby and U.S. Foreign Policy*

"Outstanding! Highly readable and fascinating summary of the longest war in U.S. history, and why it never worked. Well researched and organized, *Fool's Errand* should be mandatory reading for every military officer serving today and be placed in President Trump's hands immediately. Trump's pre-election instincts on this ugly, corrupting and unnecessary war were certainly correct. Scott Horton's well-documented timeline of waste, illogical strategies and neoconservative fantasy in Afghanistan all show why Trump's gut feelings, and those of most Americans for the past decade, have been dead-on. Using careful, fair-minded and patriotic prose, the author exposes the Afghanistan experience as a high-tech, networked Vietnam. *Fool's Errand* is the true story of the direct, undeniable result of a newer generation of 'smart' bureaucrats, in and out of uniform, their shockingly bad advice and their astonishing willingness to repeatedly lie to sitting presidents. Whether you want to wake up, stay woke or just be remembered as the president who made America great again, this book is a must read!" — Lt. Col. Karen Kwiatkowski, U.S. Air Force (ret.)

About the Libertarian Institute

Founded in 2016 by Scott Horton, Sheldon Richman and William Norman Grigg, the Libertarian Institute is a 501(c)(3) non-profit educational organization dedicated to spreading the principles of liberty.

All contributions to the Institute are tax-deductible.

Find out how you can help support the Libertarian Institute at https://libertarianinstitute.org/donate.

www.ingramcontent.com/pod-product-compliance
Lightning Source LLC
Chambersburg PA
CBHW061424040426
42450CB00007B/887